APR - 9 1994

D1338134

INTERNATIONAL SUBSCRIPTION AGENTS

Sixth Edition

Compiled by

Lenore Rae Wilkas

American Library Association

Chicago and London, 1994

The paper used in this publication meets the minimum requirements of American National Standard for Information Sciences—Permanence of Paper for Printed Library Materials, ANSI Z39.48-1984.∞

Printed on 45-pound Lakewood opaque, a pH-neutral stock, and bound in 10-point CIS by BookCrafters

Library of Congress Cataloging-in-Publication Dat

Wilkas, Lenore.
    International subscription agents / by Lenor
Rae Wilkas. -- 6th ed.
       p.   cm.
    Rev. and updated ed. of: International subscription agents / compiled by Wayne R. Perr and Lenore Wilkas. 5th ed. 1986.
    Includes index.
    ISBN O-8389-0622-2 (alk. paper)
    1. Serials subscription agencies--Directori
I. Perryman, Wayne R.   International subscript
agents.   II. Title.
Z286.P4W53   1993
070.5'025--dc20   93-29753

Printed in the United States of America.

98 97 96 95 94   5 4 3 2 1

Dedicated with deep appreciation
to my early library mentors:
Alice Leppert,
Connor Tjarks, and
Betty Martin
and to
Leigh Farrell for his understanding,
patience, and love

CONTENTS

Agents by Country

xi

UNITED STATES (continued)

INTRODUCTION

The sixth edition of <u>International Subscription Agents</u> was designed to meet the increasing demands of serials librarians as well as the monograph acquisitions librarians who may now find themselves in charge of a serials sub-unit. The questionnaire was formulated by determining what information is most important to the librarian who is in search of an agent while keeping in mind that the needs of librarians differ.

Included in this edition are phone numbers, fax numbers, cable addresses and toll-free numbers so that the librarians will have easy access to the agent for quick additional information.

Agents are listed alphabetically within an alphabetical arrangement by country of origin. Branch offices of major agents are included in the table of contents and are listed in the text by their country of location with a cross-reference to the complete entry of the parent company. Users will note the absence of many agents that appeared in the fifth edition. Many older and smaller establishments have closed their doors or were bought by larger agents. Background information is provided concerning the date of establishment, other office locations, as well as the agent's participation in library and library-related associations.

Agents were asked to specify which types of materials were handled and to state whether they or a subsidiary office handled monograph orders. This information should be helpful to the librarian interested in placing both serial and monographic orders with the same vendor.

The agent's ability to offer computerized services and the ability of its database to interface with various library systems were also queried. Some agents indicated that computerization was being planned or nearly completed. This was noted with the hope that any interested librarian would query the agent(s) for current status information.

The final part of the questionnaire dealt with the nitty-gritty business details so important to acquisitions librarians: service and handling charges, invoicing, prepayments, and transfers of orders/accounts from another vendor.

Librarians will find a copy of the questionnaire preceding the text. The questions have been numbered. The responses in each entry are numbered identically to link them to the questions that were asked. Thus, if you are interested in comparing two agents' activity in library associations, you would check the responses to questions 4 and 5. If a response was unclear, often due to language difficulty, "response unclear" was noted. If no response was given, that was also noted.

Over 700 questionnaires with a cover letter were mailed to agents literally from Afghanistan to Zimbabwe. Fifty-two were returned stating that no forwarding address was available or were marked simply "Gone away." Due to the political upheavals of the early 1990s, responses from the former countries of the U.S.S.R. are limited. Likewise, participation from African and Arab countries was less than expected.

Since the publication of the fifth edition, several agents have prospered and grown with offices worldwide, many in the countries mentioned. So the librarian may actually have increased his/her possibilities due to the rise of "mega-agents." Branch offices of all agents are listed under the countries in which the branches are located with a see-reference to the information on the main office.

Also provided is a geographic index listing agents who will provide publications from specific countries. With the geographic index, librarians can take advantage of the fact that agents frequently give the best service for serials published in the region where they do business. This index was formulated by the agents' responses to question 6. The user is urged to also look under the heading "Worldwide" for the many agents who will provide materials from any country. A short subject index provides for the specialty areas indicated by the agents in response to questions 6 and 7.

Most importantly, users are urged to use this book as a starting point in searching for an appropriate agent. Users are encouraged to consult with other librarians who may already have contact with an agent and, of course, they are encouraged to contact the agent directly. Agents listed have not received any compensation nor does their inclusion indicate approval of the American Library Association or the compiler.

The compiler wishes to thank all of the agents who made this book possible through their cooperation. Twenty years spent in the field of acquisitions, primarily serials, and spent at large libraries have put me in contact with several mentioned here. My thanks to them for what they have taught me about the business of acquisitions. Heartfelt thanks also to my always delightful editor, Herbert Bloom, and to ALA production manager, Dianne Rooney. Both were enormously helpful and their suggestions were always of great value.

THE QUESTIONNAIRE

Name of company/address:

Telephone number: Toll-free number
Fax number: Cable address:
Telex number:

1a. Date your firm was established.

1b. Are you an independent company or are you
    owned and operated by another firm?

2. Does your company have offices in other
    countries? Please specify countries and
    provide addresses and phone numbers if
    you would like all addresses listed in
    the directory.

3. Are there countries with which you will
    not do business? Specify.

4. Does your company maintain memberships in
    any library associations? Is your company
    represented regularly at these meetings?

5. Do your representatives actively
    participate in library association
    meetings in their country and/or area of
    the country they represent?

6. Do you provide materials from specific
    countries only or worldwide? Specify.

7a. What types of materials will you handle?
    Check those that apply:
    Periodicals__ Monographic standing orders
    (continuations)__ CD-ROM__ Back issues__
    Government publications__ Loose-leaf
    services__ Sets__ Microforms__
    Replacements__ Yearbooks/annuals__ (May
    client request every second or third

year?)__ Memberships__ Serials on video-
cassette__ Serials with variant publishing
(congresses, proceedings, symposia)__
Other:___

7b. Does your company also accept monographic
firm orders? Does another branch of your
company handle these? Please specify.

8. Do you communicate with back issue dealers
when supplying back issues for a client?

9. Which of the following services do you
provide? Please check:
Automatic renewal til forbid__ New order
reports__ Claim reports__ Out-of-print
searching__ Handle series with change of
publishers each year or each volume?__
Other:__

10. Are journals collected at your agency,
claimed by your agency, and then sent to
the library as a standard practice or is
this service available only on demand from
the library? If on demand, is there an
additional service charge and additional
shipping charges?

11. What computerized services do you offer
clients?

12. Is your database available to clients?
How?

13. Do you presently, or are you planning to,
interface with any library automation
systems such as NOTIS, GEAC, etc.? What
is currently available to your clients?

14. Do you issue a monthly newsletter?
Catalog? What bibliographic information
is provided in the catalog? Other
information?

15. In written and phone contacts, does a client deal with one individual assigned to the account or with different individuals depending on the nature of the inquiry?

16. Do you report back to the library on titles that you cannot supply? How long do you try to obtain material before you notify the library of unavailability?

17. Do you accept rush orders?___ Is there an added charge for these?___

18. Do you charge a service fee? Is it a standard percentage, flat fee, or determined in another manner?

19. Are service/handling charges listed separately on the invoice or are they included in the price?

20. May a client request that service charges be listed separately?

21. Do you ever pay all or part of the shipping charges?

22. How are titles entered on the invoice? (alphabetized, by order no., etc.)

23. Do you provide the purchase order number on the invoice?

24. Can you supply multiple copies of invoices? Is there a limit?

25. Can invoices be generated on computer tape or generated by other electronic means?

26. Does your company offer prepayment options and terms? Please specify.

27. If a library is interested in changing dealers or consolidating direct subscriptions, will you provide the library with quotations from their present list?

28. If a library wishes to place a major portion of or its entire account with your firm, must they cancel with present suppliers or will you assist them? How?

Directory
of
Subscription Agents

ARGENTINA

Fernando Garcia Cambeiro
Cochabamba 248, Dpto. 2
1150 Buenos Aires, Argentina

Postal address in U.S.A.:
   Box 014 Skyway USA
   7331 N.W. 35th Street
   Miami, FL 33122

Telephone number: (54) (1) 361-0473
Fax number: (54) (1) 361-0493

1. Independent firm established in 1958.
2-
3. No.

4. Maintains memberships in and is regularly represented at the annual meetings of: SALALM (Seminar of the Acquisition of Latin American Library Materials)
5. No.
6. Provides all serials and monographs from Argentina in full; provides some titles from Bolivia, Brazil, Chile, Colombia, Costa Rica, Dominican Republic, Ecuador, Guatemala, Mexico, Panama, Paraguay, Peru, Uruguay, Venezuela, and other small Latin American countries.
7a. Types of materials provided:
    Periodicals
    Monographic standing orders
    CD-ROM
    Back issues
    Loose-leaf services
    Sets
    Microforms
    Yearbooks/annuals (client may request every second or third year)
    Memberships
    Serials on videocassette
    Serials with variant publishing
7b. Books (monographic firm orders).
8. Will communicate with back issue dealers when supplying back issues for a client.
9. Services provided:
    Automatic renewal til forbid
    Claim reports
    Out-of-print searching
    Approval plans
10. Journal consolidation is standard practice.
11. Computerized services are not available for serials.
    For books in series the company produces and publishes every four months a database of books issued on CD-ROM called LATBOOK to which clients may subscribe. LATBOOK collects books from fifteen Latin American countries, from Mexico to Argentina.

```
12-
13.  No response.
14.  Will issue an Argentine serials guide in
     1993. Distributes more than thirty
     different catalogs by country,
     subject, etc., for monographs.
15.  Clients will deal directly with the
     manager.
16.  Will report back to a library on titles
     it cannot supply.
17.  Rush orders accepted only with an extra
     charge for airmail fees.
18.  No.
19.  Handling charges are included in the
     price.
20.  Handling charges will not be listed
     separately.
21.  Firm pays all shipping charges.
22-  Titles are listed on the invoice by
23.  purchase order number.
24.  Multiple copies of invoices can be
     supplied (maximum three).
25-
26.  No.
27.  Will provide a quotation for libraries
     interested in changing vendors or
     consolidating direct subscriptions.
28.  Libraries must cancel with previous
     suppliers before switching orders to
     Cambeiro.
```

Juan Manuel de Castro
Libros Argentino y Modernos
Casilla de Correo 5028-C. Central
1000 Buenos Aires, Argentina
(Postal address)

Commercial address:
    Juan Manuel de Castro
    Libros Argentinos y Modernos
    Talcahuano 416 Of. 203
    1013 Buenos Aires, Argentina

Telephone number: (54) (1) 40-7184

1. Independent company established in 1974.
2. No.
3. No response.
4. Maintains membership in and is regularly represented at meetings of:
   SALALM (Seminar of the Acquisition of Latin American Library Materials)
5. No response.
6. Provides serial materials from specific countries (none were specified in reply).
7a. Types of materials handled:
   Periodicals
   Monographic standing orders
   Back issues
   Government publications
7b-
13. No response.
14. Issues a quarterly bulletin.
15. No response.
16. Will report back to the library in three months on titles it cannot supply.
17. Rush orders are accepted at no extra charge.
18-
28. No response.

Lange & Springer
Scientific Booksellers
Florida 868, 14 G
1005 Buenos Aires, Argentina

Telephone number: (54) (1) 313-5994-6000
Fax number: (54) (1) 313-953-2763
For more information see Lange & Springer
listing under GERMANY.

Alberto Peremiansky
Casilla Correo Central 3659
1000 Buenos Aires, Argentina
(Postal address)

Commercial address:
        Alberto Peremiansky
        Av. Cordoba 2586
        Piso 10 "E"
        1120 Buenos Aires, Argentina

Telephone number: (54) (1) 962-0240

1. Independent firm established in 1980.
2-
3. No.
4. Maintains membership in:
        SALALM (Seminar of the Acquisition
            of Latin American Library Materials)
5. No.
6. Provides serials and monographs from
    Argentina, Latin America, and Spain.
7a. Types of materials handled:
        Periodicals
            Monographic standing orders
        Back issues
        Government publications
        Sets
7b. Books (monographic firm orders) accepted
    at another branch.
8. Will communicate with back issue dealers
    when supplying back issues for clients.

9. Services provided:
    New order reports
    Claim reports
    Out-of-print searching
10. Journal consolidation available only on demand.
11-
13. No response.
14. Issues catalogs and lists of Latin American rare and out-of-print books.
15. Clients will deal with one customer service representative.
16. Will report back to the library after six months on titles that cannot be supplied.
17. Rush orders accepted at no extra charge.
18. No response.
19- Service/handling charges are listed
20. separately on the invoice.
21. Will pay all or part of the shipping charges for important orders.
22- Titles are listed on the invoice by
23. purchase order number.
24. Multiple copies of invoices provided (no limit).
25. Invoices can be generated on computer tape.
26. No response.
27. Will provide quotations for libraries interested in changing dealers or consolidating direct subscriptions.
28. No response.

James Bennett Library Services
4 Collaroy Street
Collaroy, N.S.W. 2097, Australia

Telephone number: (61) (2) 982-2122
Fax number: (61) (2) 971-1309
Toll-free number: 008-226-784 (within
          Australia only)

1. Owned by B. H. Blackwell Ltd. and
    established in 1958.
2-
3. No.
4. Company maintains memberships in and is
    represented at all conferences and many
    meetings of the:
        Australian Library and Information
            Association
        New Zealand Library Association
5. Its representatives actively participate
    in library association meetings in their
    country and/or area of the country they
    represent.
6. Specializes in providing serials and
    monographs from Australia and
    New Zealand.
7a. Types of materials handled:
        Monographic standing orders
        CD-ROM
        Government publications
        Sets
        Microforms
        Yearbooks/annuals (client may request
            every second or third year)
        Serials with variant publishing
        Numbered series
        Multi-volume works
        New editions
7b. Books (monographic firm orders).
8. Not applicable (does not handle journals
    or subscriptions).

9. Services provided:
    Automatic renewal til forbid
    New order confirmations
    Progress reports (if supply is not
        as anticipated).
10. Not applicable.
11. Computer services offered:
    Lists of materials on order
    Information on forthcoming
        editions, latest edition
        supplied, etc.
12. Clients may request lists of materials
    by publisher or subject from the firm's
    database, but at this time there is no
    direct access to the database.
13. Currently considering a number of library
    automation system links. All clients may
    reach them via their ILANET mail box
    (MLN206100).
14. No.
15. Clients are assigned one customer service
    representative.
16. Will report back to the library on titles
    that they cannot supply.
17. Rush orders accepted with a nominal
    charge plus costs of telecommunications
    and air freight or courier.
18. Service fee is based on the country of
    origin list price converted to the
    appropriate currency. If an insufficient
    discount is received from the publisher,
    a normal commercial margin will be added
    to the cost of the item.
19. Service/handling charges are included in
    the price but are tagged for easy
    identification.
20. Client may not request that service
    charges be listed separately at this
    time.
21. Will pay shipping charges from the
    publisher to Bennett's. Overseas clients
    are charged freight.
22- Titles are listed on the invoice by
23. purchase order number.
24. Invoice is provided in triplicate.

25. The generation of invoice on computer tape or transference by other electronic means is now in the planning phase.
26. Prepayment and deposit accounts available. Contact firm for details.
27. For libraries interested in consolidating direct subscriptions or changing vendors, Bennett's "would provide our best estimates for the coming year or exact price for the last year. Currency conversion is a major factor in pricing for overseas libraries and we are, unfortunately, unable to predict that."
28. "We would of course write to each supplier with new order and mention replacement if sufficient information is given to do this."

B. H. Blackwell Ltd.
17/22 Darley Road
Manley, N.S.W. 2095, Australia

Telephone number: (0011) (61) (2) 977-8355
For more information see B. H. Blackwell listing under UNITED KINGDOM.

Collins Booksellers
Subscription Department
115 Elizabeth Street
Melbourne, Victoria 3000, Australia

Telephone number: (61) (3) 654-3144
Fax number: (61) (3) 670-7884

1. Independent company established in 1921.
2-
5. No.
6. Provides materials from countries worldwide.

7a. Types of materials handled:
    Periodicals
    Monographic standing orders
    CD-ROM
    Back issues
    Government publications
    Loose-leaf services
    Microforms
    Replacements
    Yearbooks/annuals (client may request
        every second or third year)
    Serials on videocassette
    Serials with variant publishing
7b. Books (monographic firm orders).
8. Will communicate with back issue dealers
    when supplying back issues for a client.
9. Services provided:
    Automatic renewal til forbid
    Claim reports
    Out-of-print searching
10. Journal consolidation is available with
    a charge for postage.
11. Computerized services:
    Invoices
    Renewal lists
    Orders
12. Database is available through specific
    lists.
13-
14. No.
15. Client will deal with different customer
    service representatives.
16. Will report back to library on titles it
    cannot supply after all avenues have
    been exhausted.
17. No.
18. Service fee is charged.
19- Service/handling charges are included
20. in the price and cannot be listed
    separately.
21. No.
22. Titles are arranged alphabetically on
    the invoice.
23. Purchase order numbers provided on the
    invoice.

24. Two copies of the invoice normally supplied; will supply additional if requested.
25. No.
26. Prepayment options and terms available.
27. Will provide quotations for libraries interested in consolidating direct orders or changing vendors.
28. Will assist libraries wishing to change vendors if libraries give them the relevant details.

EBSCO Australia
35 Mitchell Street
North Sydney, N.S.W. 2060, Australia

Telephone number: (61) (2) 922-5600
Fax number: (61) (2) 922-6659
For more informations see EBSCO Subscription Services listing under UNITED STATES.

Faxon Australia
P.O. Box 61
Higgins ACT 2615, Australia

Telephone number: (61)-62-543784
Fax number: (61)-62-543630
Also serves New Zealand.
For more information see The Faxon Co., Inc. listing under UNITED STATES.

Gordon and Gotch Ltd.
25-37 Huntingdale Road
Burwood, Vic. 3125, Australia

Postal address:
> Private Bag 290
> Burwood, Vic. 3125, Australia

Telephone number: (61) (03) 805-1650
Fax number: (61) (03) 808-0714
Telex number: AA37381

1. Operated as an independent company but owned by Independent Newspapers Ltd. (INL), established in 1853.
2. The company has offices overseas; however, the Subscription Division does not.
3-
4. No.
5. Representatives, on occasion, participate in library association meetings in their country and/or area of the country they represent.
6. Provides serials and monographs from countries worldwide.
7a. Types of materials handled:
> Periodicals
> CD-ROM
> Back issues
> Government publications
> Loose-leaf services
> Sets
> Replacements
> Yearbooks/annuals
> Memberships
> Serials on videocassette
> Serials with variant publishing
7b. Books (monographic firm orders) not presently available.
8. Goes directly to publishers when supplying back issues for a client.
9. No response.
10. Journal consolidation service is not available at present.

11. Computerized services offered:
    all orders and accounts are
        computerized
    a fully categorized listing of
        all titles will be available in
        the near future
12. Not available at present.
13. None.
14. No.
15. Clients who have overseas university and
    library accounts now deal with one
    individual assigned to their accounts.
    Non-account clients may deal with
    different individuals.
16. Will report back to the library on
    titles it cannot supply. Gordon & Gotch
    will continue to try to obtain titles
    for as long as it believes a positive
    result is possible.
17. Rush orders accepted at no added charge.
18. All rates are inclusive of service fees.
    Rates are determined on a variable
    percentage. Shipping charges included in
    the price.
19. Service/handling fees are included in
    the price.
20. Client may not request charges listed
    separately.
21. No.
22. Account summary invoices have titles
    listed alphabetically.
23. Purchase order numbers will be listed on
    the invoice if required.
24-
25. No.
26. Prepayment options and terms:
    Accounts available on 30-day terms
    All cash subscriptions must be prepaid
27. Will provide quotations for libraries
    interested in changing dealers or
    consolidating direct subscriptions.
28. If a library wishes to transfer its
    account to Gordon & Gotch, the library
    must cancel with its present supplier(s).

ISA Australia
P.O. Box 709
Toowong, Queensland 4066, Australia

Telephone number: (61) (7) 371-7500
Fax number: (61) (7) 371-5206
Toll-free numbers:
    within Australia: (008)-777-134
    from New Zealand: 0800-44-6133
    from Papua New Guinea: 05-08-61-055

1. Independent company established in 1955.
2-
3. No.
4. Firm maintains memberships in and is regularly represented at the meetings of:
   - Australian Library & Information Association
   - Australian Serials Special Interest Group
   - New Zealand Library Association
   - North American Serials Interest Group
   - United Kingdom Serials Group (UKSG)
5. No response.
6. Provides serials from countries worldwide.
7a. Types of materials provided:
   - Periodicals
   - Monographic standing orders
   - CD-ROM
   - Back issues
   - Government publications
   - Loose-leaf services
   - Microforms
   - Replacements
   - Yearbooks/annuals (client may request every second or third year)
   - Memberships
   - Serials with variant publishing
7b. No.
8. Goes directly to the publisher when supplying back issues for a client.
9. Services provided:
   - Automatic renewal til forbid
   - Claim reports

10. Journal consolidation or check-in encouraged but there are additional service and shipping charges.
11. Computerized services offered:
    Print-outs/listings
    Machine-readable invoices
12. No.
13. Presently interfaces with DATATRECK.
14. ISA Australia publishes an irregular newsletter called "Issues" two or three times per annum.
15. Client may choose to have one customer service representative or to deal with different individuals, depending on the nature of the inquiry.
16. Will report back to the library within one week of becoming aware of a title's unavailability.
17. Rush orders accepted at no added charge.
18. Service fee is a sliding scale fee: The more expensive the title, the lower the percentage margin.
19. Service/handling charges are included in the price on the invoice.
20. Customer may ask that service/handling charges appear separately on the invoice.
21. No.
22. Titles are listed on the invoice in alphabetical order.
23. Purchase order number included on invoices.
24. Multiple copies of invoices are provided (no limit).
25. Invoices can be generated on computer tape or transferred by electronic means.
26. Prepayment options and terms: If a client prepays, they receive a discount equal to the bank interest for the period.
27. Will provide quotations for libraries interested in consolidating direct orders or changing vendors.
28. Firm will assist libraries by advising each publisher of the change of vendor.

Buchhandlung Bayer
Kreuzgasse 6
A6800 Feldkirch, Austria

Telephone number: (43) (05522) 74770

1. Independent company owned by
   W. Neugebauer Verlag GmbH. and
   established in 1986.
2-
5. No.
6. Provides serials and monographs from
   countries worldwide.
7a. Types of materials handled:
   Periodicals
   Monographic standing orders
   CD-ROM
   Back issues
   Loose-leaf services
   Sets
   Microforms
   Yearbooks/annuals
   Serials on videocassette
7b. Books (monographic firm orders).
8. Will communicate with back issue dealers
   when supplying back issues for a client.
9. Services provided:
   Automatic renewal til forbid
10. No response.
11-
14. No.
15. Clients will deal with one customer
   service representative.
16. Will report back to the library on
   titles that cannot be supplied.
17. Rush orders accepted with postage as the
   only added charge.
18. No service fee charged.
19- Service/handling charges listed
20. separately on the invoice.
21. No.
22. Titles are entered on the invoice as
   requested by the client.

23. Purchase orders included on the invoices.
24. Invoices are sent in duplicate or triplicate.
25. Invoices can be faxed to the client if desired.
26. No.
27. Will provide quotations for libraries interested in consolidating direct subscriptions or changing dealers.
28. Will assist libraries in cancelling with their present suppliers if they wish to switch orders to this agency.

Gerold & Co.
Graben 31
A-1011 Vienna, Austria

Telephone number: (43) (1) 512-47-31
Fax number: (43) (1) 512-47-31-29
Telex number: 847-136157
Cable address: GEROLDBUCH

1. Independent company established in 1875.
2-
5. No.
6. Provides serials and monographs from countries worldwide.
7a. Types of materials handled:
        Periodicals
        Monographic standing orders
        CD-ROM
        Back issues
        Government publications
        Loose-leaf services
        Sets
        Microforms
        Replacements
        Yearbooks/annuals (client may request every second or third year)
        Memberships
        Serials with variant publishing
7b. Books (monographic firm orders).

8. Will occasionally communicate with back issue dealers when supplying back issues for a client.
9. Services provided:
   Automatic renewal til forbid
   New order reports
   Claim reports
10. Journal consolidation available at no added charge.
11. Computerized services:
   Complete service for journals and monographs
12-
14. No.
15. Client deals with different customer service representatives depending on the nature of the inquiry.
16. Reports back to the library on titles that cannot be supplied.
17. Rush orders accepted with an added charge.
18. Service fee is charged.
19- Service/handling charges are listed
20. separately on the invoice.
21. No.
22. Titles listed alphabetically on invoices.
23. Purchase order numbers provided on invoices.
24. Multiple copies of invoices provided.
25. No.
26. Prepayment options and terms are available. Contact the firm for details.
27. Will provide quotations for a library interested in consolidating direct subscriptions or changing dealers.
28. No.

Antiquariat V. A. Heck
Kaerntnerring 14
1010 Wien, Austria

Telephone number: (43) (0222) 505-51-52
Cable address: HECKBOOKS VIENNA

1. Independent company.
2-
3. No.
4. Maintains memberships in and is
    regularly represented at meetings of:
    Austrian League of Antiquarian
        Booksellers
    International League of Antiquarian
        Booksellers
5. Representatives actively participate in
    library association meetings in their
    country and/or area of the country they
    represent.
6. Provides serials and monographs only
    from Austria with some materials
    provided from Germany.
7a. Types of materials handled:
    Periodicals
    Monographic standing orders
    Government publications
    Loose-leaf services
    Sets
    Replacements (if available)
    Serials with variant publishing
    Yearbooks/annuals (client may request
        every second or third year)
7b. Books (monographic firm orders).
8. Will communicate with colleagues when
    supplying back issues for a client.
9. Services provided:
    Automatic renewal til forbid
    New order reports
    Claim reports
    Out-of-print searching
10. No response.
11. None.
12-
14. No response.
15. Client will usually deal with one customer
    service representative.
16. Will report back to the library as soon
    as the information is received on titles
    that cannot be supplied.
17. No response.
18- Service/handling charges include
19. postage, packing, and insurance.

20. No response.
21. No.
22- Titles are entered on the invoice by
23. purchase order number.
24. Multiple copies of invoices supplied (no limit).
25. Response unclear.
26. No response.
27. Will provide quotations for libraries interested in consolidating direct subscriptions or changing vendors.
28. May or may not assist a library wishing to transfer its orders to the company.

Georg Prachner KG
Kaerntnerstrasse 30
A1010 Vienna, Austria

Telephone number: (43) (0222) 512-85-49
Fax number: (43) (0222) 512-01-58

1. Independent company established on August 1, 1931.
2-
4. No.
5. Representatives actively participate in library association meetings in their country and/or area they represent.
6. Provides serials and monographs from Austria only.
7a. Types of materials handled:
    Periodicals
    Monographic standing orders
    CD-ROM
    Back issues
    Government periodicals
    Loose-leaf services
    Sets
    Microforms
    Replacements
    Yearbooks/annuals (client may request every second or third year)
    Serials on videocassette
    Serials with variant publishing

7b. Books (monographic firm orders).
8. Will communicate with back issue dealers when supplying back issues for a client.
9. Services provided:
    Automatic renewal til forbid
    New order reports
    Claim reports
    Out-of-print searching
10. Journal consolidation is available at no additional charge.
11. Computerized services:
    Computerized invoicing
12. No.
13. Interfacing with library automation systems not yet available.
14. Issues catalogs.
15. Clients will deal with different customer service representatives.
16. Will report back to a library within three months on titles that cannot be supplied.
17. Rush orders accepted at no extra charge.
18. No service fee charged.
19-
20. No service/handling charges.
21. No.
22. Titles are arranged alphabetically on the invoice.
23. Purchase order numbers provided on invoice.
24. Multiple copies of invoices provided (no limit).
25. Invoices can be generated on computer tape or transferred by other electronic means.
26. No.
27. Will provide quotations for libraries interested in consolidating orders or changing dealers.
28. Will assist libraries in switching orders from another vendor.

BAHAMAS

United Bookshop
No. 17 Chesapeake Road
Pyfrom Addition
P.O. Box SS-6220
Nassau, Bahamas

Telephone number: (809) 393-8770
Fax number: (809) 393-0822

Wishes to serve libraries worldwide. Will try
to supply whatever materials are needed by
libraries. Contact them directly for more
information.

BANGLADESH

International Book Trade
25/1 East Madertak, Bashaboo
Dhaka, Bangladesh

Telephone number: (880) (2) 406502
Cable address: 1BT 25/1 E. Madertak,Dhaka

1. Independent company established on
    August 1, 1965.
2-
3. No.
4-
5. Not yet.
6. Provides serials and monographs from
    Bangladesh only.
7a. Types of materials handled:
        Periodicals
        Monographic standing orders
        Government publications
        Yearbooks/annuals
        Serials on videocassette
7b. Books (monographic firm orders).
8. No.

9. Services provided:
        Automatic renewal til forbid
        New order reports
        Claim reports
        Out-of-print searching
10. Journal consolidation and claiming are the standard practice.
11-
12. Not yet.
13. No.
14. Issues occasional catalogs providing author, title, short abstract, and year of publication.
15. Clients will deal directly with the manager.
16. Will report back to the library within three or four months on titles that are unavailable.
17. Rush orders accepted at no extra charge.
18. No service charges.
19- Collection charges are shown separately
20. on the invoice.
21. No.
22. Titles are listed on the invoice alphabetically.
23. Purchase order numbers provided on invoices.
24. Multiple copies of invoices are provided (maximum four).
25. Not yet.
26. No.
27. Will provide quotations for libraries interested in consolidating direct subscriptions or changing vendors.
28. Will assist libraries in any way they desire in switching the orders to the firm.

Arani Prakashani
3-R.K. Mission Road
Dhaka-1203, Bangladesh

Telephone number: (880) (2) 253321

1. Independent firm established July 1, 1986.
2. Not applicable.
3. Will not do business with Taiwan, South Africa, and Israel.
4-
5. Not applicable.
6. Provides serials and monographs from countries worldwide.
7a. Types of materials handled:
   Periodicals
   Monographic standing orders
   Back issues
   Government publications
   Loose-leaf services
   Sets
   Replacements
   Yearbooks/annuals
   Memberships
   Serials with variant publishing
7b. Books (monographic firm orders).
8. Will communicate with back issue dealers when supplying back issues for a client.
9. Services provided:
   Automatic renewal til forbid
   New order reports
   Claim reports
   Out-of-print searching
10. No.
11. Computerized services:
   Printing of lists of published and
      grey literature
   Will prepare bibliographies upon
      request
12. Lists of various publications and occasional bibliographies are available from the database upon request.
13. No.

14. Issues a quarterly catalog which includes: title, author, page, publishers, place of publication, date of publication, price, etc.
15. Response unclear.
16. Will report back to the library on titles it cannot supply after three months.
17. Rush orders accepted at no extra charge.
18. A service fee is charged and is a standard percentage.
19- Service/handling charges are listed
20. separately on the invoice.
21. Will pay all or part of the shipping charges.
22. Titles can be listed alphabetically or by order number.
23. Purchase order numbers provided on invoice.
24. Multiple copies of invoice provided (no limit).
25. No.
26. Prepayment options and terms: prepayment sometimes required from a new customer.
27. Will provide quotations for libraries interested in changing dealers or consolidating direct subscriptions.
28. Will assist libraries "with all our service facilities" who wish to change orders from other suppliers to this firm.

BELGIUM

G.I.A.
321 Av. des Volontaires
1150 Brussels, Belgium

Telephone number: (32) (2) 751-84-70
Fax number: (32) (2) 761-06-62

1. Independent company established in 1966.

4. No.
5. Representatives actively participate at
   the International Book Fairs held in
   Brussels, Belgium; Geneva, Switzerland;
   Montreal, Canada; Paris, France; and
   Frankfurt, Germany.
6. Provides serials and monographs from
   Belgium.
7a. Types of materials handled:
       Periodicals
       Monographic standing orders
       Back issues
       Government publications
       Loose-leaf services
       Yearbooks/annuals (client may request
           every second or third year)
       Serials with variant publishing
7b. Books (monographic firm orders).
8. May communicate with back issue dealers
   when supplying back issues for a client.
9. Services provided:
       Automatic renewal til forbid
       New order reports
       Claim reports
10. Journal consolidation is available.
11. Computerized services offered to clients:
       "Any"
12. Database is not available to clients but
    G.I.A. sends specialized information to
    its clients in the fields of Philosophy
    and Letters, Law, Economics, Art, and
    other Belgian scientific books.
13. No response.
14. Issues:
       "Bulletin de l'Association des
           Editeurs Scientifiques de la
           Communaute Francaise de Belgique"
15. Client will deal with one assigned
    customer service representative.
16. Will report back to the library on
    titles it cannot supply. Will search for
    the title for nearly six months.
17. Rush orders accepted with a supplemental
    airmail cost.

18- No service fee but there is a
19. supplemental handling fee.
20. Client may request that handling charges
    be listed separately on the invoice.
21. No.
22. Titles are entered on the invoice by
    publisher.
23. Purchase order numbers are provided on
    the invoice.
24. Multiple copies of invoices provided.
25. Invoices are not yet available on
    computer tape or via other electronic
    means.
26. No.
27. Will provide quotations for libraries
    interested in changing dealers or
    consolidating direct orders; this
    service is available only for
    collections and standing orders.
28. Will assist libraries wishing to change
    dealers with regard to Belgian books.

BOLIVIA

Editorial Inca
Casilla 1514
Cochabamba, Bolivia

Mailing address in U.S.A.:
             P.O. Box 164900
             Miami, FL 33116 U.S.A.

Telephone number: (305) 279-1625
Fax number: (305) 271-2964
These numbers are for the United States.

1.   Independent company established in 1965.
2.   Has offices in Bolivia but centralizes
     all correspondence, cables, and faxes
     through the Miami address.
3.   No response.

4. Maintains membership in and regularly attends meetings of the:
    Camara Boliviana del Libro
      (Bolivian Book Chamber of Commerce)
5. Representatives, whenever possible, actively participate in library association meetings in their country and/or area they represent.
6. Provides serials and monographs from Bolivia, Colombia, Ecuador, Peru, and Venezuela.
7a. Types of materials handled:
    Periodicals
    Monographic standing orders
    Back issues
    Government publications
    Sets
    Replacements
    Yearbooks/annuals (client may request every second or third year)
    Serials with variant publishing
7b. Books (monographic firm orders).
8. Will communicate with back issue dealers when supplying back issues for a client.
9. Services provided:
    Automatic renewal til forbid
    New order reports
    Claim reports
    Out-of-print searching
10. Journal consolidation available.
11. Computerized services:
    Printout of its holdings upon request, both books and periodicals
    Specialized catalogs on specific subject areas
12. Database is available to clients through diskette.
13. Is considering interfacing with library automation systems.
14. Issues catalogs every three months for works from Bolivia, Colombia, Ecuador, Peru, and Venezuela. Information includes: author, title, editor, etc., and sometimes an annotation.

15. Clients will deal with the one individual in charge of the Miami office.
16. Reports back to the library within one to two months on titles it cannot supply.
17. Rush orders accepted. Extra charge if there is an extra charge in mailing from the country.
18. Presently do not charge service fees.
19. Shipping charges are listed in each invoice.
20. Client may request that service charges be listed separately.
21. No.
22. Titles are entered on the invoice alphabetically.
23. Purchase order numbers are included on the invoice.
24. Multiple copies of invoices provided (no limit).
25. Response unclear.
26. Prepayment options and terms are available and the firm may discount the invoice between 5% to 10%.
27. Will supply quotations for libraries interested in changing dealers or consolidating direct subscriptions.
28. Asks that libraries wishing to transfer orders to the firm first cancel with their present suppliers.

BOTSWANA

The Educational Book Service (Pty) Ltd.
P/Bag BR 42
Gaborone, Botswana

Telephone number: (267) (31) 300460
Fax number: (267) (31) 300462
Cable address: PLOT 10041, GABORONE

1. Independent company established in 1990.

2. No.
3. Does business in Zambia and Botswana only.
4. No.
5. Representatives actively participate in library association meetings in their country and/or area of the country they represent.
6. Provides serials and monographs from countries worldwide.
7a. Types of materials handled:
    Periodicals
    Monographic standing orders
    CD-ROM
    Back issues
    Government publications
    Loose-leaf services
    Replacements
    Yearbooks/annuals (clients may request every second or third year)
    Serials on videocassette
    Serials with variant publishing
7b. Books (monographic firm orders).
8. Will communicate with back issue dealers when supplying back issues for a client.
9. No response.
10. Journal consolidation is standard practice.
11. Computerized services offered:
    Up-dates on clients' orders
12-
14. No.
15. Client will deal with one individual assigned to the account.
16. Will report back to the library on titles it cannot supply. Time of reporting will vary.
17. Rush orders accepted.
18. Service fee charged is a standard percentage.
19- Service/handling charges are included
20. in the price and will not be listed separately upon client request.
21. Pays all shipping charges.
22. Titles entered on the invoice in varied formats.

23. No.
24. Multiple copies of invoices supplied (no limit).
25-
26. No.
27. Will provide quotations for libraries interested in changing vendors or consolidating direct subscriptions.
28. Will assist, if required, libraries who wish to transfer orders to this company.

BRAZIL

Susan Bach Ltda.
Rua Visconde de Caravelas, 17
22271 Rio de Janeiro, Brazil

Telephone numbers: (55) (21) 226-3590
                      (55) (21) 537-2512
Fax number: (55) (21) 246-6940

1. Independent company owned by three partners established in the 1950s.
2. Other offices:

    Susan Bach Ltda.
    Rua Icana 424
    01457 Sao Paulo, Brazil
       Telephone number: (55) (11) 211-2983
       Fax number: (55) (11) 815-4474
3. No.
4. Company maintains memberships in library associations (none were specified).
5. Representatives will eventually actively participate in library association meetings.
6. Provides serials and monographs only from Brazil.

7a. Types of materials handled:
   Periodicals
   Monographic standing orders
   Back issues
   Government publications
   Loose-leaf services
   Sets
   Replacements
   Yearbooks/annuals (client may request
      every second or third year)
   Serials with variant publishing
   Rare books
7b. Books (monographic firm orders and back
   orders).
8. Back issues: Company does its own
   searching and locating of back issues
   that they do not have in stock. It
   usually has back issues of important
   titles. "In Brazil we are possibly the
   best in locating back issues."
9. Services provided:
   Automatic renewal til forbid
   New order reports
   Claim reports
   Out-of-print searching
10. Journal consolidation is standard
   practice.
11. Computerized services: Firm is in the
   process of acquiring a system.
12. Not yet.
13. No interfaces yet.
14. Issues a monthly or bimonthly newsletter
   and special catalogs every three to
   four months. Information includes: title,
   place of publication, editor, frequency,
   format, prices, description of subjects,
   and numbers published, etc.
15. All phone calls and correspondence pass
   through the manager and co-owner who then
   answer it or assign it to the appropriate
   person.
16. Will report back to the library on titles
   it cannot supply. Because publications
   are very irregular in Brazil, the firm
   keeps trying to find the information and
   informing the client. When in doubt, the

firm sends quotes. It keeps orders open except when instructed to do otherwise.
17. Rush orders accepted with a higher postage charge assessed due to airmail rates.
18. No service charge per se. Items are priced according to cost, difficulty in obtaining, and discount given by the suppliers and publishers.
19- Postage is listed separately on the
20. invoices. The company notes that postal tariffs are now very high.
21. No.
22. Titles are listed on the invoice by order number or alphabetized as requested by the client.
23. Purchase order numbers provided on invoices.
24. Multiple copies of invoices supplied.
25. Invoices not yet available via computer tape or other electronic means.
26. Prepayment options and terms available. Specific terms depend upon negotiations with clients.
27. Will provide quotations for libraries interested in consolidating direct subscriptions or changing vendors.
28. If a library is changing vendors, Bach asks the library to cancel with its suppliers.

Libris-EBSCO Ltda.
Av. Rio Branco, 109 GR 703
20.054-Rio de Janeiro, RJ/Brazil

Telephone number: (55) (21) 252-5787
Fax number: (55) (21) 252-1421
For more information see the EBSCO Subscription Services, Inc. listing under UNITED STATES.

Faxon Brasil
Av. Paulista 1499
Conj. 701
01311 Sao Paulo SP, Brazil

Telephone number: (55) (11) 285-5416
Fax number: (55) (11) 283-0747
For more information see The Faxon Company,
Inc. listing under UNITED STATES.

BULGARIA

Martinus Nijhoff Eastern Europe
30 II Yanko Zabunov Street
1504 Sofia, Bulgaria

Telephone number: (359) (2) 431-236
Fax number: (359) (2) 464-164
For more information see Martinus Nijhoff
International B.v. listing under
The Netherlands.

CANADA

Brodart Ltd.
109 Roy Boulevard
Braneida Industrial Park
Brantford, Ontario N3T 5N3, Canada

For more information see the Brodart Company
listing under UNITED STATES.

CANEBSCO Subscription Services, Ltd.
70 McGriskin Road
Scarborough, Ontario M1S 4S5, Canada

Services all Canada except Quebec.
Telephone number: (1) (416) 297-8282
Fax number: (1) (416) 297-4848
Toll-free number: 1-800-387-5241
For more information see the EBSCO
Subscription Services, Inc. listing under
UNITED STATES.

Faxon Canada, Ltd.
P. O. Box 2382
London, Ontario N6A 5A7, Canada

Telephone number: (1) (529) 472-1005
Fax number: (1) (519) 472-1072
Telex number: 064-5666
For more information see The Faxon Company,
Inc. listing under UNITED STATES.

International Press Publications Inc.
Box 3185 Station D
Willowdale, Ontario M2R 3G6, Canada

United States address:
     International Press Publications Inc.
     P.O. Box 1064
     Amherst, NY 14226-1064
Telephone number: (1) (416) 946-9588
Fax number: (1) (416) 946-9590

1. Independent company established on
    October 1976.
2. Has affiliated offices but all
    correspondence and orders only are to go
    to the above two addresses.
3. No.

4. Maintains memberships in but does not attend meetings of the:
   American Library Association
   Canadian Library Association
5. No.
6. Provides serials and monographs from countries worldwide with emphasis on publications from Canada, United States, United Kingdom, India, China, and Hong Kong.
7a. Types of materials handled:
   Periodicals
   Monographic standing orders
   CD-ROM
   Back issues
   Government publications
   Loose-leaf services
   Sets
   Microforms
   Replacements
   Yearbooks/annuals (client may request every second or third year)
   Memberships
   Serials on videocassette
   Serials with variant publishing
   Trade/business directories
   Dictionaries, travel guides
7b. Books (monographic firm orders).
8. Carries/procures/arranges back issues if available with the publishers or tries to get them from back issue dealers, if only available from back issue dealers.
9. Services provided:
   Automatic renewal til forbid
   New order reports
   Claim reports
   Out-of-print searching
   Blanket orders
10. Journal consolidation: "We have different ways of supplying and that depends mostly on our clients' convenience and requirement. Multiple copies of the same journal to the same address, in many cases, [are] collected at our end and shipped in one consignment. Journals are either shipped by post/mail or by UPS

etc. Books/yearbooks/annuals/almanacs/
directories are stocked by us."
11. Computerized services:
    Computerized invoices
    Statements of account
    Status reports
12-
13. No.
14. Issues catalogs that give title, year,
    price, publisher, frequency etc.
15. Clients will deal with one customer
    service representative for the most part.
16. Will report back to the library on titles
    it cannot supply. It keeps on trying to
    provide until all possibilities are
    exhausted and then sends final status
    report.
17. Rush orders accepted at no extra charge.
18- No service charges generally, but if
20. there are any service charges they will
    be listed separately on the invoice.
21. No.
22- Titles appear on invoice according to
23. purchase order number.
24. Will supply multiple copies of invoices
    (no limit).
25. Invoices can be generated on computer
    tape or transferred by other electronic
    means.
26. Prepayment options and terms available.
27. Will provide quotations for libraries
    interested in consolidating direct
    subscriptions or changing vendors.
28. Will assist libraries who wish to
    transfer orders to International Press
    Publications Inc.

Troyka Ltd.
799 College Street
Toronto, Ontario M6G 1C7, Canada

Telephone number: (1) (416) 535-6693
Fax number: (1) (416) 535-3265

1. Independent firm established in 1954.
2-
5. No.
6. Provides serials and monographs from the Commonwealth of Independent States.
7a. Types of materials handled:
    Periodicals
    Serials with variant publishing
7b. Books (monographic firm orders).
8. No.
9. Services provided:
    Automatic renewal til forbid
    New order reports
    Claim reports
10. No.
11. None.
12-
13. No.
14. Issues a book catalog twice or three times a year. Also issues information regarding periodicals.
15. Client will deal with one customer service representative.
16. Will report back to the library on titles it cannot supply.
17. Rush orders accepted at no extra charge.
18. Service fee is charged only on special book orders and is a flat fee.
19- Service/handling charges are listed
20. separately on the invoice.
21. Infrequently pays all or part of the shipping charges.
22. Titles are entered on the invoice in no particular order, unless computerized when titles appear in alphabetical order.
23. Purchase order numbers are provided on the invoice.
24. Multiple copies of invoices supplied (limit three).

25-
27. No.
28. Libraries wishing to transfer orders to this firm must first cancel with their present suppliers.

CANADA - QUEBEC

Les Services d'abonnement CANEBSCO LTEE
Six Boul. Desaulniers, Suite 308
St. Lambert, Quebec J4P IL3, Canada

Telephone number: (1) (514) 672-5878
Fax number: (1) (514) 672-1232
Toll-free number: 1-800-861-7322
For more information see the EBSCO
Subscription Services, Inc. listing
under UNITED STATES.

CHILE

H. Berenguer L. Publicaciones
Casilla 16598
Correo 9
Santiago, Chile

Telephone number: (56) (2) 2317145
Fax number: (56) (2) 2319108
Toll-free number: 465517

1. Independent company established in 1968.
2-
3. No.
4. Maintains memberships in and is regularly represented at the meetings of:
    SALALM
    Camara Chilena del Libro

5. Representatives actively participate in the meetings of the Camara Chilena del Libro in Santiago.
6. Provides serials and monographs from Chile.
7a. Types of materials handled:
    Periodicals
    Monographic standing orders
    Back issues
    Government publications
    Loose-leaf services
    Microforms
    Replacements
    Yearbooks/annuals (client may request every second or third year)
    Memberships
    Serials on videocassette
    Serials with variant publishing
7b. Books (monographic firm orders).
8. Depending upon the material, the firm will communicate with back issue dealers when supplying back issues for a client.
9. Services provided:
    Automatic renewal til forbid
    New order reports
    Claim reports
    Out-of-print searching
    Bibliographies
10. Journal consolidation available on demand at no additional service charge.
11. None.
12. No.
13. Presently interface with library automation systems is not possible, but this could change during the course of the year (1992).
14. Issues periodic bibliographic bulletins.
15. Clients will be assigned one customer service representative.
16. Will report back to the library within six months on titles that it cannot supply.
17. Rush orders accepted with no extra charge.
18. No service fee.

19. Service/handling charges are included in the price on the invoice.
20. Clients may ask that service/handling charges be listed separately.
21. The company pays all shipping charges.
22. Titles on blanket order are listed alphabetically on invoice; separate orders are listed by order number.
23. Purchase order numbers included on the invoice.
24. Supplies original invoice and five copies.
25. No.
26. Prepayment options and terms available.
27. Will provide quotations for libraries interested in consolidating direct subscriptions or changing vendors.
28. Libraries wishing to transfer orders to Berenguer must cancel with their present suppliers.

Faxon Cono Sur
Padre Mariano 103
Oficina 501
Providencia
Santiago, Chile

Serves only Argentina, Bolivia, Chile, Paraguay, and Uruguay.
Telephone number: (56) (2) 2518753
Fax number: (56) (2) 499739
For more information see The Faxon Company, Inc. listing under UNITED STATES.

Servicio de Extension de Cultura Chilena, SEREC
Portugal 12, Depto. 46
Casilla 58 Correo 22
Santiago, Chile

Telephone number: (56) (2) 2221605
Fax number: (56) (2) 395360

1. Independent company established in 1974.
2-
3. No.
4. Maintains memberships in and attends meetings of:
    SALALM
    Colegio Bibliotecarios de Chile
5. Representatives participate in library association meetings in their country and/or area of the country they represent.
6. Provides serials and monographs from Chile, and occasionally from Peru, Argentina, and Bolivia.
7a. Types of materials handled:
    Periodicals
    Monographic standing orders
    CD-ROM
    Back issues
    Government publications
    Loose-leaf services
    Sets
    Replacements
    Yearbooks/annuals (clients may request every second or third year)
    Serials with variant publishing
7b. Books (monographic firm orders).
8. Will communicate with back issue dealers when supplying back issues for a client.
9. Services provided:
    Automatic renewal til forbid
    New order reports
    Claim reports
    Out-of-print searching
10. Journal consolidation available upon request.

11. Computerized services: It represents Garcia Cambeiro's LATBOOK from Chile to its clients. REDUC, from CIDE, Chile. SEREC Bibliographic Data Base.
12. Database is available to clients in diskettes.
13. Are planning future interfaces with library automation systems.
14. Issues "El Libro Chileno en Venta. NOVEDADES" every two months. Issues an annotated catalog with complete information for each title and authors.
15. Clients will be assigned one customer service representative.
16. Will report back to the library on titles that cannot be supplied. After searching for 60 days they will send a "still searching" notice and after another 60 days it will send unavailability or dispatch information.
17. Rush orders accepted. Only additional cost will be airmail cost.
18-
26. No response.
27. Will provide quotations for libraries interested in consolidating direct orders or changing vendors.
28. Response unclear.

PEOPLE'S REPUBLIC OF CHINA

China National Publishing Industry Trading Corporation
P.O. Box 782
Beijing 100011, People's Republic of China

```
Telephone number:        (86) (1) 421-5031
Fax number:              (86) (1) 421-4540
Telex number:              210215 PITC CN
Cable address:                     CNPITC
```

Office in the United States:
   China Publishing & Trading Inc.,
    (New York)
  56-11 219th Street
  Bayside, NY 11364
 Telephone number: (1) (718) 224-0463
 Fax number: (1) (718) 229-6003

1. Independent company established on October 22, 1980.
2-
4. No.
5. Representatives actively participate in library association meetings in their country and/or area of the country they represent.
6. Provides serials and monographs from the People's Republic of China.
7a. Types of materials handled:
  Periodicals
  Monographic standing orders
  Government publications
  Sets
  Microforms
  Yearbooks/annuals (client may request every second or third year)
  Serials with variant publishing
7b. Books (monographic firm orders).
8. Will communicate with back issue dealers when supplying back issues.

9. Services provided:
      Automatic renewal til forbid
      New order reports
      Claim reports
      Out-of-print searching
      Rebinds paperback books into deluxe
         editions
      Binds magazines
10. Journal consolidation is standard
    practice.
11. Computerized services: Its computers
    will provide the clients with
    information of books, periodicals,
    presses and customers.
12-
13. Not applicable.
14. It provides clients with national
    catalogs of forthcoming books on social
    sciences and natural science, provincial
    catalogs of forthcoming books, and its
    own catalogs for forthcoming books and
    available books. These are issued once or
    twice a month and are free.
15. Clients will have different customer
    service representatives for books and
    journals.
16. Will report back to the library on titles
    that cannot be supplied. It will respond
    according to the time frame determined by
    the client.
17. Rush orders accepted. Added charges:
    There will be a great difference between
    airmail postage and surface shipment
    costs.
18. Service fee:
      Serials: The export prices are the
         same in US$ as those at home in
         RMB, except postage and other
         charges.
      Books: The export prices are twice
         as much as the prices at home
         except postage and packing cost, as
         well as rebinding charge.
19. Invoices will include postage, packing
    cost, and rebinding charge (if
    applicable).

20. A client may ask that service/handling charges be listed separately on the invoice.
21. No.
22. Titles are entered on invoice number by purchase order number or ISBN.
23. Purchase orders will appear on the invoice if requested.
24. Multiple copies of invoices supplied (maximum 3).
25. No.
26. Prepayment options and terms: There is some discount for prepayment for expensive books.
27. Will provide quotations for libraries interested in consolidating direct subscriptions or changing vendors.
28. Libraries who wish to transfer orders to this company must cancel with their present suppliers.

REPUBLIC OF CHINA

Chinese Materials Center
P.O. Box 22048
Taipei 10099, Taiwan, Republic of China

Telephone number: (886) (2) 363-8032
Fax number: (886) (2) 366-0806

1. Independent company established in 1964.
2-
3. No.
4. Maintains membership in:
       CEAL
       Association of Asian Studies, Inc.
5. No.
6. Provides serials and monographs from Taiwan, People's Republic of China, and Hong Kong.

7a. Types of materials handled:
        Periodicals
        Monographic standing orders
        Back issues
        Government publications
        Sets
        Microforms
        Replacements
        Yearbooks/annuals (client may request
           every second or third year)
        Serials with variant publishing
7b. Books (monographic firm orders) handled
    by its Book Section.
8.   No.
9.   Services provided:
        Automatic renewal til forbid
        New order reports
        Claim reports
        Out-of-print searching
        Yearly confirmation lists
        Periodic reports of ceased
           publications, new periodicals,
           changes in names, publication
           schedule, etc.
10. It handles five types of delivery:
        Direct mail by publisher
        Mailed by CMC
        Airmail orders by publisher or CMC
        Non-Taiwan periodicals
        Irregularly published, CMC mailed
           publications
11. Computerized services are now being
    developed.
12-
13. No.
14. Issues periodical notifications by direct
    letter or on general booklists. Title,
    descriptions, publication schedule, and
    price information included.
15. Response unclear.
16. Will report back to the library on titles
    that cannot be supplied usually within
    two or three months.
17. Rush orders accepted at no added charge.
18. Service fee is charged.

19. Service charge is included in postage and handling fee.
20. Client may ask for service charges to be listed separately.
21. No.
22. Titles entered on invoice: First individual invoices per five types of periodical service; then by accession of order, where pricing is readily available. Where it is not, separate invoices are issued as soon as info is available. Customer order numbers cited.
23. Purchase order numbers provided on the invoice.
24. Will supply up to three copies of the invoice.
25. Company is preparing to issue invoices on computer tape and other electronic means.
26. All subscription services are prepaid upon receipt of invoice. Irregular publications are invoiced when mailed and invoices are due upon receipt of invoice, not materials.
27. Will provide quotations for libraries interested in consolidating direct orders or changing vendors.
28. Libraries wishing to transfer orders to the firm must cancel with their present suppliers.

ESS Overseas, Inc.
P.O. Box 87-713
Taipei, Taiwan, Republic of China

Serves only Taiwan, Indonesia, Malaysia, the Philippines, and Singapore.
Telephone number: (886) (2) 746-8760
Fax number: (886) (2) 761-0764
For more information see the EBSCO Subscription Services, Inc. listing under UNITED STATES.

Faxon Taiwan
9F-6, No. 40 Chang-Chuen Road
Taipei, Taiwan, Republic of China

Telephone number: (886) (2) 521-5394
Fax number: (886) (2) 565-1153
For more information see The Faxon Company,
Inc. listing under UNITED STATES.

COLOMBIA

Faxon Colombia
Carrera 13, No. 48-47
Oficina #903
Bogota, Colombia

Telephone number: (57) (1) 232-4524
Fax number: (57) (1) 285-1609
For more information see The Faxon Company,
Inc. listing under UNITED STATES.

CYPRUS

MAM
P.O. Box 1722
Nicosia, Cyprus

Telephone number: (357) (2) 472744
Fax number: (357) (2) 465411

1.   Independent firm established in 1965.
2-
3.   No.
4.   Firm cooperates with the Cyprus
     Association of Professional Librarians
     and distributes their publications.
5.   No response.
6.   Supplies materials from countries

worldwide but specializes in all types of
publications on Cyprus and in all
publications by Cypriots.
7a. Types of materials provided:
     Periodicals
     Monographic standing orders
     Back issues
     Government publications
     Loose-leaf services
     Sets
     Yearbooks/annuals (client may request
        every second or third year)
     Memberships
     Serials with variant publishing
7b. Books (monographic firm orders).
8. Also acts as a back issue dealer.
9. Services provided:
     Automatic renewal til forbid
     New order reports
     Claim reports
     Out-of-print searching
10. Stocks all journals published in Cyprus
    and will send these to clients without
    any additional charge.
11. Computerized services: Will offer these
    in the very near future.
12. Database not yet available to clients.
13. Does not interface with any library
    automation systems at the moment.
14. Planning to issue a monthly
    bibliographical listing of new Cyprus and
    Cyprological publications.
15. No response.
16. Will report back to libraries on titles
    that it cannot supply.
17. Rush orders are accepted at no added
    charge.
18-
19. No service fee/handling fee.
20. Not applicable.
21. Firm pays all shipping charges.
22- Titles appear on invoice by purchase
23. order number.
24. Multiple copies of invoices are supplied
    upon request.
25. Is presently in the planning stages to

provide invoices generated on computer tape.
26. Prepayment options and terms are sometimes offered. Contact the firm directly.
27. Will provide quotations for libraries interested in consolidating direct orders or changing vendors.
28. The firm will give full assistance to the library wishing to transfer order to it.

CZECHOSLOVAKIA

Artia Foreign Trade Company Ltd.
Ve Smeckach 30
P.O.B. 790
111 27 Praha 1, Czechoslovakia

Telephone number: (42) (2) 2137111
Fax number: (42) (2) 2137555
Telex number: 121066 ARTAC

1. Independent company established in 1953.
2-
5. No.
6. Provides materials from Czechoslovakia only.
7a. Types of materials handled:
    Periodicals
    Monographic standing orders
    Back issues
    Government publications
    Sets
    Yearbooks/annuals (client may request every second or third year)
7b. Books (monographic firm orders).
8. Communicates with back issue dealers when supplying back issues for a client.

9. Services provided:
   Automatic renewal til forbid
   New order reports
   Claim reports
   Out-of-print searching
10-
13. No response.
14. Issues annual price lists and a quarterly catalog of books published by Czechoslovak publishing houses.
15. Clients will deal with different customer service representatives depending on the nature of the inquiry.
16. Will report back to the library within six months on titles it cannot supply.
17. Rush orders accepted at no extra charge.
18. No service fee charged.
19- Service/handling charges are included in
20. the price and cannot be listed separately on the invoice.
21. No.
22- Titles are entered on the invoice by
23. purchase order number.
24. Multiple copies of invoices can be supplied (no limit).
25. No.
26. Prepayment options and terms are available. Contact the company directly for details.
27. Will provide quotations for libraries interested in consolidating direct orders or changing suppliers.
28. Libraries must cancel with present suppliers before transferring orders to this company.

DENMARK

Munksgaard
P.O. Box 2148
DK-1016 Copenhagen K, Denmark

Telephone number: (45) (3) 3128570
Fax number: (45) (3) 3129387
Telex number: 19431 DK MUNKS

1. Company is associated with
    B. H. Blackwell, Oxford, England, and was
    established in 1917.
2. No response.
3-
5. No.
6. Provides materials from countries
    worldwide.
7a. Types of materials handled:
        Periodicals
        Monographic standing orders
        CD-ROM
        Back issues
        Government publications
        Loose-leaf services
        Sets
        Replacements
        Yearbooks/annuals
        Serials with variant publishing
7b. Books (monographic firm orders).
8. Will communicate with back issue dealers
    when supplyng back issues for a client.
9. Services provided:
        Automatic renewal til forbid
        New order reports
        Claim reports
        Out-of-print searching
10. Journal consolidation available upon
    request at an additional charge.
11. Computerized services:
        Invoicing according to client
            specification
        Subscription lists
12. Its database is not available to clients
    at the moment.

13. Computer interfaces: Munksgaard is planning to associate with a Danish library automated system called DTCS.
14. Issues newsletters and catalogs on an irregular basis.
15. Clients will deal with different individuals according to the nature of the inquiry.
16. Will report back to the library on titles it cannot supply after having tried every possibility.
17. No, but all orders are executed immediately.
18. Service fee is charged only if the materials are sent from the Munksgaard address.
19- If a service/handling fee is charged
20. it is listed separately on the invoice.
21. No.
22. Titles are listed alphabetically on the invoice.
23. Purchase order numbers are provided on the invoice.
24. Multiple copies of invoices supplied (no limit).
25. Not at the moment.
26. No, usually does not require prepayment from libraries.
27. Will provide quotations for libraries interested in changing dealers or consolidating direct subscriptions.
28. If a library transfers its orders to this company, Munksgaard will specifically inform the publisher upon renewal that the subscription is now being handled by Munksgaard.

Nordic Subscription Service
ROKHOJ6
DK 8520 Lystrup, Denmark

Telephone number: (010) (45) (8) 6223188
For more information see the Nordic
Subscription Service U.K. Ltd. listing under
UNITED KINGDOM.

DOMINICAN REPUBLIC

Editora Taller, C. Por A.
Isabel la Catolica 260 y 309
Santo Domingo, Republica Dominicana

Mailing address in U.S.A.:
Editora Taller
EPS A421 Box 02-5256
2898 NW 79th Avenue
Miami, FL 33122
Telephone number: (809) 682-9369
Fax number: (809) 689-7259

1. Independent firm established in 1970.
2. Has a postal box in Miami, Florida, USA.
3. No.
4. Maintains membership in and is regularly
   represented at meetings of SALALM.
5. Representatives actively participate in
   library association meetings in their
   country and/or area of the country they
   represent.
6. Provides materials from the Dominican
   Republic.
7a. Types of materials handled:
    Periodicals
    Monographic standing orders
    Back issues
    Government publications
    Replacements
    Yearbooks/annuals
    Memberships

7a. Types pf materials handled (continued):
       Serials on videocassette
       Dominican newspapers
7b. Dominican books (monographic firm
    orders).
8. Will communicate with back issue dealers
    when supplying back issues for a client.
9. Services provided:
       Automatic renewal til forbid
       Claim reports
10. Journal consolidation only available upon
    request from the library.
11. Computerized services: Periodical list.
12. Database is not yet available to clients.
13. Would like to be able in the future to
    interface with library automation
    systems.
14. Issues a newsletter every three months
    and a catalog which provides
    information on: author, title,
    publication date, edition, cover, size,
    subject, publisher, printing name, and
    price.
15. Client will deal with different customer
    service representatives.
16. Will report back to the library on titles
    that cannot be supplied. Will try to
    obtain the item for one year.
17. Rush orders accepted at no extra charge.
18. No service fee.
19. Service/handling charges are included in
    the price.
20. Response unclear.
21. No.
22- Titles are entered on the invoice by
23. purchase order number.
24. Multiple copies of invoices provided (no
    limit).
25. No response.
26. Response unclear.
27. Will provide quotations for libraries
    interested in consolidating direct
    subscriptions or changing vendors.
28. No response.

al-Arab Bookshop
(Dar al'Arab-Boustany)
28 Faggalah Street
Cairo, Egypt

```
Telephone number: (20) (2) 908025
Fax number:       (20) (2) 771140 (Boustany)
Cable address:    ARABUKSHOP-CAIRO
```

1. Independent company established in 1900.
2-
4. No.
5. Representatives actively participate in library assocation meetings in their country and/or area of the country they represent.
6. Provides materials from the entire Middle East.
7a. Types of materials handled:
   Periodicals
   Government publications
   Yearbooks/annuals
   Serials with variant publishing
   Out-of-print periodicals
   Out-of-print monographs
7b. Books (monographic firm orders).
8. Will communicate with back issue dealers when supplying back issues for a client.
9. Services provided:
   Automatic renewal til forbid
   New order reports
   Claim reports
   Out-of-print searching
10. Journal consolidation available upon demand with no additional charges.
11. Computerized services:
   Correspondence and invoices
12-
13. No response.
14. Issues catalogs every three or four months. Entries include: author, title, publisher, year of publication, etc.

15. Client will deal with different customer service representatives depending on the nature of the inquiry.
16. Will report back to the library on titles it cannot supply.
17. Rush orders accepted at no extra charge.
18. No service fee.
19- Shipping charges listed separately on
20. invoices.
21. No response.
22- Titles listed on invoice by purchase
23. order number.
24-
25. No.
26. Individual (personal) clients must prepay.
27. No response.
28. Will assist libraries who wish to transfer orders to the firm.

FINLAND

Akateeminen Kirjakauppa
The Academic Bookstore
Lehtiryhma Subscription Services
P.O. Box 23
SF-00371 Helsinki, Finland

Telephone number: (358) (0) 121-41
Fax number: (358) (0) 121-4450

1. Part of The Stockmann Group (retail business) established in 1893.
2-
3. No.
4. Maintains memberships in library associations and is regularly represented at these meetings (none specified).
5. Representatives actively participate in library association meetings in their country and/or area of the country they represent.

6. Provides materials from countries worldwide.
7a. Types of materials handled:
Periodicals
Monographic standing orders
CD-ROM
Back issues
Government publications
Loose-leaf services
Microforms
Replacements
Yearbooks/annuals
Memberships
Serials on videocassette
Serials with variant publishing
7b. Books (monographic firm orders) handled by its bookstore.
8. Will communicate with back issue dealers when supplying back issues for a client.
9. Services provided:
Automatic renewal til forbid
New order reports
Claim reports
Out-of-print searching
10. Journal consolidation provided only upon demand and at an additional charge.
11. No computerized services at the moment.
12. There are plans to make its database available to its clients.
13. Possible interfacing with library automation systems is under consideration.
14. Issues various subject catalogs which indicate title, ISSN, frequency, country of publication, price. Also inform clients of new titles.
15. Clients will be assigned one customer service representative.
16. Will report back to the library on unavailability after having tried for one month to obtain material.
17. Rush orders accepted at no added charge.
18. Service charge: Flat fee on domestic subscriptions. Foreign determined in another manner.

19- Service/handling charges: On domestic
20. orders the service/handling charges are
listed separately; on foreign orders they
are included in the price.
21. No.
22. Titles are, in general, listed on the
invoice in alphabetical order. Upon
request, other options are possible.
23. Purchase order numbers are provided on
the invoice.
24. Multiple copies of invoices supplied
(maximum three).
25-
26. No.
27. Will provide quotations for libraries
interested in changing dealers or
consolidating direct subscriptions.
28. Will assist libraries changing suppliers
by advising publishers that orders have
previously come through another agency.

FRANCE

Aux Amateurs de Livres International
62 Avenue de Suffren
75015 Paris, France

Telephone number: (33) (1) 45-67-18-38
Fax number: (33) (1) 45-66-50-70

1. Independent firm established in 1930.
2. No.
3. The company mainly supplies
industrialized countries but will do
business with all countries.
4. Maintains memberships in library
associations. Is present at each American
Library Association convention. Was
present at the Association of College
and Research Libraries convention in
Salt Lake City in April 1992.

5. Its representatives actively participate in library association meetings in their country and/or area of the country they represent.
6. Provides publications originating in French-speaking countries: France, Belgium, Canada, Switzerland, and Africa.
7a. Types of materials handled:
    Periodicals
    Monographic standing orders
    CD-ROM
    Back issues
    Government publications
    Loose-leaf services
    Sets
    Microforms
    Replacements
    Yearbooks/annuals (client may request every second or third year)
    Memberships
    Serials on videocassette
    Serials with variant publishing
7b. Books (monographic firm orders).
8. Back issues: If it cannot find a back issue, the company will contact its correspondents.
9. Services provided:
    Automatic renewal til forbid
    New order reports
    Claim reports
    Out-of-print searching
10. Journal consolidation available upon demand at no additional charge.
11. Computerized services:
    Lists of subscriptions
    Status reports
12. No response.
13. No, at the moment.
14. No.
15. Client will have two main contacts depending upon the nature of the inquiry:
    Invoices or title/subscription information
16. Will report back to the library after two months on titles that cannot be supplied.

17. Rush orders accepted at no additional charge.
18. No service fee except for the publications for which there is no publisher's discount.
19. If there is an additional charge, it is included in the price.
20. A client may ask that the additional charge be listed separately on the invoice.
21. Pays shipping charges.
22- Titles entered on the invoice by purchase
23. order number.
24. Multiple copies of invoices supplied (maximum five).
25. Not at this time.
26. No.
27. Will provide quotations for libraries interested in changing dealers or consolidating direct subscriptions.
28. Library wishing to transfer orders to this firm must first cancel with its present suppliers. The firm will assist the library so that there is no interruption in the supply of periodicals.

C.P.E.D.E.R.F.
10 Avenue Felix Faure
75015 Paris, France

Telephone number: (33) (1) 40.60.06.27
Fax number: (33) (1) 40.60.96.90
Urgent orders Fax: France + 86.59.56.91

1. Independent company established in 1984.
2. No.
3-
5. No response.
6. Provides French-language publications published or distributed in France.

7a. Types of materials handled:
      Periodicals
      Monographic standing orders
      CD-ROM
      Back issues
      Government publications
      Loose-leaf services
      Sets
      Microforms
      Replacements
      Yearbooks/annuals
      Memberships
      Serials on videocassette
      Serials with variant publishing

7b. Books (monographic firm orders).

8. Will communicate with back issue dealers when supplying back issues for a client if the publisher cannot supply them.

9. Services provided:
      All reports requested by the client

10. Journals are sent direct to libraries at no extra charge.

11. Computerized services offered:
      Author and thematic printouts of
          available publications
      Anything the client requests

12-

13. No response.

14. Issues regular newsletters for established clients.

15. Client will deal with one customer service representative.

16. Will report back to the library on titles it cannot supply. Will try to obtain material for a length of time determined by the client library.

17. Rush orders accepted at no added charge.

18. No service fee charged.

19- Service/handling charges are listed

20. separately on the invoice. All book prices are those charged by the French publisher less the firms's rebate for clients.

21. No.

22- Titles are entered on the invoice by

23. purchase order number and title.

24. Multiple copies of invoices provided (no limit).
25. No.
26. No prepayment options and terms. Payment due upon receipt of materials.
27-
28. Response unclear.

La Cauchoiserie
Boite Postal 48
55 bis Avenue Jean Juares
78580 Maule, France

Telephone number: (33) (1) 30-90-62-26
Fax number: (33) (1) 30-90-62-32
For more information see the EBSCO
Subscription Services, Inc. under
UNITED STATES.

Dawson France SA
B.P. 40
91121 Palaiseau Cedex, France

Telephone number: (33) (1) 69-09-01-22
For more information see Dawson Holdings PLC
listing under UNITED KINGDOM.

Faxon France SA
Le Galilee
Rue Pierre Mendes France
Zac du Chemin de Croissy
77200 Torcy, France

Telephone number: (33) (1) 64800893
Fax number: (33) (1) 64620871
For more information see The Faxon Company,
Inc. listing under UNITED STATES.

Librairie Luginbuhl
International Booksellers & Subscription Agency
36, Boulevard de Latour-Maubourg
75007 Paris, France

Telephone number: (33) (1) 45-51-42-58
Fax number: (33) (1) 45-56-07-80

1. Independent firm established January 1, 1977.
2. No other offices.
3. None.
4-
5. No.
6. Provides materials from countries worldwide.
7a. Types of materials handled:
    Periodicals
    Monographic standing orders
    CD-ROM
    Back issues
    Government publications
    Loose-leaf services
    Sets
    Microforms
    Replacements
    Yearbooks/annuals (client may request every second or third year)
    Memberships
    Serials on videocassette
    Serials with variant publishing
7b. Books (monographic firm orders).
8. Will communicate with back issue dealers when supplying back issues for a client.
9. Services provided:
    Automatic renewal til forbid
    New order reports
    Claim reports
    Out-of-print searching
10. No.
11. None.
12. No.
13. Presently interfaces with library automation systems (specific systems not specified).

14. No.
15. Clients will deal with different customer service representatives depending on the nature of the inquiry.
16. Will report back to the library on titles that cannot be supplied. Will try to obtain the title for a maximum of one year.
17. Rush orders accepted with no extra charge.
18. Service fee is a standard percentage.
19- Service/handling charges are listed
20. separately on the invoice.
21. No.
22. Titles are listed alphabetically on the invoice.
23. Purchase orders appear on the invoice.
24. Multiple copies of invoice provided (maximum three).
25. Invoices can be generated on computer tape.
26. No.
27. Will provide quotations for libraries interested in changing dealers or consolidating direct orders.
28. Libraries wishing to transfer orders to this firm must first cancel with their present suppliers.

Societe Internationale de Diffusion et d'Edition, S.I.D.E.
80 Rue des Meuniers
92220 Bagneux, France

Telephone number: (33) (1) 45-36-92-22
Fax number: (33) (1) 45-36-91-92
Telex number: 632857

1. Independent firm established in 1980.
2. No offices in other countries.
3. Does no business with Africa.
4-
5. No.

6. Provides only French serials and
   monographs.
7a. Types of meterials handled:
        Periodicals
        Monographic standing orders
        CD-ROM
        Back issues
        Government publications
        Loose-leaf publications
        Sets
        Microforms
        Replacements
        Yearbooks/annuals (client may request
            every second or third year)
        Memberships
        Serials on videocassette
        Serials with variant publishing
7b. Books (monographic firm orders).
8. Will communicate with back issue dealers
   when supplying back issues for a client.
9. Services provided:
        Automatic renewal til forbid
        New order reports
        Claim reports
10. No.
11. Computerized services:
        Subscription orders to the publishers
        Claim processing
        Invoicing
        Reminders for subscription renewals
12-
14. No.
15. Client will deal with different
    individuals depending on the nature of
    the inquiry.
16. Will report back to the library within
    three weeks on titles it cannot supply.
17. Rush orders accepted at no added charge.
18. Service fee is a percentage of its net
    cost price.
19- Service and freight charges are
20. invoiced separately.
21. No.
22- Titles are entered on the invoice by
23. purchase order number.

67

24. Multiple copies of invoices supplied (limit five).
25. Invoices are generated on its computer system.
26. Prepayment is required from "not secure countries." Normal credit terms are 30 days after month of invoice.
27. Will provide quotations for libraries interested in changing dealers or in consolidating direct subscriptions.
28. Libraries wishing to transfer orders to the firm must first inform the present supplier of the cancellation of their orders from such date and then place the new orders with S.I.D.E. for renewal.

Swets Europeriodiques S.A.
Parc d'Activites de Pissaloup
B.P. 104
78191 Trappes Cedex, France

Telephone number: (33) (1) 30-62-93-86
For more information see the Swets
Subscription Service listing under
THE NETHERLANDS.

Jean Touzot Libraire-Editeur
38 Rue Saint Sulpice
75278 Paris Cedex 06, France

Telephone number: (33) (1) 43-26-03-88
Fax number: (33) (1) 46-34-77-11

1. Independent firm established in 1920.
2. No.
3. No response.
4. The firm is an exhibitor at the two annual meetings of the American Library Association.
5. No response.

6. Provides materials from France and French language countries such as Belgium, Switzerland, Canada, and all African countries. Provides French books from all countries.
7a. Types of materials handled:
    Periodicals
    Monographic standing orders
    Back issues
    Government publications
    Sets
    Microforms
    Replacements
    Yearbooks/annuals
    Serials with variant publishing
    Antiquariat
7b. Books (monographic firm orders).
8. No response.
9. Services provided:
    Claim reports
    Out-of-print searching
10. Journal consolidation is standard practice at no extra charge.
11. Computerized services offered:
    Bibliographic offer cards are sent twice a month according to the subjects selected by its customers. These offer cards are also available on floppy disk.
    Annual reports for budget and subject selection are available on demand from the libraries for approval plans.
12. Database is not yet available to its clients.
13. Agency is planning interfaces with library automation systems.
14. Slips of new books offered are published twice a month. Complete bibliographic information is provided with a subject commentary on each form.
15. Customer service representatives: There is one assigned manager for each department: approval plans, firm orders, continuation orders, and periodicals.

16. Will report on all claims. All out-of-print or unavailable books are recorded; before one year they are automatically sent or offered after.
17. Rush orders accepted at no extra charge.
18. No service charge.
19- Shipping charges are listed separately
20. on invoices for all materials, except for periodical subscriptions.
21. No.
22- Titles are entered on the invoice by
23. purchase order number.
24. Multiple copies of invoices provided (no maximum).
25. Not yet.
26. No.
27. No response.
28. Libraries transferring orders to this company must cancel with their present suppliers.

GAMBIA

Jim Heffernan
P.O. Box 203
Banjul, The Gambia, West Africa

Telephone number: (220) 28179
                  (city code not required)
Cable address: BOOKSHOP

1. Independent firm established in 1971.
2-
4. No.
5. Representatives actively participate in library association meetings in their country and/or area of the country they represent.
6. Provides materials from Gambia only.

7a. Types of materials handled:
    Periodicals
    Monographic standing orders
    Government publications
    Replacements
    Yearbooks/annuals
    Serials with variant publishing
7b. Books (monographic firm orders).
8. Will communicate with back issue dealers
    when supplying back issues for a client.
9. Services provided:
    Automatic renewal til forbid
    New order reports
    Claim reports
    Out-of-print searching
10. Journal consolidation available only upon
    demand. Only charge is the standard
    postage charge.
11. None as yet.
12. When the firm's computer system is
    operational it will issue quarterly list
    of titles available.
13-
14. No.
15. Client will deal with one individual
    assigned to its account.
16. Will report back to the library on titles
    it cannot supply and will search until
    requested to discontinue.
17. Rush orders accepted at no extra charge.
18. Service fee charged which is a standard
    percentage.
19- Service/handling charges are included
20. in the price but may be shown separately
    when requested.
21. No.
22- Titles are entered on the invoice by
23. purchase order number.
24. Multiple copies of invoices provided
    (maximum three).
25-
26. No.
27. Will provide quotations for libraries
    interested in changing dealers or
    consolidating direct subscriptions.

28. Libraries wishing to transfer orders to this firm must cancel with their present suppliers.

FEDERAL REPUBLIC OF GERMANY

B. H. Blackwell Ltd.
Slomanhaus
Baumwall 3
D-2000 Hamburg 11, Germany

Telephone number: (49) (40) 372655
For more information see the
B. H. Blackwell Ltd. listing under
UNITED KINGDOM.

Broude Europa
Postfach 1327
D-8470 Nabburg, Germany

Telephone number: (9606) 7252
For more information see Broude Brothers Ltd.
listing under UNITED STATES.

EBSCO Subscription Services - Germany
Klenzestrasse 55, RGB
W-8000 Muenchen 5, Germany

Telephone number: (49) (89) 202-1941
Fax number: (49) (89) 202-1969
For information see EBSCO Subscription
Services, Inc. listing under UNITED STATES.

Otto Harrassowitz
Taunusstrasse 5
P.O. Box 2929
D-6200 Wiesbaden, Germany

```
Telephone number:         (49) (6121) 611-5300
Toll-free/North America number:
                          1-800-348-6886
Fax number:        (49) (6121) 611-530-560
Telex number:                     4186135
E-mail:          100021.2500@COMPUSERVE.COM
```

1. Independent firm established in 1872.
2. United States office address:

> Otto Harrassowitz
> c/o Library Consultants
> P.O. Box 10
> Columbia, MD 21045-0010
>
> Telephone number: (410) 964-3011
> Toll-free US/Canada: 1-800-348-6886
> Fax number: 410-964-3013
> E-mail: 70571.1214@COMPUSERVE.COM

3. No.
4. Maintains memberships in and is regularly
    represented at the meetings of the:
    ALA: American Library Association
    CLA: Canadian Library Association
    ALIA: Australian Library
        Information Association
    Deutscher Bibliothekerstag
    ASA: Association of Subscription
        Agents
    UKSG: United Kingdom Serials Group
    Regularly represented at the meetings of
    the:
    Medical Library Association
    Music Library Association
    ARLIS: Art Library Association
    North American Serials Interest Group
    SISAC: Serials Industry Systems
        Advisory Committee
    WESS: Western European Studies Section
        (ALA)
    NAG: National Acquisitions Group (U.K.)

5. Representatives actively participate in library association meetings in their country and/or area of the country they represent.
6. Provides materials primarily from all European countries. It does have a special department which provides Asian Studies materials on a worldwide basis.
7a. Types of materials provided:
    Periodicals
    Monographic standing orders
    CD-ROM
    Back issues
    Government publications
    Loose-leaf services
    Sets
    Microforms
    Replacements
    Yearbooks/annuals (client may request every second or third year)
    Memberships
    Serials on videocassette
    Serials with variant publishing
    Music scores
7b. Books (monographic firm orders).
8. Will communicate with back issue dealers when supplying back issues for a client, but would use other contacts first.
9. Services provided:
    Automatic renewal til forbid
    New order reports
    Claim reports
    Out-of-print searching
    Approval plans
    New journal announcements
10. Journal consolidation:
    a. By contracts, for some libraries, Harrassowitz receives all journal issues and reships in consolidated shipments to the library. This is a special service provided only through specific arrangements and contracts between the library and Harrassowitz.

b. For the major German scientific/technical/medical publishers, Harrassowitz provides consolidated reshipment in order to expedite the journal issues to <u>all</u> libraries. All claiming and receipt controls are maintained by Harrassowitz for these publications at no extra cost to the libraries.

c. From time to time, a publisher in Europe may be having difficulties with its distribution procedures. When it is obvious that there are problems in this regard, in order to ensure delivery to Harrassowitz's customers, Harrassowitz will arrange for the journal issues to be mailed by the publisher to Harrassowitz and it then reships the issue to the library. If the distribution procedures should improve for the publisher involved, Harrassowitz will change these procedures as the situation warrants.

11. Computerized services:

a. **Periodicals Price Comparison (PPC):** A three-year price comparison for journal subscriptions sorted alphabetically, by country of origin, LC subject classification, publisher, ISSN, price in rank order, language of publication, fund accounting codes, or any combination of these sort of criteria.

b. **Subscriptions on Order List (SOOL) :** Listings of the complete library order data available in sorts by country of origin, LC subject classification, publisher, fund accounting codes, or alphabetically by title.

c. **Billing Status Report (BSR):**
This report identifies what titles
have not yet been billed at any
particular point in time during the
subscription year. This may help with
budget analysis during the last few
months of the fiscal year when funds
are critical.

d. **Harrassowitz Service Charge Analysis
(HASCHA):** This report documents the
total amount of periodicals
expenditures in two categories: those
with 0% service charge and those with
a service charge. The total amount
billed for the service charge is
documented for the most recent two
years.

e. **Fund Accounting Reports (FUAR):**
If the library has provided fund
information on their orders, these
reports can be issued at regular
intervals, annually, semiannually, or
quarterly.

f. **Subject Bibliographies (SUB):**
Listings of journal titles in specific
LC subject classifications and/or from
specific countries are available for
selection or collection development
analysis.

g. **Detailed Invoice Analysis (DINA):**
If an analysis for the service charge
for each title on an invoice is
required, this report can be provided
to accompany each invoice.

h. **Invoicing Data for Spreadsheet
Analysis:** The invoicing data can be
supplied on floppy disk in d-Base for
conversion to most spreadsheet
software applications.

i. **Fiscal Analysis Report (FAR):**
This is a special report for
continuation standing orders. The
report identifies the total billing
information for all of the standing
order titles during the specified
twelve-month period.

j. **Current Activity Report (CAR):**
This is a special report for
continuation standing order titles.
This documents the most recent volumes
supplied on active standing orders.
This report is most useful when a
library is reviewing its standing
order records for possible necessary
claims.

k. **Continuations on Order List (COOL):**
Listings of the complete library order
data available in sorts by country of
origin, LC subject classification,
publisher, fund, accounting codes, or
alphabetically by title.

12. The database is not yet online.

13. Interfaces are currently active for CARL,
GEAC, INNOVACQ, and NOTIS systems. Also,
Harrassowitz invoicing data have been
provided in magnetic tape format for
interfacing with automated systems since
1980. This is a "Harrassowitz Format" and
some library systems have written load
programs to use this format.

14. Newsletters and service updates are
issued on an irregular basis, whenever
there are important items to discuss or
announcements to be made. Special
catalogs are issued such as the
scientific/technical/medical (STM) titles
supplied with a 0% service charge
catalog. Harrassowitz does not issue a
complete catalog of titles available.
Specific information on titles is
provided on demand through the toll-free
telephone, E-mail, or fax. The company
also provides a New Title Announcement
Service.

15. Clients will deal with different customer
service representatives depending on the
nature of the inquiry.

16. Will report back to the library on titles
it cannot supply. Harrassowitz tries to
obtain materials until all possibilities
are exhausted (only after registered
letters are returned or all other means

are exhausted). There is no fixed time frame.

17. Rush orders accepted at no extra charge.
18. Service fee depends upon the mix of titles. Harrassowitz serves approximately 2,500 of the leading STM journals at 0% service charge. The average overall service charge for a general mix of titles is usually around 1%. The maximum service charge on any one title is 3.85%. Through special early payment arrangements, it is possible to achieve discounts of up to 5%.
19- Service/handling charges are usually
20. listed separately on the invoice, but Harrassowitz can provide invoicing that includes the service charge in each title.
21. Shipping charges: Publisher's shipping charges for periodicals are included in the subscription price. Harrassowitz pays for shipping charges from the publisher to Harrassowitz when materials are reshipped by Harrassowitz, such as continuation standing order titles. For backfiles, the publisher's postage charges are billed to the library, except in cases where special prepayment arrangements have been established.
22. Titles are usually alphabetized on the invoice, but it is possible to make other arrangements if this is required.
23. Purchase order numbers provided on invoices.
24. Multiple copies of invoices supplied (maximum six).
25. Invoices can be generated on computer tape or transferred by other electronic means.
26. Prepayment options and terms are available. Contact the firm for details.
27. Will provide a quotation based on the library's present list for a library wishing to change agents or consolidate direct orders.

28. Harrassowitz prefers that the library process its own cancellation with any previous source. The contract for the previous service is between the library and their agent(s), and any change in that arrangement should be a communication from the library to the respective agent(s). Harrassowitz can prepare the letters of cancellation for the library, on library letterhead, and supply the postage-paid envelopes and letters to the library for the appropriate signature and mailing to the respective agents. Harrassowitz feels very strongly that the actual communication should come from the library.

For all transfers, the Harrassowitz order to the publisher clearly states it is a transfer and identifies the previous source (if known).

Kubon & Sagner
Buchexport - Buchimport GmbH
P.O. Box 34 01 08
D-8000 Munich 34, Germany

Telephone number: (49) (89) 54 218-0
Fax number: (49) (89) 54 218 218
Telex number: 5 217 711 kusa d
Cable address: buchsagner muenchen

1. Independent company established in 1947.
2. No.
3. No exceptions.
4. No.
5. Firm has constant participation in German library association meetings as well as special Slavic librarians' meetings in Germany. Occasional participation in AAASS annual meetings and constant participation in ICSEES conferences every fifth year. Firm actively participates in

book fairs in the following cities: Frankfurt am Main, Leipzig, Moscow, Warsaw, Belgrade, Ljubljana, and Sofia.

6. Provides materials from all Eastern and Southeastern European countries except Greece, Germany, and Austria.

7a. Types of materials handled:
    Periodicals
    Monographic standing orders
    Back issues
    Government publications
    Loose-leaf services
    Sets
    Replacements
    Yearbook/annuals
    Serials with variant publishing

7b. Books (monographic firm orders).

8. Firm has its own sources for back issues.

9. Services provided:
    Automatic renewal til forbid
    New order reports
    Claim reports
    Out-of-print searching
    Blanket orders
    Dealer selection orders
    Approval plans

10. Journal consolidation is not being done on demand from the library, but in such cases where the supplier does not have the means to distribute the material directly to the subscriber's address.

11. Computerized services:
    Printouts of continuation orders arranged either by country or alphabet (special differentiation between periodicals and serials if wanted)
    Printouts of last calendar year's library purchases plus present status with breakdown according to monographs, periodicals and countries of publication.

12-
13. No.

14. Issues at irregular intervals approximately 150 catalogs per year, covering books in the humanities and periodicals in all fields. Countries include all Eastern and Southeastern European countries except Greece, Germany, and Austria. There are three types of catalogs: stock catalogs, NOVA for current new publications (sometimes included with stock catalogs), and antiquarian catalogs.
15. Clients will deal with an individual handling the country of publication. Phone contacts depend on language qualification.
16. Will report back immediately to the library if the item is entirely unobtainable. It searches for about two years on the understanding that no interim claims are being sent.
17. Rush orders accepted at no extra charge.
18. No service fee charges; no handling charges unless special packing or airmail is requested.
19. Neither.
20. Client need not request that charges be listed separately unless special packing or airmail is requested.
21. No.
22. Titles are listed in random order on the invoice.
23. Purchase order numbers appear on invoice.
24. Multiple copies of invoices provided (maximum four).
25. No.
26. Prepayment options and terms:
     Yearly prepayments of blanket orders are accepted but no prepayments for individual book items.
     Subscription invoices are sent out well ahead of the beginning of a subscription period and are expected to be paid in advance.
27. Will provide quotations for libraries interested in changing dealers or consolidating direct subscriptions.

28. Libraries wishing to transfer orders to the firm must first cancel with their present suppliers.

Kunst und Wissen
Wilhelmstrasse 4
D-6700 Stuttgart 1, Germany

Telephone number: (49) (711) 210770
Fax number: (49) (711) 247439
Telex number: 721929
For more information see The Faxon Company, Inc. listing under UNITED STATES.

Lange & Springer Wissenschaftliche
Buchhandlung
(Scientific Booksellers)
Otto-Suhr-Allee 26/28
D-1000 Berlin 10, Federal Republic of Germany

Telephone number: (49) (030) 34005-0
Fax number: (49) (030) 3420611
Telex number: 183-195-1sbn d

1. Owned by Springer-Verlag Heidelberg Berlin New York. Is an independently operated firm under German law.
2. Other offices in the United States, Russia, Poland, Italy, and Argentina (for addresses see Lange & Springer listing under specific countries).
3. No.
4. Maintains memberships in and is regularly represented at meetings of:
   ASPB (Arbeitsgemeinschaft
         Spezialbibliotheken)
   DGD (Deutsche Gesellschaft fuer
        Dokumentation)
5. Representatives actively participate in library association meetings in their country and/or area of the country they represent.

6. Provides materials from countries worldwide.
7a. Types of materials handled:
    Periodicals
    Monographic standing orders
    CD-ROM
    Back issues
    Government publications
    Loose-leaf services
    Sets
    Microforms
    Replacements
    Yearbooks/annuals (client may request every second or third year)
    Memberships
    Serials on videocassette
    Serials with variant publishing
7b. Books (monographic firm orders) handled by its book department.
8. Will communicate with back issue dealers when supplying back issues for a client.
9. Services provided:
    Automatic renewal til forbid
    New order reports
    Claim reports
10. Journal consolidation is available upon demand. Charges depend on the size and nature of the account. Prices are available upon request.
11. Computerized services:
    Subscription lists
    Exchanges and renewals via magnetic tape or disk
    Placement of claims by tape or disk
12. Database is available to clients upon request.
13. No, not planned.
14. No. Bibliographic information is provided upon request.
15. Client will deal with one customer service representative per department: books, journals, continuations, CD-ROM, bookkeeping.
16. Will report back to the library on titles it cannot supply. Will notify library after all available bibliographic means

are exhausted and when contacting the
publisher yields no results.

17. Rush orders accepted at no extra charge.
18. There is no separate service fee as all
    charges are calculated in an inclusive
    price.
19- Charges can be listed separately upon
20. request.
21. Shipping charges:
    Journals: Customer pays publishers
        postage charges.
    Books/continuations: A portion of the
        shipping charge is paid by the
        customer.
22. Titles are entered on the invoice as
    requested by the customer: alpha-
    betically, by order number, by end
    user.
23. Purchase order number is always supplied
    on the invoice.
24. Multiple copies of invoices provided (no
    limit).
25. Invoices can be generated on computer
    tape or transferred by other electronic
    means.
26. Prepayment terms and options information
    are available upon request.
27. Will provide quotations upon request to
    libraries interested in changing vendors
    or consolidating direct subscriptions.
28. Firm can help libraries cancel with their
    present suppliers in some cases,
    depending on the account.

Neuwerk-Buch-und-Musikalienhandlung GmbH
Heinrich-Schutz-Allee 35
D-3500 Kassel-Wilhelmshoehe, Federal Republic
of Germany

Telephone number: (49) 0561/3105-262
Fax number: (49) 0561/3105-240

1. Owned by Baerenreiter-Verlag, Kassel,
    Germany. Established in 1986.

2-
5. No response.
6. Provides materials from countries worldwide.
7a. Types of materials handled:
     Periodicals
     Monographic standing orders
     Government publications
     Loose-leaf services
     Yearbooks/annuals
     Serials with variant publishing
     Music (handled by Music Shop)
7b. Books (monographic firm orders) handled by its bookstore.
8. No response.
9. Services provided:
     Automatic renewal til forbid
     New order reports
     Claim reports
     Out-of-print searching
10. Journal consolidation available upon demand.
11-
14. No response.
15. Client will deal with one customer service respresentative assigned to the account.
16. Will report back to the library on titles it cannot supply. Will try to obtain materials for three to six months before notifying library of unavailability.
17. No response.
18- Usually there is not a service fee;
20. however, if there is one the service/handling charges are listed separately on the invoice.
21. No response.
22- Titles are listed on the invoice by
23. purchase order number.
24. Multiple copies of invoices provided (maximum two).
25-
26. No response.
27. Will provide quotations for libraries interested in changing vendors or consolidating direct subscriptions.

28. Libraries wishing to transfer orders to this firm must cancel with their present suppliers.

Sautter & Lackmann Fachbuchhandlung
Admiralitatstrasse 71/72
Postfach 110431
D-2000 Hamburg 11, Germany

Telephone number: (49) (40) 37 31 96
Fax number: (49) (40) 36 54 79

1. Independent firm established in 1970.
2-
5. No.
6. Provides materials from: Austria, Germany, Switzerland, Scandinavia, and The Netherlands.
7a. Type of materials handled:
     Periodicals
     Monographic standing orders
     CD-ROM
     Back issues
     Loose-leaf services
     Microforms
     Yearbooks/annuals
     Serials with variant publishing
7b. Books (monographic firm orders).
8. No.
9. Services provided:
     Automatic renewal til forbid
     New order reports
     Claim reports (on request)
10. Journal consolidation available on demand at no extra service charge. There is, however, a postage charge for postage from the publisher to Sautter and from Sautter to the customer.
11. Computerized services under development.
12-
14. No.
15. Client will deal with one customer service representative.

16. Will report back to the library on titles
    it cannot supply. How long Sautter will
    try to obtain materials before notifying
    the library depends on the circumstances.
17. Rush orders accepted at no extra charge
    unless special delivery (airmail etc.)
    is requested.
18. Service fee is generally not charged; it
    depends on the publisher's discount
    margin to Sautter.
19- Service/handling charges are listed
20. separately on the invoice.
21. No.
22. Titles are entered on the invoice
    according to customer's instructions,
    usually by purchase order number.
23. Purchase order numbers provided on
    invoice.
24. Multiple copies of invoices provided (no
    limit).
25. Invoices can be faxed.
26. Prepayment options and terms: According
    to customer's request.
27. Will provide quotations for libraries
    interested in changing dealers or in
    consolidating direct subscriptions.
28. Sautter prefers that libraries
    transferring orders to it should cancel
    with their present suppliers. Sautter &
    Lackmann will notify publishers when it
    places the order that it has taken over
    the subscription.

Schmidt Periodicals GmbH
Dettendorf
D-8201 Bad Feilnbach 2, Germany

Telephone number: (49) 08064-221
Fax number: (49) 08064-557
Telex number: 525 959 period

1. Independent company established in 1962.

2. Branch offices:
   Marcello S.N.C.
   via P. Canal 12/1
   I-35137 Padova, Italy
   Telephone number: (39) (49) 8721455
   Fax number: (39) (49) 42854

   Libreria Especializada PONS
   Paseo Fernando el Catolico 37
   P.O.B. 648
   500 80 Zaragoza, Spain
   Telephone number: (34) (76) 359037
   Fax number: (34) (76) 356072
3. No.
4. Company does not maintain memberships in any library associations but is regularly represented at the Deutscher Bibliothekarstag.
5. Representatives actively participate in library association meetings in their country and/or area of the country they represent.
6. Provides materials from countries worldwide.
7a. Types of materials handled:
    Back issues
    Reprints of journals and series
    Holds a large stock of back sets and reprints
7b. No.
8. Communicates with back issue dealers when
 . supplying back issues for a client.
9. Services provided:
    Out-of-print searching
10. Response unclear.
11. None.
12-
13. No.
14. Catalogs of reprints and backsets are issued once a year.
15. Clients will deal with different customer service representatives.
16. Will report back to libraries on titles that they cannot supply. They search the antiquarian market worldwide.
17. Rush orders accepted at no extra charge.

18. No service fee.
19- Service/handling charges are listed
20. separately on the invoice.
21. No.
22. Titles are invoiced alphabetically;
    invoices will show order numbers.
23. Purchase order numbers provided on the
    invoice.
24-
25. No.
26. No prepayments requested.
27. Will provide quotations for back volumes
    only.
28. No response.

Slavic Verlag Dr. A. Kovac
(formerly Dr. R. Trofenik)
Elisabethstrasse 22
D-8000 Muenchen 40,
Federal Republic of Germany

Telephone number: (49) (89) 272 56 12
Fax number: (49) (89) 271 65 94

1. Firm was established in 1960 by Dr.
   Rudolf Trofenik; partially taken over in
   1987 and since 1991 wholly owned by
   Dr. A. Kovac.
2. Has offices in other countries (none
   specified).
3. No response.
4. Maintains membership in and is regularly
   represented at the Yugoslavian library
   association meetings.
5. Representatives actively participate in
   library association meetings in their
   country/and or area of the country they
   represent.
6. Provides materials from Southeast Europe:
   former Yugoslavia (Croatia, Bosnia, &
   Herzegovina, Slovenia, Macedonia, and
   Montenegro), Hungary, Romania, Bulgaria,
   and Germany.

7a. Types of materials handled:
        Periodicals
        Monographic standing orders
        Yearbooks/annuals
        Serials with variant publishing
7b. Books (monographic firm orders) handled
    by its printed books department.
8. No response.
9. Services provided:
        Automatic renewal til forbid
        New order reports
        Claim reports
        Out-of-print searching
10. Journal consolidation is the standard
    practice.
11. No response.
12-
13. No.
14. Issues a catalog. Bibliographic
    information is provided according to MLA
    standards.
15. Clients will deal with one customer
    service representative.
16. Will report back to the library on titles
    it cannot supply. Time is dependent on
    the type of material ordered.
17. Rush orders accepted at no additional
    charge.
18. Service fee is charged.
19- Service/handling charges are listed
20. separately on invoices.
21. No response.
22- Titles are listed by purchase order
23. number on invoices.
24. Multiple copies of invoices provided
    (maximum two).
25. No response.
26. Prepayment options and terms are
    available and are client specific.
27. Will provide quotations for libraries
    interested in changing vendors or
    consolidating direct subscriptions.
28. Libraries wishing to transfer orders to
    this firm must cancel with their present
    suppliers.

Buchhandlung Staeheli & Co.
Am Marketplatz 20
D-7208 Spaichingen
Federal Republic of Germany

For more information see Staeheli's Bookshops Ltd. listing under SWITZERLAND.

Stern-Verlag Janssen & Company
Booksellers & Subscription Agents
Friedrichstrasse 24-26
D-4000 Duesseldorf
Federal Republic of Germany

Telephone number: (49) (211) 38-81201
Fax number: (49) (211) 38-5376

1. Privately owned, independent company established in 1900.
2-
3. No response.
4. Company maintains memberships in but is not regularly represented at the meetings of:
    American Library Association
    Association of College & Research
        Libraries
    American Theological Library
        Association
5. Representatives actively participate in the following meetings:
    France: Annual Congress of the
        Association of French Library
        Directors
    Germany: Annual Congress of the
        German Library Association
6. Provides materials from countries worldwide.
7a. Types of materials handled:
    Periodicals
    Monographic standing orders
    CD-ROM
    Back issues
    Government publications

7a. Types of materials handled (continued):
Loose-leaf services
Sets
Microforms
Replacements
Yearbooks/annuals (client may request
every second or third year)
Memberships
Serials on videocassette
Serials with variant publishing

7b. Books (monographic firm orders).

8. No response.

9. Services provided:
Automatic renewal til forbid
New order reports
Claim reports
Out-of-print searching
Approval plans
Blanket orders

10. Journal consolidation is available on demand. Service charges depend on the kind and quantity of periodicals ordered by the library concerned.

11. Computerized services:
Its in-house SERIDATA electronic control system provides effective control of our serial records.
Its in-house MONODATA electronic control system provides the same service for monographic orders.

12. Database availability: Stern-Verlag is planning to make its database available to clients.

13. No response.

14. Issues catalogs and monthly newsletters containing new publications in different fields. Also issues antiquarian catalogs.
MOSES: Monographic Selection Services provides title slips in a standard library format on new and forthcoming publications in different fields.

15. Client will deal with one individual assigned to the account.

16. Will report back to the library on outstanding orders on a regular basis. Stern-Verlag tries to obtain material until the customer cancels.
17. Rush orders accepted at no extra charge.
18. Service fee is charged for periodicals, depending on the kind and quantity of the periodicals ordered by the library concerned.
19. Service/handling charges may be included in the price or listed separately depending on customer request.
20. Client may request that service charges be listed upon request.
21. Payment of all or some of the shipping charges by Stern-Verlag depends on the volume of business it does with the customer.
22. Titles are entered on the invoice in random order.
23. Purchase order numbers included on the invoice. Stern-Verlag provides complete order references on the invoice.
24. Multiple copies of invoices supplied: Limited to one original invoice and three copies of the invoice.
25. Stern-Verlag is now in process of planning to generate invoices via computer tape.
26. No response.
27. Will provide quotations for libraries interested in changing vendors or in consolidating direct subscriptions.
28. Will assist a library who wishes to transfer its subscriptions to Stern-Verlag. It will cancel current subscriptions with the publishers concerned if the library authorizes Stern-Verlag with a formal letter to do so.

Swets & Zeitlinger GmbH
Bockenheimer Anlage 13
D-6000 Frankfurt am Main-1
Federal Republic of Germany

Telephone number: (49) (69) 531099
For more information see Swets Subscription
Service listing under THE NETHERLANDS.

HONDURAS

Mario R. Argueta
Apartado Postal 20185
Comayaguela, Honduras

Telephone number: (504) 31-14-41
          (no city code needed)

1. Independent company established in 1971
    run by a well-known author, librarian and
    historian.
2-
5. No.
6. Provides serials and monographs from
    Honduras, Guatemala, El Salvador, Costa
    Rica, and Nicaragua.
7a. Types of materials handled:
          Periodicals
          Monographic standing orders
          CD-ROM
          Back issues
          Government publications
          Loose-leaf services
          Sets
          Microforms
          Replacements
          Yearbooks/annuals
          Memberships
          Serials on videocassette
          Serials with variant publishing
          Out-of-print, rare materials
7b. Books (monographic firm orders).

8. Will communicate with back issue dealers when supplying back issues for a client.
9. Services provided:
   Automatic renewal til forbid
   New order reports
   Claim reports
   Out-of-print searching
10. Journal consolidation available upon demand with no additional charge.
11. Computerized services:
    Searches for out-of-print materials
12-
13. No response.
14. Issues a monthly catalog. Bibliographic information included: author, title, edition, place of publication, date, pages, and comments on important items.
15. Clients will deal directly with the owner.
16. Will report back to the library on titles that cannot be supplied. Will try to obtain material for a year.
17. Rush orders accepted at no extra charge.
18. No service fee.
19- Handling charges listed separately on
20. invoice.
21. Will sometimes pay all or part of the shipping charges.
22. Titles appear alphabetically on invoices.
23. Purchase orders provided on the invoice.
24. Multiple copies of invoices provided (no limit).
25. Invoices can be generated on computer tape or transferred by other electronic means.
26. Payment due upon receipt of materials.
27. Will provide quotations for libraries interested in changing dealers or consolidating direct subscriptions.
28. Will assist libraries wishing to change dealers in any way possible.

Apollo Book Company Ltd.
(Japanese Book Centre)
27-33 Kimberley Road
2nd floor, "A" Wing Lee Building
Kowloon, Hong Kong

Telephone number: (852) 367-8482
(no city code needed)
Fax number: (852) 369-5282
Cable address: APOBOOK HONG KONG

1. "Owned company" established in 1945.
2-
5. No.
6. Provides serials and monographs from countries worldwide, specializing in materials from Mongolia, Russia, North Korea, and Vietnam.
7a. Types of materials handled:
    Periodicals
    Monographic standing orders
    CD-ROM
    Back issues
    Government publications
    Loose-leaf services
    Sets
    Microforms
    Replacements
    Yearbooks/annuals (client may request every second or third year)
    Serials on videocassette
    Serials with variant publishing
7b. Books (monographic firm orders).
8. Usually deals directly with the publisher when supplying back issues for a client.
9. Services provided:
    Automatic renewal til forbid
    New order reports
    Claim reports
10. Journal consolidation is standard practice. A 20% service charge will be added on those items on which one cannot obtain a trade discount from the supplier. An additional postage fee will

be applied on every subscription which needs to be delivered by post.
11. No.
12. Database is available to clients upon request.
13. No.
14. Issues a new books list.
15. Clients will be assigned a customer service representative and an independent account number.
16. Will report back to the library on titles which are not available. Will try to obtain materials for six months before returning orders.
17. Rush orders accepted with no extra service charges "except speedy delivery charges on actual expenses."
18. There is no service fee except for newspapers which have 10% added to the newspapers' selling price. Others are charged at the cover price.
19. Mailing and packing charges are listed separately on the invoice.
20. Client may request that service charges be listed separately on the invoice.
21. No.
22- Titles are listed on the invoice by
23. purchase order number.
24. Multiple copies of invoices supplied.
25-
26. No.
27. Will provide quotations for libraries interested in changing vendors or consolidating direct subscriptions.
28. No response.

Chiao Liu Publication Trading Co. Ltd.
P.O. Box 50324
Sai Ying Pun Post Office, Hong Kong

Telephone number: (852) 858-0645
                           (no city code needed)
Fax number: (852) 858-6379
Cable address: CHIAO LIU

1. Independent company established in 1955.
2-
5. No.
6. Provides serials and monographs from countries worldwide.
7a. Types of materials handled:
      Periodicals
      Monographic standing orders
      Back issues
      Government publications
      Loose-leaf services
      Sets
      Microforms
      Replacements
      Yearbooks/annuals (client may request every second or third year)
      Serials on videocassette
      Serials with variant publishing
7b. Books (monographic firm orders).
8. Will communicate with back issue dealers when supplying back issues for a client.
9. Services provided:
      Automatic renewal til forbid
      New order reports
      Claim reports
      Out-of-print searching
10. Journal consolidation is standard practice.
11. None.
12-
13. No.
14. Issues an annual catalog.
15. Client will deal with different customer service representatives.
16. Will report back to the library within three months on titles it cannot supply.
17. Rush orders accepted at no extra charge.

18. Service fee is not a standard percentage nor a flat fee. It is determined in another manner (not specified).
19. Service/handling charges are included in the price.
20. Service/handling charges will not be listed separately upon client request.
21. In some cases, it pays all or part of the shipping charges.
22. Titles are entered on the invoice according to its code number.
23. Purchase order numbers are supplied on the invoice.
24. Multiple copies of invoices provided (no limit).
25. Invoices can be generated on computer tape and generated by other electronic means.
26. Prepayment is required.
27. Will provide quotations for a library interested in changing dealers or consolidating direct subscriptions.
28. If a library wishes to transfer its orders to Chaio Liu, the library must cancel with its present suppliers.

ESS Overseas, Inc.
Room 704, 7th floor
Winning Commercial Building
46-48 Hillwood Road
Tsimshatsui, Kowloon, Hong Kong

Telephone number: (852) (3) 368-4397
Fax number: (852) (3) 312-0584
Serves Hong Kong and the People's Republic of China.
For more information see EBSCO Subscription Services, Inc. listing under UNITED STATES.

ICELAND

Mal og Menning
Postholf 392
191 Reykjavik, Iceland

Telephone number: (354) (1) 24240
Fax number: (354) (1) 623523

1. Independent company established in 1937.
2-
5. No.
6. Provides serials and monographs from Iceland only.
7a. Types of materials handled:
    Periodicals
    Monographic standing orders
    Back issues
    Government publications
    Yearbooks/annuals (clients may request every second or third year)
    Memberships
    Serials with variant publishing
7b. Books (monographic firm orders).
8. Will communicate directly with publishers or secondhand booksellers when supplying back issues for a client.
9. Services provided:
    Automatic renewal til forbid
    New order reports
10. Journal consolidation available only upon demand at no additional charge.
11. Computerized services:
    List of Icelandic books
12. Database available to clients in printed form only.
13. No.
14. Issues a yearly catalog.
15. Client is assigned one customer service representative.
16. Will report back to the library on items that cannot be supplied. Will report back after two months of searching.
17. Rush orders accepted at no extra charge.
18. No service fee.

19. Postage charges are listed separately on invoices.
20. No response.
21. No.
22. Titles appear at random on the invoice.
23. Purchase order numbers are included on the invoice.
24. Multiple copies of invoices supplied (no limit).
25. No.
26. Prepayment is required for new orders from new clients.
27. Will provide quotations on Icelandic periodicals only for libraries interested in changing vendors or consolidating direct subscriptions.
28. No response.

INDIA

Asia Books & Periodicals Co.
11/3 Darya Ganj
Ansari Road
New Delhi 110002, India

Telephone number: (91) (11) 3273347
Fax number: (91) (11) 3275542
Telex number: 31 61087 PRIN-IN
Cable address: INDOLOGY

1. Independent company established in 1973.
2. No
3. Will not do business with Fiji.
4. In India we maintain liaisons with libraries.
5. Representatives actively participate in library association meetings in their country and/or area of the country they represent.
6. Provides serials and monographs from India and Nepal.

7a. Types of materials handled:
        Periodicals
        Monograpic standing orders
        Back issues
        Sets
        Replacements
        Yearbooks/Annuals (client may request
            every second or third year)
        Memberships
        Serials with variant publishing
7b. Books (monographic firm orders).
8. Will communicate with back issue dealers
    when supplying back issues for a client.
9. Services provided:
        Automatic renewal til forbid
        New order reports
        Claim reports
        Out-of-print searching
10. Journal consolidation available at no
    extra charge. Issues are supplied via
    Registered Book Post to avoid
    unnecessary claims.
11-
13. Not applicable.
14. Issues a monthly newsletter providing
    bibliographic information and other
    details.
15. Clients will deal with one customer
    service representative assigned to the
    account.
16. Will report back to the library on titles
    it cannot supply. Will try to obtain
    material for one month before notifying
    library of unavailability.
17. Rush orders accepted at no extra charge.
18. No service fee.
19- If there are handling charges they
20. are listed separately on the invoice.
21. Will pay all or part of the shipping
    charges.
22- Titles are entered on the invoice by
23. purchase order number.
24. Multiple copies of invoices supplied (no
    limit).

25. Invoices can be generated on computer tape or transferred by other electronic means.
26. Prepayment options available. Contact the company.
27. Will provide quotations for libraries interested in changing dealers or consolidating direct subscriptions.
28. Libraries wishing to change vendors must cancel with their present suppliers.

Bhatkal & Son
16 Southern Avenue
Calcutta 700026, India

Telephone number: (91) (33) 460812

1. Independent company established in 1990.
2-
3. Not applicable.
4. Does not maintain memberships in any library associations but does participate in conferences. Participated at the 1992 IFLA Conference.
5. Representatives will participate at IFLA.
6. Provides serials and monographs from countries worldwide, especially from the United Kingdom and the USA.
7a. Types of materials handled:
    Periodicals
    CD-ROM
    Government publications
    Yearbooks/annuals
    Serials on videocassette
    Serials with variant publishing
7b. Books (monographic firm orders).
8. No.
9. Services provided:
    Automatic renewal til forbid
10-
13. No response.
14. Issues an annual catalog.
15. Client will deal with one individual assigned to the account.

16. No response.
17. Rush orders not accepted.
18. No service fee.
19-
20. No response.
21. Pays all or part of the shipping charges.
22- Titles entered on the invoice by
23. purchase order number.
24. Multiple copies of invoices provided (no limit).
25-
26. No.
27. Will provide quotations for libraries interested in changing dealers or consolidating direct subscriptions.
28. No response.

Biblia Impex Pvt. Ltd.
2/18 Ansari Road
New Delhi 110002, India

Telephone number: (91) (11) 3278034
Fax number: (91) (11) 3282047
Cable address: ELYSIUM

1. Independent company established in 1980.
2-
5. No.
6. Provides serials and monographs from India.
7a. Types of materials handled:
    Periodicals
    Monographic standing orders
    CD-ROM
    Back issues
    Government publications
    Loose-leaf services
    Sets
    Microforms
    Replacements
    Yearbooks/annuals (client may request every second or third year)
    Memberships
    Serials on videocassette

7a. Types of materials handled (continued):
    Serials with variant publishing
7b. Books (monographic firm orders).
8. Will communicate with back issue dealers when supplying back issues for a client.
9. Services provided:
    Automatic renewal til forbid
    New order reports
    Claim reports
    Out-of-print searching
10. Journal consolidation: Almost all of the journals are collected at our office for onward dispatch to our clients at no extra cost. Only daily and weekly periodicals are mailed by the publishers directly to the clients.
11. No.
12. Not applicable.
13. No.
14. Issues a monthly newsletter of books only, providing author/editor, title, pagination, plates, place and year of publication, and price.
15. Client will deal with different customer service representatives depending upon the inquiry.
16. Will report back to the library within one to three months on titles it cannot supply depending upon the title.
17. Rush orders accepted at no extra charge.
18. Service fee: "We charge only the publishers' prices in most cases except about 10% where the publishers do not allow discount. In such case, we add 20% as our charges."
19. Service/handling fees are included in the prices.
20. Client may request that charges be listed separately.
21. Pays all of the shipping charges.
22. Titles are entered on the invoice according to the client's instructions.
23. Purchase order numbers supplied on invoices.
24. Multiple copies of invoices supplied (no limit).

25. No.
26. Prepayment options and terms: "Clients can prepay on the basis of subscription rates and on terms settled with them in advance."
27. Will provide quotations for libraries interested in changing vendors or consolidating direct subscriptions.
28. Libraries wishing to transfer orders to this firm must cancel with their present suppliers. Any assistance asked for from Biblia Impex will be provided.

D.K. Agencies (P) Ltd.
A-15/17, Mohan Garden
Najafgarh Road
New Delhi 110059, India

Telephone numbers: (91) (11) 5598897
                      (91) (11) 5598899
Fax number: (91) (11) 5598898
Telex number: 031-76106 DK IN
Cable address: DIKAYBOOK, NEW DELHI-
                      110059

1. Independent company established in 1968.
2-
4. No.
5. Not applicable.
6. Provides serials and monographs published in India.
7a. Types of materials handled:
        Periodicals
        Monographic standing orders
        Back issues
        Government publications
        Loose-leaf services
        Sets
        Microforms
        Replacements
        Yearbook/annuals (clients may request every second or third year)
        Serials with variant publishing
7b. Books (monographic firm orders).

8. Will communicate with back issue dealers when supplying back issues for a client.
9. Services provided:
    Automatic renewal til forbid
    New order reports
    Claim reports
    Out-of-print searching
10. Journal consolidation is standard practice with no additional service charges.
11. Computerized services offered:
    Listings of new journals
    Listings of current periodicals by subject
12-
13. No.
14. Issue occasional listings by subject of current Indian journals.
15. Client will deal with different customer service representatives depending on the nature of the inquiry.
16. Will report back to the library on titles it cannot supply. Generally continues to search for the title for two years.
17. Rush orders accepted at no extra charge unless client wants the material sent by airmail or courier. The client then will pay for the additional mailing costs.
18. No service/handling charges.
19-
20. Not applicable.
21. Firm pays all shipping charges. If sent airmail or by courier, these charges are paid by the client.
22. Titles are entered on the invoice per client's instructions.
23. Purchase order numbers are provided on invoices.
24. Multiple copies of invoice provided (no limit).
25. No.
26. Prepayment options and terms: Orders can be recorded as on "renewal basis" or on "Until forbidden" basis. For "until forbidden" the firm continues to supply the materials even if they have not

received payment. If on "renewal basis" the firm supplies the material only after the receipt of renewal [payment].

27. Will provide quotations for libraries interested in changing vendors or consolidating direct subscriptions.
28. If library is transferring orders to this firm, the firm asks that the library cancel its orders with its present supplier.

Globe Publications Pvt. Ltd.
C-62, Inderpuri
New Delhi 110012, India

Telephone numbers:	(91) (11)	5719333
	(91) (11)	5727319
Fax number:	(91) (11)	5737306
Telex number:		+31 77310

1. Independent company established in 1991.
2-
4. No.
5. Representatives actively participate in library association meetings in their country and/or the area of the country they represent.
6. Provides serials and monographs from countries worldwide.
7a. Types of materials handled:
     Periodicals
     Monographic standing orders
     CD-ROM
     Government publications
     Yearbooks/annuals
     Serials with variant publishing
7b. Books (monographic firm orders).
8. No.
9. Services provided:
     Automatic renewal til forbid
     New order reports
     Claim reports
10. Journal consolidation is standard practice at no additional charge.

11. Computerized services: All aspects are computerized.
12. Database availability to clients: Not available at the moment but Globe has initiated processes to make its database available to clients online.
13. No.
14. Issues a catalog; informs clients of new journals and lists publishers' journals with all information about them--available for specific publishers.
15. Client will deal with one individual assigned to its account.
16. Will report back to the library after six months on titles it cannot supply.
17. Rush orders accepted at no added charge.
18. No service fee.
19. Service/handling charges are included in the price.
20. Client may request that service/handling charges be listed separately.
21. Will pay all or part of the shipping charges.
22- Titles are entered on the invoice by
23. "order number (first priority) and then alphabetized currency wise."
24. Multiple copies of invoices provided (maximum four).
25. Invoices cannot as yet be generated on computer tape or transferred by other electronic means but it should soon be possible.
26. No.
27. Will provide quotations for libraries interested in changing vendors or in consolidating direct subscriptions.
28. Will assist libraries wishing to transfer orders to Globe.

India Book Distributors
107/108 Arcadia
195 Nariman Point
Bombay 400021, India

Telephone numbers: (91) (22) 225220
                      (91) (22) 224691
Fax number: (91) (22) 2872531
Telex number: 0-11-86085 IBD IN
Cable address: PAPERBACK

1. Independent firm established in June 1980.
2. Has an office in the United States:
   Latcorp, Inc.
   10 Norden Lane
   Huntington Station, NY 11746
   U.S.A.
3. None.
4-
5. No.
6. Provides serials from countries worldwide.
7a. Types of materials handled:
   Periodicals
   Yearbooks/annuals
7b.-
8. No response.
9. Services provided:
   Automatic renewal til forbid
   New order reports
   Claim reports
10. No response.
11. Computerized services offered:
   Direct marketing
   Database marketing
12. Database is available to clients "to enter into joint promo efforts."
13. No.
14. Issues a monthly newsletter providing information on new books and magazines.
15. Client will deal with different customer service representatives depending upon nature of the inquiry.
16. Will report back to the library on titles it cannot supply within thirty days.

17. Rush orders accepted. There is an extra charge.
18. Service fee is a flat fee.
19- Service/handling charges are listed
20. separately on the invoice.
21. No.
22- Titles are listed on the invoice by
23. purchase order number.
24. Multiple copies of invoices provided (no limit).
25. Invoices can be generated on computer tape or transferred by other electronic means.
26. Prepayment options and terms are available; contact the firm.
27-
28. No response.

Informatics (India) Pvt. Ltd.
P.B. No. 2025
Seshadripuram, India

Telephone number: (91) (812) 344-598
Fax numbers: (91) (812) 320-840
                   (91) (812) 346-185
Telex number: 845-2041 (INFO IN)
For more information see The Faxon Company
Inc. listing under UNITED STATES.

K. Krishnamurthy, Books & Periodicals
23 Thanikachalam Road
Madras 600017, India

Telephone number: (91) (44) 444-519
Cable address: READERSHIP, Madras

1. Independent company established in 1944.
2. No.
3. Will not do business where there are official government restrictions.
4. Member of I.A.S.L.I.C.
5. No.

111

6. Provides serials and monographs from most countries in the world, with emphasis in the United States, United Kingdom, Europe, Japan, and Hong Kong.

7a. Types of materials handled:
Periodicals
Back issues
Government publications
Yearbooks/annuals
Memberships

7b. Books (monographic firm orders).

8. Will deal with some back issue jobbers in trying to supply back issues for a client.

9. Services provided: Renewal notices are sent with reminders sent afterwards. Due to exchange control problems, there are no automatic renewals without firm orders and payments.

10. Agent receives journals from the United States and United Kingdom by consolidated air freight and re-mails them to only a few special clients.

11. Computerized services:
Renewal notices
Account statements

12. "Free information, such as periodicity, subscription etc. furnished to clients, from our extensive files."

13. "Not prevalent in India so far."

14. Ad hoc answers to customer queries and occasional descriptive lists and fliers on groups of journals or selected individual titles are mailed to clients.

15. Client deals with several customer service representatives handling journal inquiries.

16. Will report back to the library if titles cannot be supplied.

17. No (but we do not know which question it answers).

18. Agent charges a percentage for service fee. It was 10% but has now increased to 15% due to higher costs.

19- Service/handling charges are listed
20. separately on the invoice.

21. Shipping charges: "Where we offer a consolidation and air freighting service, we round the costs on a 'per issue' basis."
22- Titles are entered on the invoice by
23. customer order reference.
24. Purchase order numbers provided on invoices.
25. Two copies of the invoice are normally supplied, more if requested.
26. Prepayments: All journal subscriptions are payable strictly in advance.
27. Will provide quotations to libraries interested in consolidating direct subscriptions or changing vendors.
28. Agent offers such help as the client needs to effect a smooth transfer from previous suppliers.

Prints India
Prints House
11, Darya Ganj
New Delhi 110002, India

```
Telephone numbers: (91) (11) 3268645
                   (91) (11) 3273347
                   (91) (11) 3271378
Fax number:        (91) (11) 3275542
Telex number:       31 61087 PRIN-IN
Cable address:              INDOLOGY
```

1. Independent company established in 1966.
2. No.
3. Will not do business in Fiji.
4. "In India we maintain liaisons with libraries."
5. Representatives actively participate in library association meetings in their country and/or area of the country they represent.
6. Provides serials and monographs from India and Nepal.

7a. Types of material handled:
     Periodicals
     Monographic standing orders
     Back issues
     Government publications
     Replacements
     Yearbooks/annuals
     Serials with variant publishing
7b. Books (monographic firm orders).
8. Will communicate with back issue dealers when supplying back issues for a client.
9. Services provided:
     Automatic renewal til forbid
     New order reports
     Claim reports
     Out-of-print searching
10. Journal consolidated available at no extra charge.
11-
13. Not applicable.
14. Issues a monthly newsletter with bibliographic and other details provided.
15. Client will deal with one customer service representative.
16. Will report back to the library on titles it cannot supply after searching for one month.
17. Rush orders accepted at no extra charge.
18. No service fee.
19- If any service/handling charges are
20. necessary, they are listed separately on the invoice.
21. Will pay all or part of the shipping charges.
22- Titles are listed on the invoice by
23. purchase order number.
24. Multiple copies of invoices provided (no limit).
25. Invoices can be generated on computer tape or transferred by other electronic means.
26. Prepayment options available, no special terms. Contact firm directly.
27. Will provide quotations for libraries interested in changing suppliers or consolidating direct subscriptions.

28. Firm asks that libraries wanting to
    transfer orders to the firm first cancel
    with their present suppliers.

K. K. Roy (Private) Ltd.
55 Gariahat Road
P.O. Box 10210
Calcutta 700029, INDIA

Telephone numbers: (91) (33) 75-4872
                   (91) (33) 75-5069
Cable address: Helbell

1. Independent company established in 1954.
2. Only resident representatives.
3-
4. No.
5. Representatives actively participate in
   library association meetings in their
   country and/or area of the country they
   represent.
6. Provides serials from: India, Nepal,
   Myamar (Burma), Sri Lanka, Bangladesh,
   Maldives, and Bhutan.
7a. Types of materials handled:
        Periodicals
        Monographic standing orders
        Back issues
        Government publications
        Loose-leaf services
        Sets
        Replacements
        Yearbooks/annuals (client may request
            every second or third year)
        Serials with variant publishing
7b. No.
8. Will communicate with back issue dealers
   when supplying back issues for a client.
9. Services provided:
        Automatic renewal til forbid
        New order reports
        Claim reports
        Out-of-print searching

10. Journal consolidation available upon demand with extra service and shipping charges.
11. None at present.
12. No.
13. Not in the near future.
14. Issues catalogs once a year.
15. Clients will deal with different customer service representatives depending on the nature of the inquiry.
16. Will report back to the library on unavailable titles usually within six months.
17. Rush orders accepted at no added charge.
18. Service fee charge is a standard percentage.
19. Service fee is included in the price.
20. Clients may ask that service charges be listed separately.
21. Firm pays all shipping charges.
22. Titles are entered by purchase order number on the invoice.
23. Purchase order numbers provided on the invoice.
24. Multiple copies of invoice can be supplied.
25. No.
26. Prepaid orders are not subject to service charges.
27. Will provide quotations for libraries interested in consolidating orders or changing vendors.
28. Libraries wishing to transfer orders to this firm must cancel with their present suppliers.

Scientific Publishers
Subscription Division
P.O. Box 91
Jodhpur 342001, India

Telephone number: (91) 33323
Cable address: Publishers-Jodhpur 342001

1. Independent firm established in 1978.
2. No.
3. Not applicable.
4. No.
5. Representatives actively participate in library association meetings in their country and/or area of the country they represent.
6. Provides serials and monographs from countries worldwide.
7a. Types of materials handled:
  Periodicals
  Monographic standing orders
  CD-ROM
  Back issues
  Loose-leaf services
  Sets
  Yearbooks/annuals (client may request every second or third year)
  Memberships
  Serials with variant publishing
7b. Books (monographic firm orders).
8. Will communicate with back issue dealers when supplying back issues for a client.
9. Services provided:
  Automatic renewal til forbid
  New order reports
  Claim reports
  Out-of-print searching
10. Journal consolidation is standard practice at no additional service or shipping charges.
11. Computerized services offered:
  Billing
  Renewal notices
  Claim reports
  Packing slips
12. No response.

13. No.
14. Issues a journals bulletin containing publication date, price for new journals, and relevant information regarding Indian journals.
15. Client will deal with different customer service representatives depending on the nature of the inquiry.
16. Will report back to the library on titles it cannot supply after confirming with the publishers, distributors, and other sources.
17. Rush orders accepted at no extra charge.
18. No service fee.
19- Service/handling charges are included
20. in the price and will not be listed separately even if requested.
21. Firm pays all shipping charges.
22- Titles are listed on invoice by
23. purchase order number.
24. Multiple copies of invoices supplied (no limit).
25. No response.
26. Prepayment options and terms are available. Contact firm for details.
27. Will provide quotations for libraries interested in changing suppliers or consolidating direct subscriptions.
28. Will assist libraries wishing to changes suppliers "as far as possible."

UBS Publishers' Distributors Ltd.
5 Ansari Road
New Delhi 110002, India

Telephone numbers:	(91) (11) 3273601
	(91) (11) 3266646
Fax number:	(91) (11) 3276593
Telex number:	31-65106 UBS IN
Cable address:	ALL BOOKS

1. Independent firm established in June 1963.

2.   Has additional office in England:

>   UBS Publishers' Distributors Ltd.
>   475 North Circular Road
>   Neasden
>   London NW2 7QG, England
>   Telephone number: (44) (81) 450-8667
>   Fax number: (44) (81) 452-6612
>   ATTN UBS

3.   Will not do business with South Africa.
4.   No.
5.   Representatives actively participate in
     library association meetings in their
     country and/or area of the country they
     represent.
6.   Provides serials and monographs from
     countries worldwide.
7a. Types of materials handled:
         Periodicals
         Monographic standing orders
         Back issues
         Government publications
         Loose-leaf services
         Sets
         Replacements
         Yearbooks/annuals
         Serials with variant publishing
7b. Books (monographic firm orders).
8.   Will communicate with back issue dealers
     when supplying back issues for a client.
9.   Services provided:
         Automatic renewal til forbid
         New order reports
         Claim reports
         Out-of-print searching
10. Journal consolidation is standard
     practice. Customer chooses type of
     shipping (registered book post
     airmail/sea-mail/airfreight) and pays for
     the specified type of shipping.
11. Computerized services offered:
         Complete order processing
12-
13. No.
14. Not for journals.

15. Client will deal with one customer service representative.
16. Will report back to the library on titles that it cannot supply within one month.
17. Rush orders accepted.
18. Service fee charges are dependent upon the nature of the journal.
19. Service/handling charges are listed separately on the invoice.
20. Yes.
21. Payment of all or part of the shipping charges by the agent is dependent upon the value of the orders.
22. Titles are listed on the invoice as specified by the client.
23. Purchase order numbers are provided on the invoice.
24. Multiple copies of invoices supplied.
25. Invoices can be generated on computer.
26. Prepayment options and terms: Prepayment preferred.
27. Will provide quotations for libraries interested in changing dealers or consolidating direct subscriptions.
28. Libraries wishing to transfer orders must cancel with their present suppliers.

United Publishers
Panbazar Main Road
P.O. Box No. 82
Guwahati 781001, Assam, India

Telephone number: (91) (361) 32059
Fax number: (91) (361) 24791
Telex number: (0235) 2219 UNIT IN.
Cable address: UNIPUB, GUWAHATI 781 001

1. Independent company established in 1969.
2-
5. Not applicable.
6. Provides serials and monographs from countries worldwide.

7a. Types of materials handled:
    Periodicals
    Government publication
    Yearbooks/annuals
    Serials on videocassette
    Other: Presently offering print media
        and audio and video cassettes
7b. Books (monographic firm orders).
8. Will communicate with back issue dealers
    when supplying back issues for a client.
9. Services provided:
    Automatic renewal til forbid
    New order reports
    Other: Orders for current
        subscriptions on minimum annual
        basis
10. Journal consolidation available only upon
    demand with additional service and
    shipping charges.
11. Computerized services offered:
    Presently reviewing computerization
12-
13. Not applicable.
14. Information provided on specific request.
15. Client will deal with one customer
    service representative.
16. Will report back to the library within
    one month on titles it cannot supply.
17. Rush orders accepted at no extra charge.
18. Service fee is determined on a volume
    basis.
19. Service/handling fees can be listed
    separately on the invoice or included in
    the price.
20. Client may request that they be listed
    separately.
21. Never.
22- Titles are entered on the invoice by
23. purchase order number.
24. Multiple copies of invoices provided
    (limit) three.
25. No.
26. Prepayment terms and options: Only
    subscriptions are on a prepayment
    basis.

27. May offer quotations to libraries wishing to change dealers or consolidate direct subscriptions. "Depends."
28. Volume of orders to be transferred by a library to this firm will determine the assistance offered by the firm.

Universal Subscription Agency Pvt. Ltd.
18-19 Community Centre
P.O. Box 8, Saket
New Delhi 110017, India

Telephone numbers:	(91) (11) 668167	
	(91) (11) 668192	
Fax number:	(91) (11) 6866138	
Telex number:	31-73021	
Cable address:	WORLD MAGS	

1. Independent firm established on May 27, 1985.
2-
4. No.
5. Representatives selectively participate in library association meetings in their country and/or the area of the country they represent.
6. Provides serials and monographs from countries worldwide.
7a. Types of materials handled:
    Periodicals
    Monographic standing orders
    CD-ROM
    Back issues
    Microforms
    Replacements
    Yearbooks/annuals
    Serials with variant publishing
7b. Books (monographic firm orders) are handled by a sister company.
8. Will communicate with back issue dealers when supplying back issues for a client.
9. Services provided:
    Automatic renewal til forbid
    Claim reports

10. Journal consolidation is available on demand from the library. There are no additional service or handling charges.
11. Computerized services offered: All departments and services are fully computerized (subscriptions, order processing, remittance, claims, distribution, marketing).
12. Database will soon be available to clients via WAN.
13. No.
14. Issues a yearly catalog for publishers represented with basic journal/title details.
15. Client will be assigned a "zonal" specific customer service agent.
16. Will report back to the library within eight to twelve weeks on titles it cannot supply.
17. Rush orders accepted at no added charge.
18-
19. No service fee; no service charges.
20. Not applicable.
21. Firm pays all shipping charges.
22. Titles appear alphabetically on invoices.
23. Purchase order numbers are provided on invoices.
24. Generally supplies up to four copies of the invoice or will provide whatever number desired.
25. Invoices on customized formats can be generated via computer tape or via e-mail networks. International formats are not available.
26. Prepayment options and terms are offered, but rarely. Contact the firm for details.
27. No.
28. Will negotiate a mutually acceptable assistance for libraries wishing to transfer orders to this firm from another supplier.

Vedams Books International
12A/11 W.E. Area
Post Box 2674
New Delhi 110005, India

Telephone number: (91) (11) 572 4053
Fax number: (91) (11) 574 5114

1. Independent company established in 1970.
2. No.
3. None.
4-
5. No.
6. Provides serials and monographs from India only.
7a. Types of materials handled:
    Periodicals
    Monographic standing orders
    Back issues
    Government publications
    Yearbooks/annuals
    Serials with variant publishing
7b. Books (monographic firm orders).
8. Will contact publisher and/or back issue dealers when supplying back issues for a client.
9. Services provided:
    Automatic renewal til forbid
    Claim reports
    Out-of-print searching
10. Journal consolidation is standard practice. Journals are ordered, monitored, collated, and sent regularly by registered airmail.
11. None.
12. Database availability: Vedams will supply customers with a printout of journals it supplies.
13. No.
14. Issues catalogs for monographs in botany, zoology, geology, physical sciences, arts, anthropology and other subjects in the humanities. The catalogs list entire table of contents of the book and also excerpts from the jacket/preface and the position of the author.

15. Client will deal with either Mr. Achal Rajagopal or Mr. Achal Madhavan.
16. Will report back to the library after four months on titles it cannot supply.
17. Rush orders accepted at no extra charge.
18. No service/handling charges. Discount of 10% extended on both monographs and journals to libraries which buy all of their Indian monographs and journals from Vedams.
19-
20. Not applicable.
21. All journals are sent by registered airmail. Vedams pays all shipping charges.
22. Titles can be entered alphabetically and by order number.
23. Purchase order numbers provided on the invoice.
24. Multiple copies of invoices supplied (no limit).
25. Invoices can be sent by fax, if required.
26. Prepayment options and terms: Vedams sends the first issue of a year's subscription with an invoice.
Customer payment due after receipt of the first issue and the invoice.
27. Will provide quotations for libraries interested in changing dealers or consolidating direct subscriptions.
28. If a library wishes to transfer its orders to Vedams, Vedams asks that the order be placed for the entire year's subscription as publishers seldom supply a partial year's subscription.

C. V. Toku Buku Tropen
113, Jln. Pasar Baru
Jakarta Pusat 10710, Indonesia

```
Telephone numbers:      (62) (21) 326695
                        (62) (21) 363543
Fax numbers:            (62) (21) 3800566
                        (62) (21) 327092
Telex number:              44122 Tropen IA
Cable address: TROMOL POS 3604-JAKARTA
                                     10002
```

1. Independent company established in 1939.
2. Singapore office:

>Intermail Enterprise Pte. Ltd.
>Block 805, Tampines Ave. 4
>#07-27
>Singapore 1852, Republic of
>   Singapore
>Telephone number: (65) 7835935
>Fax number: (65) 7857015

3. No.
4. Maintains memberships in and is regularly represented at the meetings of the:
>Indonesia Library Association
>   Jakarta Branch (Indonesia
>   Capital Territory)

5. Representatives actively participate in library association meetings both in their country and in the area of the country they represent.
6. Provides serials from countries worldwide: Europe, U.S.A., Australia, Asia.
7a. Types of materials handled:
>Periodicals
>CD-ROM
>Back issues
>Government publications
>Loose-leaf services
>Sets
>Microforms
>Replacements

7a. Types of materials handled (continued):
    Yearbooks/annuals (clients may request
        every second or third year)
    Memberships
    Serials with variant publishing
7b. No.
8. Will communicate with back issue dealers
    when supplying back issues for a client.
9. Services provided:
    New order reports
    Claim reports
10. Journal consolidation is available (did
    not state whether standard practice or on
    demand). There is an additional charge
    for this service.
11. Computerized services: Provides printouts
    from the database by subject for clients.
12. Will print database for clients by
    subject.
13. Interfaces with library automation
    systems but did not specify which system
    or how.
14. No.
15. Client will deal with one assigned
    customer service representative.
16. Will report back to the library on titles
    it cannot supply.
17. Rush orders accepted and there is an
    added charge.
18. Service fee is charged and it is a flat
    fee.
19- Service/handling charges are listed
20. separately on the invoice.
21. Pays all of the shipping charges.
22. Titles are alphabetized on the invoice.
23. Purchase order numbers appear on the
    invoice.
24. Multiple copies of invoice supplied (no
    limit).
25. Invoices can be generated on computer
    tape or transferred by other electronic
    means.
26-
27. No.
28. Will assist libraries wishing to transfer
    orders from their present suppliers.

ISRAEL

Israbook
P.O. Box 6056
Jerusalem, Israel 91060

Telephone number: (972) (2) 380247
Fax number: (972) (2) 388423

1. Owned by Gefen Publishing House Ltd.
2. Has office in New York (U.S.A.), but all mail should be sent to Israel.
3. No.
4. Company is present at meetings of the:
   ABA
   American Library Association
   AJL
5. Representatives actively participate in library association meetings in Israel and the United States.
6. Provides serials only from Israel.
7a. Types of materials handled:
   Periodicals
   Monographic standing orders
   Back issues
   Government publications
   Loose-leaf services
   Sets
   Yearbooks/annuals (client may request every second or third year)
   Serials on videocassette
   Serials with variant publishing
7b. No.
8. Will communicate with back issue dealers if necessary when supplying back issues for a client. Usually deals directly with publishers for back issues.
9. Services provided:
   Automatic renewal til forbid
   New order reports
   Claim reports
   Out-of-print searching
10. Journal consolidation available at no extra charge.

11. Computerized services:
    Its entire back list is computerized.
    Listing of all new books published in
    Israel
12. Database is available to clients upon
    request.
13. Not yet.
14. Issues a catalog and will be starting a
    monthly or quarterly listing.
15. Clients, in most cases, will deal with
    one customer service representative.
16. Will report back to the library on titles
    it cannot supply. Will search for the
    titles for a time period specified by the
    library.
17. Rush orders accepted. Only additional
    charge is postage.
18. No service fee.
19. Service/handling charges are listed
    separately on the invoice.
20. Not applicable.
21. No.
22- Titles are listed on invoice by
23. purchase order number.
24. Multiple copies of invoices provided.
25. No.
26. Prepayment options and terms availability
    depend on specific orders. Contact the
    firm directly for information.
27. No.
28. Will do their best to assist libraries
    wishing to change suppliers depending
    upon the situation.

Rassem Yusuf Jebarah
Taybah-Netanya, Israel 40400

Telephone number: (972) (52) 993021
Fax number: (972) (52) 993021

1. Jebarah is a librarian and representative
    of the United States Library of Congress.
2-
5. No.

6. Provides serials and monographs from Israel and the West Bank (Occupied Territories).
7a. Types of materials handled:
    Periodicals
    Monographic standing orders
    Government publications
    Yearbooks/annuals
    Serials with variant publishing
7b. Books (monographic firm orders).
8. Will communicate with back issue dealers when supplying back issues for a client.
9. Services provided:
    Automatic renewal til forbid
    New order reports
    Claim reports
    Out-of-print searching
10. Journal consolidation is standard practice.
11. No response.
12. No.
13. In the future.
14. Issues a catalog which indicates author, title, place, publisher, date.
15. Response unclear.
16. Will report back to the library within two months on titles it cannot supply.
17. No response.
18. Service fee is charged.
19- Service/handling charges are listed
20. separately on the invoice.
21. No.
22. Titles appear alphabetically on the invoice.
23. Purchase order numbers provided on the invoice.
24. Multiple copies of invoices supplied (no maximum).
25. Invoices can be generated on computer tape and transferred by other electronic means.
26-
27. No.
28. No response.

Jerusalem Books Ltd.
P.O.B. 18189
Jerusalem, Israel

Telephone number: (972) (2) 826373
Fax number: (972) (2) 826373

1. Independent company established in March 1982.
2. Has office in the United States:

> Jerusalem Books Ltd.
> 1190 Ridge Road
> Highland Park, IL 60035 U.S.A.
> Telephone number: (1) (708) 831-3293
> Fax number: (1) (708) 831-3293

3. No.
4. Company maintains membership and is regularly represented at the annual convention of the:
   Association of Jewish Libraries
5. Representatives actively participate in library association meetings in their country and/or area of the country they represent.
6. Provides serials and monographs published in Israel.
7a. Types of materials handled:
   Periodicals
   Monographic standing orders
   CD-ROM
   Back issues
   Government publications
   Loose-leaf services
   Sets
   Microforms
   Replacements
   Yearbooks/annuals (client may request every second or third year)
   Serials with variant publishing
7b. Books (monographic firm orders).
8. Will communicate with back issue dealers when necessary when supplying back issues for a client.

9. Services provided:
    Automatic renewal til forbid
    New order reports
    Claim reports
    Out-of-print searching
10. Journal consolidation is the standard practice and there is no additional charge.
11. Computerized services:
    Lists of publications supplied to its clients
    Lists of publications supplied to its clients according to date (i.e., last year, half-year)
    Lists of publications supplied to its clients according to its subject categories
12. Printouts of all monographs supplied to its various client libraries.
13. No.
14. Issues a catalog every four to six months which lists author, title, date and place of publication, number of pages, publisher.
15. Client will deal with one customer service representative.
16. Will report back to libraries on titles it cannot supply after searching for six months.
17. Rush orders accepted. The only additional charges are airmail charges if airmail service is requested.
18. Service fee is a standard percentage.
19. Service/handling charges are included with postal charges and insurance.
20. No response.
21. No.
22. Titles are listed on invoices in alphabetical order.
23. Purchase order numbers are provided on the invoice.
24. Multiple copies of invoices provided: one sent by mail and one is sent in the parcel.
25. Photocopies.

26. Prepayment options and terms: Discount for a large advance payment ($10,000) is negotiated according to current interest rates.
27. Will provide quotations for libraries interested in changing suppliers or consolidating direct subscriptions.
28. Requests that libraries wishing to change suppliers cancel with their present suppliers.

Rubin Mass Ltd.
Publishers & Booksellers
P.O. Box 990
Jerusalem, Israel 91000

Telephone number: (972) (2) 632565
Fax number: (972) (2) 632719

1. Independent firm established in 1927.
2. No.
3. Will not do business with Arab countries.
4. No.
5. Not regularly.
6. Provides serials and monographs only from Israel.
7a. Types of materials handled:
   Periodicals
   Monographic standing orders
   Back issues
   Government publications
   Sets
   Replacements
   Yearbooks/annuals (clients may request every second or third year)
   Serials with variant publishing
7b. Books (monographic firm orders).
8. Will communicate with back issue dealers when supplying back issues for a client.
9. Services provided:
   Automatic renewal til forbid
   New order reports
   Claim reports
   Out-of-print searching

10. Journal consolidation is standard practice.
11. Computerized services:
    Catalogs and invoices
12-
13. No.
14. Issues a catalog. Bibliographic information included: title, author, subtitle, pages, ISBN, year, publisher.
15. Clients will deal with different customer service representatives.
16. Will report back to the library within six months on titles that cannot be supplied.
17. Rush orders accepted at no extra charge.
18. No service fee charged.
19- Handling charges are included in the
20. price. Will not be listed separately.
21. No.
22. Titles are listed on the invoice by its catalog number.
23. Purchase order numbers are provided on the invoice.
24. Multiple copies of invoices provided (limit four).
25-
26. No.
27. Will provide quotations for libraries interested in consolidating direct subscriptions or changing suppliers.
28. Will assist libraries in changing suppliers.

Ludwig Mayer Ltd., Bookstore
P.O. Box 1174
4 Shlomzion Hamalka Street
Jerusalem, Israel 91010

Telephone number: (972) (2) 252628
Fax number: (972) (2) 290774

1. Independent company established in 1908.
2. No.
3. Will not do business with the Arab world.

4-
5. No response.
6. Provides serials and monographs from countries worldwide.
7a. Types of materials handled:
   - Periodicals
   - Monographic standing orders
   - Back issues
   - Sets
   - Microforms
   - Replacements
   - Government publications
   - Yearbooks/annuals
   - Serials with variant publishing
7b. Books (monographic firm orders).
8. Will communicate with back issue dealers when supplying back issues for a client.
9. Services provided:
   - Automatic renewal til forbid
   - New order reports
   - Claim reports
   - Out-of-print searching
10. Journal consolidation not available.
11-
13. No response.
14. Issues an annual catalog of all books published in Israel.
15. Clients will deal directly with Mr. Raphael Mayer.
16. Will report back to the library on titles it cannot supply within one month.
17. Rush orders accepted at no extra charge.
18. No service fee.
19- Service/handling charges are listed
20. separately on the invoice.
21. Seldom.
22- Titles are entered on the invoice by
23. customer purchase order number.
24. Multiple copies of invoices provided (no limit).
25. No.
26. Prepayment options and terms: Prepayment if wanted, otherwise after receipt.
27. Will provide quotations for libraries interested in changing dealers or in consolidating direct subscriptions.

28. Will assist as far as possible libraries wishing to change dealers.

On Time
P.O.B. 46646
Haifa, Israel 31465

Fax number: (972) (4) 668878

1. Firm established in 1982.
2. No.
3. Will only do business with Arab countries through a third party.
4. No.
5. No response.
6. Provides serials from Israel only.
7a. Types of materials provided:
        Periodicals
        Monographic standing orders
        Back issues
        Government publications
        Loose-leaf services
        Sets
        Replacements
        Yearbooks/annuals (clients may request every second or third year)
        Serials with variant publishing
7b. No response.
8. Will communicate with back issue dealers if necessary when supplying back issues for a client.
9. Services provided:
        Automatic renewal til forbid
        New order reports
        Out-of-print searching
10. Journal consolidation is standard practice with no additional charge.
11. Computerized services: Provides diskette containing client's orders and catalog.
12-
14. No.
15. Client will deal with one customer service representative.

16. Will report back to the library on items it cannot supply.
17. Rush orders accepted. Added charges depend upon the way the library wishes it delivered.
18. Service fee is a standard percentage.
19- Service/handling charges are listed
20. separately.
21. Included.
22. Titles entered on the invoice by FIFO (first in, first out).
23. Purchase order numbers are provided on the invoice.
24. Multiple copies of invoices are provided (no limit).
25. No.
26. Prepayment options and terms: Prepayments required for subscriptions.
27. Will provide quotations for libraries interested in changing dealers or consolidating direct subscriptions.
28. Will assist libraries wishing to transfer orders to it by use of a follow-up system on its computer.

Yozmot Ltd.
P.O.B. 56055
Tel Aviv, Israel 61560

Telephone number: (972) (3) 5285397
Fax number: (972) (3) 5285397

1. Independent company established on January 1, 1990.
2-
3. No.
4. Maintains memberships in Israeli library associations and is regularly represented at the meetings of these associations.
5. Representatives actively participate in library association meetings in their country and/or area of the country they represent.

6. Provides serials from countries worldwide.
7a. Types of materials provided:
    Periodicals
    CD-ROM
    Back issues
    Government publications
    Loose-leaf services
    Sets
    Replacements
    Yearbooks/annuals (clients may request every second or third year)
    Memberships
    Serials on videocassette
    Serials with variant publishing
    Medical and scientific books
7b. No.
8. Will communicate with back issue dealers when supplying back issues for a client.
9. Services provided:
    New order reports
    Claim reports
    Out-of-print searching
10. Journal consolidation is standard practice.
11. Computerized services:
    Mailing lists according to subject requested
12-
13. No.
14. Issues quarterly catalog with booklists according to subject.
15. Clients will deal with different customer service representatives depending upon nature of the inquiry.
16. Will report back to the library on titles that it cannot supply. It will report only after the firm is satisfied that it cannot be supplied.
17. Rush orders accepted. The only added charge is the delivery charge.
18. No service fee; only charges are delivery charges.
19- Handling charges are included in the
20. price and will not be listed separately.

21. Will pay all or part of the shipping charges.
22- Titles are listed on invoice by purchase
23. order number.
24. Multiple copies of invoices supplied (no limit).
25. No.
26. Prepayment options and terms are available. Contact the firm directly for details.
27. Will provide quotations for libraries interested in changing dealers or consolidating direct subscriptions.
28. Will assist libraries wishing to transfer orders from other suppliers.

ITALY

Casalini Libri
Via Benedetto da Maiano, 3
50014 Fiesole (FI), Italy

Telephone number: (39) (55) 599941
Fax number: (39) (55) 598895

1. Independent company established in 1959.
2-
3. No response.
4. Maintains membership in the:
    American Library Association and
        various sub-sections of the ALA
    ARLIS
    Casalini Libri has a booth at the ALA
        Annual Conference and also at the
        ALA Midwinter Meeting
5. The firm has various staff members, responsible for different countries, who regularly attend library association meetings in their sectors.
6. Provides serials and monographs from Italy, the Vatican, San Marino, Malta, and the Italian Canton of Switzerland.

7a. Types of materials handled:
    Periodicals
    Monographic standing orders
    CD-ROM
    Back issues
    Government publications
    Loose-leaf services
    Sets
    Microforms
    Replacements
    Yearbooks/annuals (clients may request
        every second or third year)
    Memberships
    Serials on videocassette
    Serials with variant publishing
7b. Books (monographic firm orders).
8. Will contact the publisher in question
    when client requests back issues.
9. Services provided:
    Automatic renewal til forbid
    New order reports
    Claim reports
    Out-of-print searching
    Binding
    Blanket order/Approval plan service
10. Journal consolidation is standard
    practice. A charge to cover a percentage
    of the total annual postage costs is
    added.
11. Computerized services: Completely
    computerized service is offered.
12. Database is available to clients but not
    yet available online. Its bibliographic
    data are available to its customers on
    MARC format via tape or diskette.
13. Are planning interfaces with other
    library automation systems.
14. Issues at monthly intervals
    bibliographical cards for new
    publications, free of charge.
15. Clients will deal with one customer
    service representative assigned to the
    account.

16. Will report back to the library if it cannot supply a title. The firm tries until it is certain the title is unavailable.
17. Rush orders accepted at no added charge.
18. No service fee.
19- Postage and handling charges are
20. listed separately on the invoice.
21. No.
22. Titles are listed on the invoice as specified by the client.
23. Purchase order numbers provided on the invoice.
24. Multiple copies of invoices provided (no limit).
25. Presently are studying the possibility of generating invoices on computer tape or transferring them by other electronic means. The firm hopes to do so in the near future.
26. Prepayment options and terms are available. Deposit account facilities available whereby customers make advanced payments, annually or at six-month intervals, against future acquisitions. Interest is given on the deposit sum.
27. Will provide quotations for libraries interested in changing dealers or consolidating direct subscriptions.
28. Casalini Libri asks that libraries wishing to transfer orders to the firm cancel with their previous dealer(s).

The Courier, s.a.s.
Italian Books and Journals
Via L.A. De Bosis, 25
50145 Firenze, Italy

Telephone number: (39) (55) 300010
Fax number: (39) (55) 300036

1. Independent company established in 1986.
2-
5. No.

6. Provides serials and monographs from Italian publishers.
7a. Types of materials handled:
    Monographic standing orders
    Government publications
    Serials with variant publishing
    Back issues
7b. Books (monographic firm orders).
8. Will communicate with back issue dealers when supplying back issues for a client.
9. Services provided:
    Automatic renewal til forbid
    New order reports
    Claim reports
10. No response.
11. Computerized services:
    Various reports/printouts
12. Its database is available to clients through printouts.
13. No.
14. Issues a newsletter with the following bibliographic information: title, pages, pictures, plates, size, price, publisher, and subject.
15. Clients will deal with one customer service representative.
16. Will report back to the library if it cannot supply a title.
17. Rush orders accepted at no added charge.
18. No service fee; it charges only postage and packing.
19- Handling charges are listed separately
20. on the invoice.
21. Will pay shipping charges for shipments through the mail; will not pay for shipments by courier.
22- Titles are listed by purchase order on
23. the invoice.
24. Multiple copies of invoices supplied (no limit).
25. Invoices are generated on the computer.
26. No response.
27. Will provide quotations on books for libraries interested in changing dealers or consolidating direct subscriptions.

28. Will assist libraries that wish to
    transfer their orders to The Courier.

D.E.A. Librerie Internazionali
Via Lima 28
00198 Roma, Italy

Telephone number: (39) (6) 8551441
Fax number: (39) (6) 8543228

1. Independent firm established in 1949.
2. The firm has six branches.
3. No.
4. Maintains memberships in and is regularly
   represented at library association
   meetings (not specified).
5. Representatives actively participate in
   library association meetings in their
   country and/or area of the country they
   represent.
6. Provides serials and monographs from
   countries worldwide.
7a. Types of materials handled:
        Periodicals
        Monographic standing orders
        CD-ROM
        Back issues
        Government publications
        Loose-leaf services
        Sets
        Microforms
        Replacements
        Yearbooks/annuals (client may request
           every second or third year)
        Memberships
        Serials on videocassette
        Serials with variant publishing
7b. Books (monographic firm orders).
8. Will communicate with back issue dealers
   when supplying back issues for a client.

9. Services provided:
   Automatic renewal til forbid
   New order reports
   Claim reports
   Out-of-print searching
10. Journal consolidation is standard practice at no additional charge.
11. Computer services offered: Check-in of all journals before shipment. A delivery list is printed for each shipment and sent with the shipment.
12. Database not yet available to clients.
13. No.
14. Issues a monthly newsletter.
15. Response was "Yes" but does not indicate which part of the question it answers.
16. Will report back to libraries on titles it cannot supply.
17. Rush orders accepted with an added charge.
18. Service fee is a standard fee depending on the value of the order.
19. Service/handling charges are included in the price on the invoice.
20. Client may request that service/handling charges be listed separately.
21. Will pay all or part of the shipping charges.
22- Titles are entered on the invoice by
23. purchase order numbers.
24. Multiple copies of invoices supplied.
25. Invoices can be generated on computer tape or transferred by other electronic means.
26. Prepayment options and terms are available. Contact the firm directly.
27. Will provide quotations for libraries interested in changing dealers or consolidating direct subscriptions.
28. Libraries wishing to transfer orders to this firm must cancel with their present suppliers.

EBSCO Italia S.r.l.
Corso Brescia 75
10152 Torino, Italy

Telephone number: (39) (11) 248-0870
Fax number: (39) (11) 248-2916
For more information see EBSCO Subscription
Services, Inc. listing under UNITED STATES.

Lange & Springer
Agente per l'Italie
Ms. Eva Lindenmeyer
Via San Vidale 13
I-40125 Bologna, Italy

Telephone number: (39) (51) 238069
Fax number: (39) (51) 262982
For more information see Lange & Springer
listing under FEDERAL REPUBLIC OF GERMANY.

Marcello S.N.C.
via P. Canal 12/1
I-35137 Padova, Italy

Telephone number: (39) (49) 8721455
Fax number: (39) (49) 42854
For more information see the Schmidt
Periodicals GmbH listing under FEDERAL
REPUBLIC OF GERMANY.

Libreria gia Nardecchia S.r.l.
Via di Tor di Nona 39
00186 Roma, Italy

Telephone number: (39) (6) 6877617
Fax number: (39) (6) 68300010

1. Independent company established in 1895.
2-
5. No.

6. Provides serials and monographs only from Italy, including the Vatican.
7a. Types of materials handled:
    Periodicals
    Monographic standing orders
    Back issues
    Government publications
    Sets
    Replacements
    Yearbooks/annuals (client may request every second or third year)
    Serials with variant publishing
7b. Books (monographic firm orders).
8. Nardecchia is also a back issue dealer but it will sometimes communicate with back issue dealers when supplying a back issue for a client.
9. Services provided:
    Automatic renewal til forbid
    New order reports
    Claim reports
    Out-of-print searching
10. Journal consolidation is standard practice with no additional charges.
11. None.
12. No.
13. Interfaces with library automation systems are planned for the future.
14. Supplies photocopies of title pages and indexes of new interesting publications.
15. Client will deal with different customer service representatives depending on the nature of the inquiry.
16. Will report back to the library on titles it cannot supply but will try for six months to obtain them.
17. Rush orders accepted at no added charge.
18. No service fees.
19-
21. No response.
22. Not applicable. Titles are alphabetized on the invoices.
23. Purchase order numbers are provided on the invoice.
24. Multiple copies of invoices supplied (no limit).

25. Invoices not yet available on computer tape or through other electronic means.
26. No.
27. If there is any.
28. Libraries wishing to transfer orders to Nardecchia must cancel with their present suppliers.

JAPAN

Faxon Asia Pacific Company, Ltd.
4-17-10 Hara-Machida
Machida-Shi, Tokyo 194, Japan

Telephone number: (81) (427) 21-2252
Fax number: (81) (427) 21-2214
For more information see The Faxon Company, Inc. listing under UNITED STATES.

Nankodo Company, Ltd.
Subscription Department
42-6, Hongo 3-Chome,
Bunkyo Tokyo 113, Japan

Telephone number: (81) (3) 3811-9950
Fax number: (81) (3) 3811-5031
Telex number: 2722203
Cable address: BOOKNANKODO TOKYO

1. Independent company established on Feb. 13, 1879.
2. No.
3. Will not do business with North Korea.
4. No.
5. Representatives participate actively in some library association meetings in Japan.
6. Provides serials from countries worldwide, mainly United States and European countries.

147

7a. Types of materials handled:
     Periodicals
     Monographic standing orders
     CD-ROM
     Back issues
     Government publications
     Yearbooks/annuals
     Serials with variant publishing
7b. No.
8. Communicates with back issue dealers when supplying back issues for a client.
9. Services provided:
     Claim reports
10. Journal consolidation is available upon request at an additional charge.
11. Computerized services:
     Subscriptions and anything associated
12. Its database is not directly accessible.
13. No.
14. Issues annual catalog.
15. Regular clients are assigned one customer service representative. Irregular clients deal with various representatives.
16. Will report back to the library on titles that cannot be supplied after it has tried for six months.
17. Rush orders accepted with additional charge.
18. A service fee is charged and is a standard percentage.
19. Service/handling charges are included in the price.
20. Charges will not be listed separately on the invoice.
21. Will pay all or part of the shipping charges.
22. Titles are listed alphabetically on the invoice.
23. Purchase orders provided on the invoice.
24. Multiple copies of invoices provided if number is within reason.
25. Invoices can be generated on computer tape or transferred by other electronic means.
26. Response unclear.

27. Will provide quotations for libraries interested in changing dealers or consolidating direct subscriptions.
28. Will assist a library wishing to transfer orders to this firm.

Nihon Faxon Co., Ltd.
4th floor, Kurihara Building
7-8-13 Nishi Shinjuku
Shinjuku, Tokyo 160, Japan

Telephone number: (81) (3) 3367-3081
Fax number: (81) (3) 3366-0295
Telex number: 232-5149
For more information see The Faxon Company, Inc. listing under UNITED STATES.

Nihon Swets Inc.
World Times Building 5F
10-7 Ichiban-cho
Chiyoda-ku, Tokyo 102, Japan

Telephone number: (81) (3) 262-0701
For more information see the Swets Subscription Service listing under THE NETHERLANDS.

KENYA

Africa Book Services (EA) Ltd.
P.O. Box 45245
Nairobi, Kenya

Telephone number: (254) (2) 223641
Fax number: (254) (2) 330272

1. Independent company established in 1972.

2-
3. No.
4. Company maintains a membership in and is regularly represented at the meetings of the:
   Kenya Library Association, Nairobi
5. Representatives actively participate in library association meetings in their country and/or are of the country they represent.
6. Provides serials from Africa and the world.
7a. Types of materials handled:
   Periodicals
   Monographic standing orders
   Government publications
   Loose-leaf services
   Yearbooks/annuals
   Serials with variant publishing
7b. No response.
8. Will communicate with back issue dealers when supplying back issues for a client.
9. Services provided:
   Automatic renewal til forbid
   New order reports
   Claim reports
   Out-of-print searching
10. Journal consolidation is a standard practice.
11. Computerized services being planned.
12-
13. No.
14. Issues information containing title, author, editors, publishers, duration, and price.
15. Client will normally deal with one customer service representative.
16. Will report back to the library on titles it cannot supply.
17. Rush orders accepted at no extra charge.
18. Service fee is charged and is a standard percentage.
19. Service/handling charges may be listed separately or included in the price on the invoice.

20. Client may request that service/handling charges be listed separately on the invoice.
21. No.
22- Titles are entered on the invoice by
23. purchase order number.
24. Multiple copies of invoices supplied (no limit).
25. No.
26. Prepayment options and terms: Overseas periodicals are supplied on prepayment basis. Local titles are generally supplied on a monthly account.
27. Will provide quotations for libraries interested in changing vendors or in consolidating direct subscriptions.
28. Libraries wishing to transfer their orders to Africa Book Services must cancel with their present suppliers.

Book Sales (K) Ltd.
P.O. Box 20373
Nairobi, Kenya

Telephone numbers: (254)(2) 226543
                      (254)(2) 221031

1. Independent firm established in 1976.
2-
5. No.
6. Provides serials from countries worldwide: "whoever/where ever"
7a. Types of materials handled:
        Periodicals
        Government publications
7b. No response.
8-
13. Not applicable.
14. No.
15. Clients will deal with one customer service representative.
16. Will report back to the library on titles it cannot supply.

17. Rush orders accepted with an additional charge.
18-
20. Not applicable.
21. Pays all of the shipping charges.
22. Titles are entered on the invoice as listed on the order.
23. Purchase order number provided on the invoice.
24. Multiple copies of invoices provided (no limit).
25. Not applicable.
26-
28. No response.

KOREA

ESS Overseas, Inc.
S.L. Yeong Dong
P.O. Box 749
Seoul, Korea

Telephone number: (82) (2) 548-3541
Fax number: (82) (2) 511-4046

For more information see the EBSCO Subscription Services, Inc. listing under UNITED STATES.

Faxon Korea
DAE-OH Bldg., Suite 1507
26-5 Yoido-Dong
Youngdeungpo-Ku
Seoul 150, Korea

Telephone number: (82) (2) 780-8648
Fax number: (82) (2) 785-7218
For more information see The Faxon Company, Inc. listing under UNITED STATES.

Universal Publications Agency, Ltd.
UPA Building
54, Kyonji-Dong, Chongno-Ku
C.P.O. Box 1380
Seoul, Korea

Telephone number: (82) (2) 7347611
Fax number: (82) (2) 7390054
                    (82) (2) 7206505
Telex number: K28504 UNIPUB
Cable address: CHANGHOSHIN SEOUL

1. Independent company established in 1958.
2-
3. No.
4. Maintains memberships in local library
    associations and attends meetings
    regularly.
5. Representatives actively attend library
    association meetings held in Korea.
6. Provides serials and monographs from
    countries worldwide, including [former]
    Communist countries.
7a. Types of materials handled:
        Periodicals
        Monographic standing orders
        CD-ROM
        Back issues
        Government publications
        Loose-leaf services
        Sets
        Microforms
        Replacements
        Yearbooks/annuals (client may request
            every second or third year)
        Memberships
        Serials on videocassette
        Serials with variant publishing
7b. Books (monographic firm orders).
8. Communicates with back issue dealers when
    supplying back issues for a client.
9. Services provided:
        Automatic renewal til forbid
        New order reports
        Claim reports
        Out-of-print searching

10. "We render hand-delivery service, except [for] some libraries in provinces who receive post-delivery service, but without additional charge."
11. None.
12-
14. No.
15. Client deals with one customer service representative assigned to the account.
16. Will report back to the library after two months if it cannot supply a title.
17. Rush orders accepted at no extra charge.
18. Service fee is a standard percentage "unless requested specially."
19. Service/handling charges are normally included in the price.
20. Client may request that service charges be listed separately.
21. Pays all shipping charges.
22- Titles are entered on the invoice by
23. purchase order number.
24. Multiple copies of invoices supplied (no limit).
25. Invoices generated by computer or typewriter.
26. Prepayment options and terms: Prepayment is requested normally.
27. Will provide quotations for libraries wishing to change dealers or consolidate direct subscriptions.
28. If a library wishes to place a portion or its entire account with this firm, Universal Publications Agency will contact suppliers first for alternatives on behalf of clients.

Will Journal Inc.
54 Kyonji-Dong, Chongno-ku
Seoul 110-170, Korea

Telephone numbers:	(82) (2) 735-8755
	(82) (2) 735-8756
Fax number:	(82) (2) 722-5723
Telex number:	UNIPUB K28504
Cable address:	54 KYONJI-DONG, CHONGNO-KU, SEOUL

1. Independent company (affiliated with Universal Publications Agency, Ltd.) established on December 28, 1990.
2-
4. No.
5. Not applicable.
6. Provides serials and monographs from countries worldwide.
7a. Types of materials handled:
    Periodicals
    Monographic standing orders
    Back issues
    Government publications
    Yearbooks/annuals (client may request every second or third year)
    Memberships
    Serials with variant publishing
7b. Books (monographic firm orders).
8. No.
9. Services provided:
    New order reports
    Out-of-print searching
10. Journal consolidation is standard practice.
11. None.
12. No.
13. Not applicable.
14. No.
15-
16. Not applicable.
17. No.
18. Service fee is a standard percentage.
19. Service/handling charges included in the price.

20. Client may ask that service/handling charges be listed separately on the invoice.
21. Pays all shipping charges.
22- Titles are entered on the invoice by
23. purchase order number.
24-
25. No.
26. Prepayment options and terms are available. Contact the company directly.
27. No.
28. Not applicable.

LEBANON

Sulaiman's Bookshop
P.O. Box 11-8258
Beirut, Lebanon

Telephone number: 292755
    (Direct dialing not available from
    U.S.A.—call operator)

1. Independent company established in 1970.
2. Has addresses in Cyprus and the U.S.A. which are used only when there is no mail service to and from Lebanon.
3. No.
4. Company maintains membership in and regularly attends the meetings of:
    MELA (Middle East Studies Assn.)
5. Representatives actively participate in library association meetings in their country and/or area of the country they represent.
6. Provides serials and monographs from Arab countries, mainly Lebanon and Syria.

7a. Types of materials handled:
     Periodicals
     Monographic standing orders
     CD-ROM
     Back issues
     Sets
     Replacements
7b. Books (monographic firm orders).
8. No.
9. Services provided:
     Automatic renewal til forbid
     New order reports
     Claim reports
     Out-of-print searching
10. Journal consolidation is standard practice.
11. Computerized services: None available now but probably will have computerization by the end of 1993.
12. No response.
13. No.
14. Issues bimonthly lists of new titles and annual lists of all available titles. Bibliographic information included: title, volumes, year, issues, price.
15. Client will deal with one customer service representative.
16. Will report back to the library on titles it cannot supply. Length of time in reporting depends on the time given by the library and sometimes on the political situation in Lebanon.
17. Rush orders accepted at no extra charge.
18. No service fee; it charges the price listed by publishers. There is no handling charge.
19-
20. Not applicable.
21. Pays all shipping costs: The price listed by the publisher includes handling and postage. Price of subscriptions includes all shipping charges.
22- Titles are listed on the invoice in
23. alphabetical order with order numbers before each title.

24. Multiple copies (usually 3) of invoice provided (no limit).
25. Hopes to provide invoices generated on computer tape or by other electronic means in the future.
26. Prepayment options and terms are only available to local clients.
27. Will provide quotations for libraries interested in changing dealers or consolidating direct subscriptions.
28. Sulaiman's Bookshop asks libraries wishing to transfer orders from another supplier to cancel with their former supplier.

MALAYSIA

Academic Library Services (M) Sdn. Bhd.
Malaysia

For more information see Academic Library Services listing under SINGAPORE.

Parry's Book Center SDN. BHD.
No. 60 Jalan Negara
Taman Melawati
53100 Kuala Lumpur, Malaysia

Telephone number: (60) (3) 4087235
Fax number: (60) (3) 4079180
Telex number: PARRY'S MA 33243
Cable address: PABOKCENT

1. Independent company established in 1973.

2. Another office in Singapore:
       Parry's Book Center Pte. Ltd.
       #03-04, Golden Wall Auto Centre
       89 Short Street
       Singapore 0718, Republic of Singapore
           Telephone number: 02-3394572
           Fax number: 02-3387320
3. No.
4. Company maintains membership in library
   associations and is regularly represented
   at their meetings (associations not
   specified).
5. Representatives of the company actively
   participate in library association
   meetings in their country and/or area of
   the country they represent.
6. Provides serials and monographs from
   countries worldwide.
7a. Types of materials handled:
       Periodicals
       Monographic standing orders
       CD-ROM
       Back issues
       Government publications
       Sets
       Microforms
       Replacements
       Yearbooks/annuals (client may request
           every second or third year)
       Memberships
       Serials on videocassette
       Serials with variant publishing
7b. Books (monographic firm orders).
8. Will communicate with back issue dealers
   when supplying back issues for a client.
9. Services provided:
       Automatic renewal til forbid
       New order reports
       Claim reports
       Out-of-print searching
10. Journal consolidation available only upon
    demand with no additional charges.

11. Computerized services:
    Invoicing
    Ordering
    Sending of claims and reminders
    Confirmations of orders
    Correspondence
12. No.
13. Is planning to interface with library automation systems.
14. Issues a monthly newsletter and catalog with full bibliographic information.
15. Client will deal with different customer service representatives depending upon the nature of the inquiry.
16. Will report back to the library within three months on titles it cannot supply.
17. Rush orders accepted at no extra charge.
18. Does charge a service fee depending on whether it is a journal issue or a book order.
19- Service/handling charges are included
20. in the price on the invoice. Will not be listed separately upon request.
21. Will pay part of the shipping charges.
22- Titles are entered on the invoice by
23. the purchase order numbers.
24. Multiple copies of invoices supplied (no limit).
25. Invoices can be generated on computer tape.
26. Prepayment options and terms are available. Contact the firm for details.
27. Will provide quotations for libraries interested in changing dealers or consolidating direct subscriptions.
28. If a library wishes to transfer a portion of its account to this firm, Parry's notes that it is not necessary for the library to cancel with its present supplier.

MEXICO

DIRSA
Georgia #10-8
Col. Napoles
03810 Mexico, D.F., Mexico

Telephone number: (52) (5) 543-46-29
Fax number: (52) (5) 536-12-93
Telex number: 176-4639

1. Independent company established in 1977.
2-
3. No.
4. Maintains memberships in and regularly attends meetings of:
> SALALM
> AMBAC
5. No.
6. Imports serials from countries worldwide; exports materials from Mexico.
7a. Types of materials handled:
> Periodicals
> Monographic standing orders
> CD-ROM
> Back issues
> Government publications
> Loose-leaf services
> Sets
> Microforms
> Replacements
> Yearbooks/annuals (client may request
>   every second or third year)
> Memberships
> Serials on videocassette
> Serials with variant publishing
7b. Books (monographic firm orders).
8. Will communicate with back issue dealers when supplying back issues for a client.
9. Services provided:
> Automatic renewal til forbid
> New order reports
> Claim reports
> Out-of-print searching
> Photocopying of out-of-stock issues

10. Journal consolidation is standard practice at no extra charge.
11. Computerized services: All of its processes are computerized; orders, claim reports, etc., are offered on diskette.
12-
13. No.
14. Issues "Catalogo General de Publicaciones Periodicas Mexicanas" every two years. This includes approximately 3,500 titles of Mexican magazines.
15. Client will deal with different customer service representatives depending on nature of the inquiry.
16. Will report back to the library every four months on titles it cannot supply. Will continue searching if library requests.
17. Rush orders accepted. Airmail or courier charges are added.
18. Service fee depends on the price and which type of postage.
19. Service/handling charges are included in the price on the invoice.
20. Client may request that service charges be listed separately.
21. Pays all shipping charges.
22. Titles are entered alphabetically on the invoice. Subscriptions are separated according to regularly issued, irregularly issued, and those invoiced issue by issue.
23. Purchase order numbers always appear on the invoice.
24. Multiple copies of invoices can be supplied according to client specification.
25. Not yet.
26. Prepayment options and terms: All subscriptions must be prepaid. Deposit accounts available starting with $1000 U.S. dollars. Client will receive a monthly statement of the account.
27. Will provide quotations for libraries interested in changing dealers or consolidating direct subscriptions.

28. DIRSA requests that libraries transferring orders please cancel with their former suppliers.

Mexican Academic Clearing House/MACH
Apartado Postal 13-319
Deleg. Benito Juarez
03500 Mexico, D.F., Mexico

Telephone number: (52) (5) 674-07-79
Fax number: (52) (5) 673-62-09

1. Independent company established in 1969.
2-
3. No.
4. Maintains memberships in and is regularly represented at the meetings of SALALM.
5. Representatives actively participate in library association meetings in their country and/or area of the country they represent.
6. Provides serials and monographs from Mexico only.
7a. Types of materials handled:
        Periodicals
        Monographic standing orders
        CD-ROM
        Back issues
        Government publications
        Loose-leaf services
        Sets
        Microforms
        Replacements
        Yearbooks/annuals
        Serials on videocassette
7b. Books: Monographic firm orders and blanket orders.
8. Will communicate with back issue dealers when supplying back issues for a client.
9. Services provided:
        Automatic renewal til forbid
        New order reports
        Claim reports
        Out-of-print searching

10. Journal consolidation is the standard practice.
11. No response.
12. Database is available to clients "by price agreed."
13. No.
14. Issues a bimonthly annotated catalog called "MACH Booklist."
15. Client will deal with different customer service representatives depending upon nature of the inquiry.
16. Will report back after several months to the library on titles it cannot supply.
17. Rush orders accepted at no added charge.
18. Service fee is charged.
19. Service fee is included in the price. Packing and mailing charges are listed separately on the invoice.
20. Client may request that service charges be listed separately on the invoice.
21. No.
22. No response.
23. Purchase order numbers are provided on the invoice.
24. Multiple copies of invoices are provided: usually the original and two copies.
25-
26. No.
27. Will provide quotations for libraries interested in changing dealers or consolidating direct subscriptions.
28. If libraries wish to transfer orders to MACH, they must first cancel with the present supplier.

Puvill Mexico Division
Attn.: Miss Carmen Garcia Moreno
Empresa 109
Mixcoac
03910 Mexico, D.F., Mexico

For more information see Puvill Libros listing under SPAIN.

Librairie Internationale
10 rue T'ssoule
B.P. 302
Rabat (Souissi), Morocco

Telephone number: (212) (7) 75-01-83
Fax number: (212) (7) 76-76-67

1. Independent company established in 1960.
2-
3. No.
4. Maintains memberships in library
   associations and is regularly represented
   at the meetings (not specified).
5. Representatives actively participate in
   library association meetings in their
   country and/or area of the country they
   represent.
6. Provides serials and monographs from
   countries worldwide and is the only
   dealer which exports Moroccan
   periodicals.
7a. Types of materials handled:
        Periodicals
        Monographic standing orders
        CD-ROM
        Back issues
        Government publications
        Loose-leaf services
        Sets
        Microforms
        Replacements
        Yearbooks/annuals
        Serials on videocassette
7b. Books (monographic firm orders).
8. Will communicate with back issue dealers
   when supplying back issues for a client.
9. Services provided:
        Automatic renewal til forbid
        New order reports
        Claim reports
        Out-of-print searching

10. Journal consolidation is available. Did not state whether it was standard practice or on demand.
11. Computerized services: Provides computerized lists of new titles by subjects to clients on demand.
12. Its database is available to clients on demand.
13. Interfacing with library automation systems does not yet exist in Morocco.
14. Regularly send clients a computerized "belletinage." It also distributes to libraries pamphlets, etc., received from publishers.
15. Client will deal with one customer service representative assigned to the account.
16. Will report back to the library on titles it cannot supply after searching for one year. It sends copies of all correspondence concerning the search.
17. Rush order accepted with an added charge.
18. Service fee is a standard 5%.
19. Service/handling charges are included in the price.
20. Client may request that service charges be listed separately.
21. Agency pays all shipping charges.
22. Titles appear alphabetically on the invoice.
23. Purchase order numbers appear on the invoice.
24. Multiple copies of invoices supplied (limit 5-7).
25. Invoices can be generated on computer tape.
26. Prepayment options and terms: Available for private clients but "most clients are universities and ministries with whom prepayment is impossible in Morocco."
27. Will provide quotations for libraries interested in changing dealers or consolidating direct subscriptions.
28. Response unclear.

International Standards Books and Periodicals (P) Ltd.
Worldwide Publishing Systems
P.O. Box 3000-ISB
Kathmandu-3, City
Kathmandu-44601-3000, Nepal

Telephone number: (977) 270289
                    (no city codes needed)
Toll-free number: (977) 224005

1. Independent company established in 1991.
2-
5. No.
6. Provides serials from: Nepal, India, Pakistan, Bangladesh, Sri Lanka, China, Bhutan, United States of America, United Kingdom, Germany, and Canada.
7a. Types of materials handled:
    Periodicals
    Monographic standing orders
    Back issues
    Government publications
    Loose-leaf services
    Sets
    Yearbooks/annuals (client may request every second or third year)
    Memberships
    Serials with variant publishing
7b. No.
8. Will communicate with back issue dealers when supplying back issues for a client.
9. Services provided:
    Automatic renewal til forbid
    New order reports
    Claim reports
    Out-of-print searching
10. Journal consolidation is standard practice.
11. None.
12-
13. No.
14. Issues a monthly newsletter and catalog.
15. No.

16. Will report back to the library within three months of receipt of order on titles it cannot supply.
17. Rush orders accepted at no extra charge.
18. Service fee is charged. Prices will be quoted or published in our price list.
19- Service/handling charges are included
20. in the price with shipping extra and will not be listed separately upon request of client.
21. No.
22. Response unclear.
23. Purchase order numbers are provided on the invoice.
24. Multiple copies of invoices provided.
25. No.
26. Prepayment options and terms are available. Contact the firm directly.
27. Will provide quotations for libraries interested in changing dealers or consolidating direct subscriptions.
28. Response unclear.

THE NETHERLANDS

EBSCO Subscription Services - Western Europe
P.O. Box 204
1430 AE Aalsmer, The Netherlands

Telephone number: (31) (29) 77-23949
Fax number: (31) (29) 77-23156
Serves Western Europe with the exception of Italy, France, Germany, Spain, and Turkey. For more information see EBSCO Subscription Services listing under UNITED STATES.

Faxon Europe, B.v.
Postbus 197
1000 AD Amsterdam, The Netherlands

Telephone number: (31) (20) 565-9300
Fax number: (31) (20) 691-1735
Telex number: 14651

Office serves Europe, the Middle East, and
Africa. For more information see The Faxon
Co., Inc. listing under UNITED STATES.

NEDBOOK International B.v.
P.O. Box 3113
1003 AC Amsterdam, The Netherlands

Telephone number: (31) (20) 632 1771
Fax number: (31) (20) 634 0963
Telex number: 16727
Cable address: NEDBOOK

1. Independent company established 1986.
2. Other offices:

> NEDBOOK NEW YORK
> 24 Hudson Street
> Kinderhook, NY 12106
> Telephone number: (1) (518) 758-9512
> Fax number: (1) (518) 758-9514
>
> NEDBOOK SCANDINAVIA
> Holandargatan 31
> 113 59 Stockholm, Sweden
> Telephone number: (46) (8) 348 881
> Fax number: (46) (8) 332 613

3. No.
4. Company maintains memberships in library
    associations and is regularly represented
    at meetings (associations not specified).
5. Representatives participate in library
    association meetings, mostly in trade
    exhibits, in their country and/or area of
    the country they represent.

6. Provides materials from Western Europe, including the United Kingdom, Scandinavia, and North America.
7a. Types of materials handled:
    Periodicals
    Monographic standing orders
    CD-ROM
    Back issues
    Government publications
    Loose-leaf services
    Sets
    Microforms
    Replacements
    Yearbooks/annuals (client may request every second or third year)
    Serials on videocassettes
    Serials with variant publishing
7b. Books: Monographic firm orders and approval plans.
8. Will communicate with back issue dealers when supplying back issues for a client.
9. Services provided:
    Automatic renewal til forbid
    New order reports
    Claim reports
10. Journal consolidation available only upon demand with an additional charge.
11. No response.
12. No.
13. Currently it does not interface with library automation systems but "will certainly offer such interfaces in the future."
14. Issues biweekly bibliographic information on new and forthcoming (English language) titles published in The Netherlands. Bibliographic services regarding The Netherlands, Belgium, and Luxembourg are included in Nedbook's Approval Plan covering these countries.
15. "Customer services are, in principle, centralized but depending on the specifics of the inquiry the answer may be given by the appropriate department (for instance, CD-ROM)."

16. Will report back to the library on titles it cannot supply. Agent will hold order until cancelled by the library in cases of monographs and standing orders. Journal subscriptions and CD-ROM are regularly reported on if a subscription is not being issued as expected.
17. Rush orders accepted at no extra charge.
18. Service fee charged is not a standard percentage. The fee depends on the quality of the subscriptions. No service fee for continuations/standing orders. Will only charge a service fee for monographs if it receives no discount or a marginal discount from the publisher. The same applies for CD-ROM.
19. The service charge for journal subscriptions is listed separately on the invoice or can be included in the price, as requested. For CD-ROM the publisher's price applies in principle unless the publisher's price discount is nothing or insufficient, then the price is adjusted.
20. A client may request that service charges be listed separately for journal subscriptions, but not for CD-ROM.
21. Will pay all or part of the shipping charges for monographs and continuations from Amsterdam to the client. Will not pay for shipping charges for subscriptions and CD-ROM from the publisher to the client.
22. Titles are entered on the invoice by order number for monographs and continuations, alphabetically for journal subscriptions, and per title for CD-ROM.
23. Purchase order numbers always appear on the invoice.
24. Multiple copies of invoices supplied (limit three copies).
25. Invoices will be generated by computer tape or transferred by other electronic means in the near future.

26. Prepayment options and terms are available upon request and depending on the client. Contact the company directly for further details.
27. Will provide libraries interested in changing dealers or consolidating direct subscriptions with a quotation.
28. A library wishing to transfer their accounts to Nedbook must cancel with present suppliers. Nedbook will advise the library on how best to accomplish the transfer which often depends on the package and the library's ability to provide management information on its own holdings.

Martinus Nijhoff International B.v.
P.O. Box 269
2501 AX The Hague, The Netherlands

Telephone number: (31) (79) 684400
Fax number: (31) (79) 615698
Telex number: 34164

1. Independent firm established in 1853.
2. Other offices:

> Martinus Nijhoff North America
> 175 Derby Street
> Suite 13
> Hingham, MA 02043 USA
> Telephone number: (1) (617) 749-8805
> Toll-free number: (1) (800) 346-3662
> Telefax number: (1) (617) 749-8920
>
> Martinus Nijhoff Eastern Europe
> 30 II Yanko Zabunov Street
> 1504 Sofia, Bulgaria
> Telephone number: (359) (2) 431 236
> Telefax number: (359) (2) 464 164

Martinus Nijhoff
G.P.O. Box 2991
Bangkok 10501, Thailand
Telephone number: (66) (2) 247 1032
Telefax number: (66) (2) 247 1033

3. Will not do business with Latin American
    countries.
4. Company maintains memberships in and is
    regularly represented at the meetings of
    the:
        American Library Association
        Association of Subscription Agents
        North American Serials Interest Group
        IFLA
        Association of College & Research
            Libraries
5. Representatives actively participate in
    library association meetings in their
    country and/or the part of the country
    they represent.
6. Provides serials and monographs from
    countries worldwide, except Latin
    America.
7a. Types of materials handled:
        Periodicals
        Monographic standing orders
        CD-ROM
        Back issues
        Government publications
        Loose-leaf services
        Sets
        Microforms
        Replacements
        Yearbooks/annuals (client may request
            every second or third year)
        Memberships
        Serials on videocassette
        Serials with variant publishing
7b. Books (monographic firm orders).
8. Will communicate with back issue dealers
    when supplying back issues for a client.

9. Services provided:
   Automatic renewal til forbid
   New order reports
   Claim reports
   Bibliographic reports: title
      changes, frequency changes
   Reports on major price differences
   Supplies annual renewal checklist in
      June
10. Journal consolidation available on
    request. There is an additional
    consolidation charge and the shipping
    charges are also additional.
11. Computerized services offered: Complete
    computerized services.
12. Beginning in 1993, database and
    management information reports will be
    available to clients through an online
    connection.
13. Presently interfaces with the following
    library automations systems:
       NOTIS
       GEAC
       INNOVACQ
       and tailor-made interfaces
14. Issues two monthly catalogs:
    Nijhoff Information, New
          Publications from the
          Netherlands
    Nijhoff Information, New
          Publications from Germany,
          Austria, and Switzerland
    Issues an annual title file on microfiche
       and a biannual MNI COURANT, a
       newsletter.
15. Clients deal with one customer service
    representative regarding journals,
    continuations, standing orders,
    proceedings, government documents, and
    monographs.
16. Will report back to the library when it
    cannot supply a title. Will search for
    out-of-print books when requested.
17. Rush orders accepted at no additional
    charge.

18. Service fee: The titles from the major Western publishers are supplied at list price, thus with no service charge at all. The rest of the titles, in general, are supplied at a 3% service charge.
19- Service/handling charges are listed
20. separately on the invoice, but may also be included in the price upon request.
21. Shipping charges are included in the subscription prices.
22. Titles may be listed on the invoice in several ways. Client may choose.
23. Purchase order numbers as well as fund numbers are provided on the invoice.
24. Multiple copies of invoices NOT provided.
25. Invoices can be generated on computer tape or diskette (5 1/4" and 3 1/2").
26. Prepayment options and terms: A one-line invoice or a specified title-by-title invoice can be produced at any time. Nijhoff offers a discount schedule for early payments. The rate differs from year to year depending on the official interest rates.
27. Will provide quotations for libraries wishing to change dealers or consolidate direct subscriptions. Are always prepared to send any listing which the library needs.
28. Nijhoff asks that libraries cancel their orders with their present agents if interested in transferring those orders to Nijhoff. Nijhoff will support the libraries by informing publishers about the change of agent.

Swets Subscription Service
A Division of Swets & Zeitlinger BV
P.O. Box 830
2160 SZ Lisse, The Netherlands

Telephone number: (31) 2521-35111
Fax number: (31) 2521-15888
Telex number: 41325
Toll-free number: 1-800-447-9387
Cable address: Swezeit Lisse

1. Swets & Zeitlinger BV is an independent, family-owned company, established in 1901.
2. Other offices:

> Swets & Zeitlinger, Inc.
> P.O. Box 517
> Berwyn, PA 19312 U.S.A.
> Telephone number: (1) (215) 644-4944
>
> Swets UK Ltd.
> 32 Blacklands Way
> Abingdon Business Park
> Abingdon, Oxfordshire OX14 1SX,
> United Kingdom
> Telephone number: (44) 0235-30809
>
> Swets & Zeitlinger GmbH
> Bockenheimer Anlage 13
> D-6000 Frankfurt am Main-1, Germany
> Telephone number: (49) (69) 531099
>
> Swets Europeriodiques SA
> Parc d'Activites de Pissaloup
> B.P. 104
> 78191 Trappes Cedex, France
> Telephone number: (33) (1) 30-62-93-86
>
> Nihon Swets Inc.
> World Times Building 5F
> 10-7 Ichiban-cho
> Chiyoda-ku, Tokyo 102, Japan
> Telephone number: (81) (3) 262-0701

Swets Subscription Service
Box 30244
S 43403 Kungsbacka, Sweden
Telephone number: (46) 300-28314

3. No.
4. Swets maintains memberships in and
    regularly attends the meetings of the:
       IFLA - International Federation of
                Library Associations
       ALA - American Library Association
       MLA - Medical Library Association
       NASIG - North American Serials
                Interest Group
5. Representatives actively participate in
    library association meetings in their
    country and/or the area of the country
    they represent.
6. Operates worldwide and provides serials
    and monographs from countries worldwide.
7a. Types of materials handled:
       Periodicals
       Monographic standing orders
       CD-ROM
       Back issues
       Government publications
       Loose-leaf services
       Sets
       Microforms
       Replacements
       Yearbooks/annuals
       Memberships
       Serials on videocassette
       Serials with variant publishing
7b. Books (monographic firm orders).
8. No.
9. Services provided:
       Automatic renewal til forbid
       New order reports
       Claim reports
       Three-year price analysis reports
            for subscriptions maintained
            over the last three years
       Subscription checklists in various
            formats (upon request)

9. Services provided (continued):
    Pre-printed claim forms can be
        supplied free of charge
    Requests for sample copies handled
        free of charge
    Monographic orders are handled as
        part of the subscriptions
        account a library has with
        Swets. The library may choose
        to have monographic firm orders
        treated separately on a "book-
        and-bill" basis, with the
        material being forwarded from
        Swets along with a corresponding
        invoice.
10. Journal consolidation: FAST, Swets'
    consolidated shipment service, operates
    online on its premises in Holland and the
    USA. It includes check-in, claiming,
    control, management reports, scheduled
    delivery, and online file maintenance.
    This service is available only on demand
    at an additional fee, with delivery
    charges being billed at cost.
11. Computerized services: Complete
    computerized services.
12. Database availability: Online access to
    the Swets Subscription Service database
    through DataSwets, its interactive
    information and communication system
    enabling clients to search for
    bibliographic information, to look up
    their subscriptions, and to initiate
    administrative transactions. Clients dial
    in via the public data network of their
    choice.
13. Interfacing (invoicing) available for
    libraries using:
        NOTIS
        INNOVACQ/INNOPAC
        GEAC
14. Issues the annual Swets Serials
    Catalogue listing approximately 35,000
    titles for customers. Bibliographic data
    included (when available) : ISSN, year of
    publication, volume number(s), issue

number(s), frequency, subject, publisher or agent/distributor assigned by publisher, country of publication, publisher's price in original currency, postage included. When a publisher has separate domestic and foreign prices, these are indicated.

15. Each library customer is assigned a specific customer service staff member responsible for day-to-day account maintenance and dealing with all correspondence and inquiries pertaining to the account in question.

16. Will report back to the library on titles it cannot supply if and when the reason(s) for its inability to supply is/are known. Whenever this is not the case, Swets will expect its customers to monitor progress and initiate follow-up at regular intervals, in response to which Swets will continue pursuing until supply or a conclusive response ensues.

17. Rush orders accepted at no added charge.

18. Service fee: For foreign periodicals and continuations, 0% service charge for all titles published by eight major West-European publishers; a flat 3% service charge for all other periodicals and continuations.

For domestic periodicals and continuations, service charge percentage to be assessed on the basis of the mix of titles.

19- Service/handling charges are listed
20. separately on all invoices.
21. No.
22. Titles can be entered on the invoice in several ways upon client request:
     Alphabetically
     Alphabetically listed by order
          number
     Alphabetically listed by budget
          number
     Alphabetically, sorted by year
          of material being charged

23. Purchase order numbers provided on the invoice.
24. Multiple copies of invoices supplied (limit 5).
25. Invoicing is available on magnetic tape for libraries using NOTIS, GEAC, INNOVACQ/INNOPAC. Invoicing also available on floppy disk. Alternatively, libraries may also use the Swets standard tape format.
26. Prepayment options and terms: Swets offers libraries its One-Line invoice plan, whereby it charges, in April/May of each year, an estimated, unspecified lump-sum amount for next year's subscriptions. The library earns a basic 2 1/2% discount for payment posted in our records before October 1st, and an additional 1/2% discount for each month prior to October 1st by which payment is posted.

    The total discount earned in this way is granted on the specific definite prices shown on our Definite Invoice issued in November of the same year, resulting in a balance in Swets' favor or in favor of the library.
27. Will supply free quotations for libraries wishing to change dealers or consolidate direct subscriptions.
28. If a library wishes to transfer orders to Swets, it must cancel with its present supplier(s). Swets will include as part of each of its orders to the pertinent publishers a reference drawing their attention to the previous source of supply.

NEW ZEALAND

EBSCO New Zealand Ltd.
Private Bag 99914
Newmarket
Auckland, New Zealand

Telephone number: (64) (09) 524-8067
For more information see EBSCO Subscription
Services listing under UNITED STATES.

NIGERIA

Lat-Kay Commercial Enterprises
P.O. Box 52175, Falomo
Ikoyi, Lagos, Nigeria

Telephone number: (234) (1) 846932

1. Independent company established on
   September 19, 1991.
2. No.
3. Will not do business with South Africa.
4-
5. Not yet.
6. Provides serials and monographs from
   countries worldwide.
7a. Types of materials handled:
   Periodicals
   Monographic standing orders
   Back issues
   Government publications
   Replacements
   Yearbooks/annuals (client may request
      every second or third year)
   Serials with variant publishing
   Legal and religious publications
7b. Books (monographic firm orders).
8. Will communicate with back issue dealers
   when supplying back issues for a client.

9. Services provided:
   Automatic renewal til forbid
   New order reports
   Claim reports
   Out-of-print searching
10. Response unclear.
11-
13. Not applicable.
14. Not yet.
15. Client deals with different individuals depending on the nature of the inquiry.
16. Will report back to the library within 8 to 12 weeks on titles it cannot supply.
17. Rush orders accepted at no extra cost.
18. Processing and handling charges are charged depending on the size and quantity of orders.
19- Service/handling charges are listed
20. separately on the invoice.
21. Pays all shipping charges.
22. Titles may be entered on the invoice alphabetically or by order number.
23. Purchase order numbers appear on invoices.
24. Multiple copies of invoices provided (maximum 3).
25. Not yet.
26. Prepayment options and terms are available on annual subscriptions, contact agent for details.
27. Will provide quotations for libraries wishing to change dealers or consolidate direct subscriptions.
28. Upon request, it will assist libraries interested in changing suppliers.

Mabrochi International Co., Ltd.
143 Apapa Road
Ebute Metta (West)
P.O. Box 1509 Surulere P.O.
Lagos State, Nigeria

Telephone number: (234) (1) 847603

1. Independent company established in 1981,
    registered as a Limited Liability Co. in
    1987.
2. Other offices:

> Mabrochi International Co. Ltd.
> Y.11 Ibadan Street/Zaria Road
> Kaduna, Nigeria

3-
5. No.
6. Provides serials and monographs from
    countries worldwide (without trade
    restrictions).
7a. Types of materials handled:
    Periodicals
    Monographic standing orders
    CD-ROM
    Back issues
    Government publications
    Loose-leaf services
    Sets
    Microforms
    Replacements
    Yearbooks/annuals (client may request
        every second or third year)
    Memberships
    Serials on videocassette
    Serials with variant publishing
7b. Books (monographic firm orders).
8. Will communicate with back issue dealers
    when supplying back issues for a client.
9. Services provided:
    Automatic renewal til forbid
    New order reports
    Claim reports
    Out-of-print searching

10. Journal consolidation available on demand with additional charges.
11-
13. No.
14. Issues a periodic catalog of books available, new publications and out-of-print books.
15. No.
16. Will report back to the library on titles it cannot supply. Time period will depend upon the instructions of the library.
17. Rush orders accepted.
18. Service fee is charged and is between 10% and 15%.
19- Service/handling charges are listed
20. separately on the invoice.
21. Will pay part or all of the shipping charges if previously agreed.
22- Titles are entered on the invoice by
23. purchase order number.
24. Multiple copies of invoices provided.
25. No.
26. Prepayment options and terms: Agent asks for prepayment for expensive items not stocked by us.
27. Will provide quotations for libraries interested in changing dealers or consolidating direct subscriptions.
28. Will assist libraries wishing to change dealers upon request.

NORWAY

Erik Qvist Bokhandel A/S
Drammensveien 16
N-0255 Oslo, Norway

Telephone number:	(47) (2) 46 68 36
Fax number:	(47) (2) 55 89 88

1. Independent company established in 1905.
2. No.

3. The greater part of its business concentrates on European countries and America.
4-
5. No.
6. Provides serials and monographs from Norway, Denmark, Sweden, and England.
7a. Types of materials handled:
       Monographic standing orders
       Back issues
       Government publications
       Sets
       Replacements
       Yearbooks/annuals (client may request every second or third year)
7b. Books (monographic firm orders).
8. Will communicate with back issue dealers when supplying back issues for a client.
9. Services provided:
       Automatic renewal til forbid
       New order reports
       Claim reports
       Out-of-print searching
10. No.
11-
12. No response.
13. Interfaces with library automation systems:
       CD-ROM Bookbank
14. Issues a yearly booklist.
15. Client will be assigned one customer service representative if requested.
16. Will report back to libraries within two months on titles it cannot supply.
17. Rush orders accepted. Added charges only apply if order is supplied by airmail.
18. No service fee.
19. No service/handling charges.
20. No response.
21. No.
22. Titles are entered on the invoice by order number; will be entered alphabetically, if requested.
23. Purchase order numbers provided on the invoice.

24. Multiple copies of invoices supplied
    (maximum two).
25. Not yet.
26. No.
27. Will provide quotations for libraries
    interested in changing dealers or
    consolidating direct subscriptions.
28. If a library wishes to transfer its
    orders to Qvist, the library must cancel
    with its present supplier.

PAKISTAN

Mizra Book Agency
65, Shahrah-e-Quaid-e-Azam
Lahore 54000, Pakistan

Telephone number: (92) (42) 66839
Telex number: 44886 UBL PK
                     ATT: MIZRA BK
Cable address: Knowledge

1. Independent company established on
   July 1, 1949.
2. Other offices: None at present but will
   shortly be opening an office in the
   United States.
3. Will not do business in countries subject
   to regulations: Communist countries and
   India.
4. Company maintains memberships in and is
   regularly represented at the meetings of
   the:
        Pakistan Library Association
        Bangladesh Library Association
5. Representatives actively participate in
   library association meetings in their
   country and/or area of the country they
   represent.
6. Provides materials from countries
   worldwide except India and Communist
   countries.

7a. Types of materials handled:
   Periodicals
   Monographic standing orders
   Back issues
   Government publications
   Sets
   Replacements
   Yearbooks/annuals
   Serials with variant publishing
7b. Response unclear.
8. Communicates with back issue dealers when supplying back issues for a client.
9. Services provided:
   New order reports
   Claim reports
10. In process of negotiating journal consolidation.
11. None.
12-
14. No.
15. Client will deal with the subscription department concerning customer service matters.
16. Will report back to libraries on titles it cannot supply depending on publisher/distributor response.
17. Rush orders accepted. Added charge depends on clients; usually it does not add charges.
18. Service fee rates are fixed by the government and are charged accordingly.
19-
21. No response.
22. Titles appear on invoices according to customer requirements.
23. Purchase order numbers appear on the invoice.
24. Multiple copies of invoices supplied, normally three.
25. No.
26. Prepayment options and terms: Prepayment is required on subscriptions.
27. Will provide quotations for libraries interested in changing dealers and in consolidating direct subscriptions.

28. Will assist libraries wishing to transfer
    orders to the company.

NGM Communication
Ghufran House, 1st floor
1-22-C Area, Liaquatabad
(Post Box No. 2614)
Karachi-75900, I.R. Pakistan

Telephone number: (92) (21) 428625
Fax number: (92) (21) 613854.KNZ.PK.52
Cable address: ANJEEAMCOM

1. Independent company established on
    March 1, 1980.
2. No.
3. Will not do business with South Africa
    and Israel.
4-
5. No.
6. Provides serials and monographs from
    countries worldwide.
7a. Types of materials handled:
        Periodicals
        CD-ROM
        Back issues
        Government publications
        Loose-leaf services
        Sets
        Replacements
        Yearbooks/Annuals (client may request
          every second or third year)
        Memberships
        Serials with variant publishing
        Publications from research institutes
7b. Books (monographic firm orders).
8. No.
9. Services provided:
        Automatic renewal til forbid
        New order reports
        Claim reports
        Out-of-print searching
10. Journal consolidation available upon
    demand at an additional charge.

11. None.
12-
13. No.
14. Issues a monthly NGM Newsletter regularly and a price list of publications at a regular interval.
15. Clients will deal with one individual.
16. Will report back to the library on titles it cannot supply after the firm has made three attempts to obtain the materials.
17. No.
18. Service fee is charged.
19- Service/handling charges are included
20. in the price and will not be separately identified.
21. Pays all shipping charges.
22- Titles are entered on invoice by purchase
23. order number.
24. Multiple copies of invoices provided (limit two).
25. No.
26. Prepayment options and terms are available. Contact agent for details.
27. Will provide quotations for libraries wishing to change dealers or consolidating direct subscriptions.
28. Libraries wishing to transfer orders to the firm must first cancel with their present suppliers.

Pakistan Law House
Pakistan Chowk
P.O. Box 90
Karachi 1, Pakistan

Telephone number: (92) (21) 212455
Fax number: (92) (21) 219762
Cable address:
         PRILECT,KARACHI,PAKISTAN

1. Independent firm established in 1950.
2. No.
3. Will not do business with Israel due to government regulations.

4-
5. No.
6. Provides serials and monographs from the United Kingdom, United States, Holland, Germany, India, Australia, and Singapore.
7a. Types of materials handled:
       Periodicals
       Monographic standing orders
       Back issues
       Government publications
7b. Books (monograph firm orders).
8. No.
9. No response.
10. Journal consolidation upon demand with no additional service charge but additional postage will be charged.
11. None.
12-
13. No.
14. Publishes an irregular catalog of Pakistani law books and periodicals which provides author, title, price.
15. Clients will deal with one customer service representative.
16. Will report back to the library on titles it cannot supply. Length of time before reporting back depends on the nature of the material ordered.
17. Rush orders accepted at no extra charge.
18. Service fee is charged only if the firm does not receive a discount itself from the publisher.
19. Service/handling charges are included in the price.
20. Client may request that service charges be listed separately on the invoice.
21. No.
22-
23. No response.
24. Multiple copies on invoices provided.
25. No.
26. Prepayment is required for all orders.
27. No.
28. Libraries wishing to transfer order to the firm must first cancel with their present suppliers.

Paradise Subscription Agency
112, Depot Lines, Saddar
P.O. Box 3956
Karachi, Pakistan

Telephone numbers: (92) (21) 7780625
(92) (21) 7780629
Fax number: (92) (21) 5682704
Telex number: 23220 P.B.S. MG PK.

1. Independent company established in 1962.
2. No.
3. Will not do business with Israel and South Africa.
4-
5. No.
6. Provides serials and monographs from countries worldwide with the exception of Israel and South Africa.
7a. Types of materials handled:
    Periodicals
    Yearbooks
    Government publications
7b. Books (with the exception of anti-Islamic and vulgar).
8. Very rarely communicates with back issue dealers when supplying back issues for a client.
9. Services provided:
    Automatic renewal
    New order reports
    Claim reports
10. Journals are delivered by its own courier in Karachi, Lahore, Rawalpindi, and Islamabad. Some customers collect their journals from its office.
11. Computerized services: Paradise is planning to computerize its operation very soon. It will offer this service to its clients with regard to journal renewals, new arrivals, magazine and book promotion.
12. Database will be available to customers upon completion of its computerization.
13. No.

14. Issues information regarding book and magazine promotion.
15. Client will deal with different customer service representatives depending on the nature of the inquiry.
16. Will report back within three months to the library on titles it cannot supply.
17. Rush orders accepted. Paradise will charge shipping cost if material is not available at the agency and has to be ordered from any foreign country.
18. Service fee is charged (flat fee).
19- Service/handling charges are included in
20. the price on the invoice and will not be separated.
21. No.
22- Titles are listed on the invoice by
23. purchase order number.
24. Multiple copies of invoices supplied (limit five).
25. Invoices are generated by electronic means (not on computer tape).
26. Prepayment options and terms are available. Contact agency for details. Paradise will also issue proforma invoices at the client's request.
27. Will provide quotations for libraries interested in changing dealers or in consolidating direct subscriptions.
28. Response unclear.

Sipra Book Company
A-12, Street #2, Awami Chowk
Manzoor Colony
Karachi-44-03, Pakistan Zip 75460

Telephone number: (92) (21) 545086
Fax number: (92) (21) 437656
Telex number: 23531 INDMN PK.
                    (ATTN. SIPRA)

1. Independent, individually owned company established in 1980.
2. No.

3. No response.
4. Is a member of the Publishers and Booksellers Association and regularly attends its meetings.
5. Representatives actively participate in library association meetings in their country and/or area of the country they represent.
6. Provides serials and monographs from countries worldwide.
7a. Types of materials handled:
    Periodicals
    Monographic standing orders
    Back issues
    Government publications
    Loose-leaf services
    Sets
    Replacements
    Yearbooks/annuals
    Memberships
    Serials with variant publishing
7b. Books (monographic firm orders, handled by another branch).
8. Will communicate with back issue dealers when supplying back issues for a client.
9. Services provided:
    Automatic renewal til forbid
    New order reports
    Claim reports
    Out-of-print searching
10. Journal consolidation is standard practice. Client may choose to receive journals directly and firm will process client's claims. No additional charges.
11. Computerized services:
    Search of journal and books
12. Database availability: Will search for clients and supply printouts.
13. No.
14. Issues quarterly price lists "entering subject-wise listing of journals and books."
15. Client deals with two or three customer service representatives, depending upon the nature of the inquiry.

16. Will report back to the library after three months on titles it cannot supply.
17. Rush orders accepted with a 1% added charge.
18. Service fee: "On subscription of any journal we do not charge a service fee; our charge is included in discounts available from publishers."
19- Service/handling charges included in the
20. invoice price and will not be listed separately upon request.
21. Will pay all or part of the shipping charges.
22. Titles may be listed alphabetically or by purchase order number as requested by the client.
23. Purchase order numbers appear on all invoices.
24. Multiple copies of invoices provided (limit three).
25. Computerized invoices are issued.
26. Prepayment required for journals.
27. Will provide quotations for libraries wishing to change dealers or to consolidate direct subscriptions.
28. Will assist the library wishing to transfer a major part of its account to the firm.

PARAGUAY

Mayer's International
P.O. Box 1416
Gral. Diaz, 629
Asuncion, Paraguay

Telephone number: (595) (21) 448 246
Fax number: (595) (21) 444 719

1. Independent firm established on February 2, 1980.

2-
5. No.
6. Provides serials from countries worldwide.
7a. Types of materials handled:
    Periodicals
    Government publications
    Yearbooks/annuals (client may request every second or third year)
7b. No response.
8. Will communicate with back issue dealers when supplying back issues for a client.
9. Services provided:
    Automatic renewal til forbid
    New order reports
10. Journal consolidation available only on demand with additional shipping charges.
11. No response.
12-
14. No.
15. Clients will deal with different customer service representatives.
16. No.
17. Rush orders accepted at no additional charge.
18. Service fee is a standard percentage.
19. Depending upon total of the invoice, service/handling charges will be included in the price.
20. Client may request to have service charges listed separately on the invoice.
21. All shipping charges are paid by the vendor.
22- Titles are listed on the invoice by
23. purchase order number.
24. Multiple copies of invoices supplied (no limit).
25. Invoices can be generated on computer tape or transferred by other electronic means.
26. Prepayment options and terms: Customers who prepay are offered a reasonable discount.
27-
28. No response.

E. Iturriaga & Cia. S.A.
Jr. Ica 441-A Oficina 109
Casilla 4640
Lima, Peru

Telephone Number: (51) (14) 28-1979
Fax number: (51) (14) 46-9141

1. Independent company established in March 1947.
2-
3. No.
4. Maintains memberships in and is regularly represented at the meetings of:
   Camara Peruana del Libro en Peru
   SALALM
5. Representatives actively participate in library association meetings in their country and/or area of the country they represent only when it is required.
6. Provides serials amd monographs from Peru to worldwide.
7a. Types of materials handled:
   Periodicals
   Monographic standing orders
   Back issues
   Government publications
   Loose-leaf services
   Sets
   Replacements
   Yearbooks/annuals (client may request every second or third year)
   Serials with variant publishing
   Newspapers
7b. Books (monographic firm orders).
8. Will communicate with back issue dealers when supplying back issues for a client.
9. Services provided:
   Automatic renewal til forbid
   New order reports
   Claim reports
   Out-of-print searching

10. Journal consolidation available upon demand with no additional service charges. Peruvian shipping charges will be charged.
11. Computerized services are in the process of being developed.
12. Database is not yet ready for customer availability.
13. Planning to interface with NOTIS.
14. Issues a bimonthly catalog of current books with complete bibliographic information.
15. Client will deal with one assigned customer service representative.
16. Will report back to the library on titles it cannot supply. The firm will try to obtain it for two years.
17. Rush orders accepted at no added charge.
18. No service fee.
19. Service/handling charges are included in the price.
20. Only the postal charge may be listed separately on the invoice upon client request.
21. No.
22. Titles are listed "according to the purchase order number in alphabetical form."
23. Purchase order numbers appear on the invoice.
24. Multiple copies of invoices provided (maximum 2).
25. Invoices may be generated on computer tape or transferred by other electronic means.
26. Prepayment options and terms: According to the client's requirement.
27. Will provide quotations for libraries wishing to change dealers or to consolidate direct subscriptions.
28. Response unclear.

Libreria "Studium" S.A.
Plaza Francia 1164
Lima, Peru

Telephone numbers: (51) (14) 275960
                    (51) (14) 326278
Fax number: (51) (14) 321260

1. Independent company established in 1937.
2-
3. No.
4. Company maintains memberships in library associations and is regularly represented at these meetings. Firm did not specify which library associations.
5. Representatives actively participate in library association meetings in their country and/or area of the country they represent.
6. Provides materials from countries worldwide.
7-
15. No response.
16. Will report back to the library within one month on titles it cannot supply.
17. Rush orders NOT accepted.
18. Service fee is charged.
19. Response unclear.
20. Client may request that service charges be listed separately on the invoice.
21. No.
22. Titles are entered on the invoice by area and alphabetical order.
23. Purchase order number is provided on the invoice.
24. Multiple copies of invoices supplied.
25-
26. No response.
27. Will provide quotations for libraries wishing to change dealers or to consolidate direct subscriptions.
28. No response.

Lange & Springer
Ksiegarnia Naukowa
Przedstawicielstwo w Poznaniu
Dr. Zdzislaw Piotr Szkutnik
Ul. Ostroroga 30/1
60-349 Poznan, Poland

Telephone number: (48) (61) 671239
Fax number: (48) (61) 617293
For more information see the Lange & Springer
listing under FEDERAL REPUBLIC OF GERMANY.

Lange & Springer
Ksiegarnia Naukowa
Przedstawicielstwo: Magdalena Sliwka
Ul. Gombrowicza 11, no. 6
70-785 Szczecin, Poland

Telephone number: (48) (91) 609085
Fax number: (48) (91) 609085
For more information see the Lange & Springer
listing under FEDERAL REPUBLIC OF GERMANY.

RUSSIA & THE COMMONWEALTH
OF INDEPENDENT STATES

East View Publications
Contact: Mr. Usachev

(no address given)
Telephone number: (7) (95) 114-31-66
For additional information see the East View
Publications listing under the UNITED STATES.

Faxon International Moscow/ICSTI
Ul, Kuusinena 21B
Moscow 125252, Russia

Telephone number: (7) (95) 198-7431
Fax number: (7) (95) 943-0089
For additional information see the Faxon
Company, Inc. listing under the
UNITED STATES.

Lange & Springer
Biblioteka Po Estestvennym Naukam AN
Ul. Frunze 11
Moscow 121019, Russia

Telephone number: (7) (95) 291-2289
Fax number: (7) (95) 291-0003
For additional information see Lange &
Springer listing under FEDERAL REPUBLIC
OF GERMANY.

Lange & Springer
Biblioteka Po Estestvennym Naukam AN
Ul. Voschod 15
630200 Novosibirsk, Russia

Telephone number: (7) 3832-667197
Fax number: (7) 3832-660308
For additional information see Lange &
Springer listing under FEDERAL REPUBLIC
OF GERMANY.

SIERRA LEONE

New Horizons
7 Bultney Street
PMB 391
Freetown, Sierra Leone

Telephone number: (232) (22) 226289
Fax number: (232) (22) 224387

1. Independent firm established in 1981.
2. No.
3. Will not do business with Israel.
4-
5. No.
6. Provides serials and monographs from Sierra Leone.
7a. Types of materials handled:
    Periodicals
    Monographic standing orders
    Back issues
    Government publications
    Loose-leaf services
    Yearbooks/annuals (client may request every second or third year)
7b. Books (monographic firm orders).
8. No.
9. Services provided:
    Automatic renewal til forbid
    New order reports
10. Journal consolidation available. The firm did not indicate whether or not it was standard practice.
11. Computerized services:
    Address lists
12-
14. No.
15. Client will deal with one customer service representative.
16. Will report back to the library within one month on titles it cannot supply.
17. Rush orders accepted at no added charge.
18. No service fee charged.
19-
20. No.
21. Firm pays all of the shipping charges.

22- Titles are entered on the invoice by
23. purchase order number.
24. Multiple copies of invoices supplied
    (maximum three).
25. No.
26. Prepayment options and terms: All
    transactions on a prepayment basis.
27. Will provide quotations for libraries
    wishing to change vendors or consolidate
    direct subscriptions.
28. "Our market is limited and _entire_ account
    does not add to any such big figure so
    the situation does not arise."

SINGAPORE

Academic Library Services
30 East Coast Road #03-21/22
Paramount Shopping Center, Singapore 1542

Telephone numbers: (65) 2872705
                          (65) 2825017
              (no city codes needed)
Fax number: (65) 2871862
Telex number: RS 38615 MANAGE

1. Independent company established in March
    1986.
2. Other offices:

        Academic Library Services (M) Sdn.Bhd.
        Malaysia
3-
4. No.
5. Representatives actively particapte in
    library association meetings in their
    country and/or area of the country they
    represent.
6. Provides serials from countries
    worldwide.

7a. Types of materials handled:
    Periodicals
    Monographic standing orders
    CD-ROM
    Back issues
    Government publications
    Yearbooks/annuals
    Videocassettes
7b. No.
8. Will communicate with back issue dealers when supplying back issues for a client.
9. Services provided:
    Automatic renewal til forbid
    New order reports
    Claim reports
10-
11. No response.
12-
13. No.
14. Issues a monthly newsletter.
15. Client will deal with different customer service representatives depending on the nature of the inquiry.
16. Will report back to the library on titles that it cannot supply within four to six weeks.
17. Rush orders accepted at no additional charge.
18. Service fee is charged.
19- Service/handling charges are listed
20. separately on the invoice.
21. Pays all or part of the shipping charges.
22- Titles are entered on the invoice by
23. purchase order number.
24. Multiple copies of invoices provided.
25. No.
26. Prepayment options and terms are available. Contact firm directly for details.
27. Will provide quotations for libraries wishing to change dealers or to consolidate direct subscriptions.
28. Will assist libraries that wish to transfer its account from another vendor.

Chopmen Publishers
865 Mountbatten Road #05-28
Katong Shopping Centre, Singapore 1543

Telephone number: (65) 3441495
Fax number: (65) 3440180
           (no city code needed)
Cable address: NIRMALJI, SINGAPORE

1. Independent company established in 1963.
2-
4. No.
5. Representatives actively participate in library association meetings in their country and/or area of the country they represent.
6. Provides serials and monographs from countries in the Asia Pacific area only.
7a. Types of materials provided:
    Periodicals
    Monographic standing orders
    CD-ROM
    Back issues
    Government publications
    Loose-leaf services
    Sets
    Microforms
    Replacements
    Yearbooks/annuals (client may request every second or third year)
    Memberships
    Serials on videocassette
    Serials with variant publishing
    Out-of-print items (if not available, will provide xerox copies)
7b. Books (monographic firm orders).
8. Will communicate with back issue dealers when supplying back issues for a client.
9. Services provided:
    Automatic renewal til forbid
    New order reports
    Claim reports
    Out-of-print searching
10. Journal consolidation is standard practice.
11. None.

12-
14. No.
15. Client will usually deal with one customer service representative.
16. Will report back to the library within six months on titles it cannot supply.
17. Rush orders acccepted at no extra charge.
18. No separate service fee.
19. Service/handling charges are included in the price. Postage and packing are shown on the invoice as separate items.
20. It would be difficult to list service charges separately if a client requested this.
21. No.
22- Titles are entered on the invoice by
23. purchase order number.
24. Multiple copies of invoices supplied (no limit).
25. No.
26. Prepayment options and terms available. For details, contact Chopmen directly.
27. Will supply a quotation for a library interested in changing dealers or consolidating direct subscriptions.
28. Libraries wishing to transfer orders to Chopmen should cancel with their present suppliers.

Faxon Singapore
7500-A Beach Road
#04-319 The Plaza, Singapore 0719

Telephone number: (65) 293-2341
Fax number: (65) 293-2348
            (no city codes needed)
For additional information see the Faxon Co., Inc. listing under the UNITED STATES.

Intermail Enterprise Pte. Ltd.
Block 805, Tampines Ave. 4
#07-27, Singapore 1852

Telephone number: (65) 7835935
Fax number: (65) 7857015
              (no city codes needed)
For additional information see the C. V. Toko
Buku Tropen listing under INDONESIA.

Parry's Book Center Pte. Ltd.
#03-04 Golden Wall Auto Centre
89 Short Street, Singapore 0718

Telephone number: (65) 02-3394572
Fax number: (65) 02-3387320
For additional information see Parry's Book
Center SDN. BHD. listing under MALAYSIA.

SPAIN

Dawson Iberica
c/o Base, Aribau 282-284
Piso 7-Oficina 3
E 08006 Barcelona, Spain

Telephone number: (34) (3) 4142000
For additional information see Dawson
Holdings PLC listing under UNITED KINGDOM.

EBSCO Subscription Services - Spain
Apartado de Correos 40-001
28080 Madrid, Spain

Telephone number: (34) (1) 433-0228
Fax number: (34) (1) 433-7009
For additional information see EBSCO
Subscription Services, Inc. listing under
UNITED STATES.

IBERBOOK International, S. L.
C/Torpedero Tucuman, 16
28016 Madrid, Spain

Telephone numbers: (34) (1) 250-82-62
                   (34) (1) 458-24-46
Fax number: (34) (1) 250-82-60

1. Independent firm established in 1986.
2-
3. No.
4. Attends the twice yearly meetings of the
    American Library Association.
5. Representatives actively participate in
    library association meetings in their
    country and/or area of the country they
    represent.
6. Provides serials and monographs from
    Spain.
7a. Types of materials handled:
        Periodicals
        Monographic standing orders
        CD-ROM
        Back issues
        Government publications
        Loose-leaf services
        Sets
        Microforms
        Replacements
        Yearbooks/annuals (client may request
            every second or third year)
        Memberships
        Serials on videocassette
        Serials with variant publishing

7b. Books (monographic firm orders).
8. Will order back issues requested by clients from the publisher.
9. Services provided:
    Automatic renewal til forbid
    New order reports
    Claim reports
    Out-of-print searching
    Blanket orders/Approval plans
    Bibliographic information
10. Journal consolidation is the standard practice.
11. Computerized services: All services completely computerized.
12. Database not available to clients but will be in the future.
13. Planning interfaces with other library automation systems.
14. Produce bibliographical cards every two months which are sent free of charge to clients.
15. Clients will deal with one customer service representative assigned to the account.
16. It keeps orders active in its files until it is certain that it cannot supply or until the client gives instructions to cancel.
17. Rush orders accepted at an extra charge.
18. No service charge.
19- Postage and handling charges only are
20. added and are listed separately on the invoice.
21. No.
22. Titles are entered on the invoice per client's instructions.
23. Purchase order number appears on the invoice.
24. Multiple copies of invoices can be supplied with no limit.
25. Is currently working on generating invoices on computer tape.
26. Prepayment options and terms: Deposit account facilities are available.

27. Will provide quotations for libraries wishing to consolidate direct subscriptions.
28. Client wishing to change suppliers must cancel with its present supplier.

Libreria Passim, S.A.
Bailen, 134
08009 Barcelona, Catalonia, Spain

Telephone number: ((34) (3) 4574757

1. Independent company established in 1963.
2-
5. No.
6. Provides serials and monographs from Spain.
7a. Types of materials handled:
    Periodicals
    Monographic standing orders
    CD-ROM
    Government publications
    Sets
    Microforms
    Replacements
    Yearbooks/annuals (client may request every second or third year)
    Serials with variant publishing
7b. Books (monographic firm orders).
8. No response.
9. Services provided:
    Automatic renewal til forbid
    New order reports
    Claim reports
    Out-of-print searching
10. Journal consolidation available only on demand with additional shipping charges.
11. None.
12-
13. No response.

14. Issues catalogs which contain all bibliographic information. A brief abstract is included if the title is not clear enough or when it could cause confusion.
15. The customer service representative with whom the client will work will depend upon the language of the client.
16. Will report back to the library on titles it cannot supply. Passim will not report back until they have a report of unavailability from the publisher. This sometimes may take six months, depending upon the publisher.
17. Rush orders accepted at no extra charge.
18. Service charge is charged only when the discount percentage to Passim from the publisher is not sufficient.
19- Service/handling charges are included in
20. the price. When Passim does the shipping (such as for annual publications or serials supplied by the volume), charges are listed separately.
21. Passim will pay the shipping charges only in the case of very expensive items.
22. Titles are entered on the invoice by purchase order number, if available. If not, titles are entered alphabetically.
23. Purchase order number provided on the invoice.
24. Multiple copies of invoices supplied (limit five).
25-
27. No response.
28. If libraries wish to transfer orders to Libreria Passim, the library must cancel with its present supplier.

Puvill Libros
Boters 10 y Paja 29
08002 Barcelona, Spain

Telephone numbers: (34) (3) 3182986
                       (34) (3) 3181848
Fax number: (34) (3) 4123140

1. Independent company established in 1928.
2. Other offices:

> Mr. Dror Faust
> Puvill U.S. Representative
> 264 Derrom Avenue
> Paterson, NJ 07504 U.S.A.
>
> Puvill Mexico Division
> Attn.: Miss Carmen Garcia Moreno
> Empresa 109, Mixcoac
> 03910 Mexico, D.F., Mexico

3. No.
4. Maintains memberships in and is regularly represented at the meetings of:
    SALALM
    NACS
    Also attends more than 15 meetings hosted by other associations.
5. Representatives offer information and customer services.
6. Provides serials and monographs from Spain, Portugal, Mexico, and other Latin American countries.
7a. Types of materials handled:
    Periodicals
    Monographic standing orders
    CD-ROM
    Back issues
    Government publications
    Loose-leaf services
    Sets
    Microforms
    Replacements
    Yearbooks/annuals (client may request
        every second or third year)
    Memberships

7a. Types of materials handled (continued):
Serials on videocassette
Serials with variant publishing
7b. Books (monographic firm orders and
approval plans).
8. Will communicate with back issue dealers
when supplying back issues for a client.
9. Services provided:
Automatic renewal til forbid
Claim reports
Out-of-print searching
10. Journal consolidation is standard
practice.
11. Computerized services:
Bibliographical cards
Computerized database for
subscriptions and other orders
12. No.
13. Is presently investigating interfacing
with some library automation systems.
14. Offers a wide selection of regularly
published catalogs as well as issuing
bibliographical cards.
15. Clients will deal directly with
Mr. Jose Puvill, the director.
16. Will report back to the library after an
adequate period of time on titles it
cannot supply. The length of time depends
on the nature of the inquiry.
17. Rush orders accepted and there is an
added charge.
18. Service fee charged is a standard
percentage of the price.
19. Service/handling charges are included in
the price on the invoice.
20. Client may request that service/handling
charges be listed separately on the
invoice.
21. Will pay all of part of the shipping
charges "if adequate."
22- Titles appear alphabetically on the
23. invoice with purchase order numbers.
24. Multiple copies of invoices provided (no
limit).

25. Invoices are generated by a computer but are not generated on computer tape or any transferable means.
26. Prepayment options and terms are available. Contact the firm directly for details.
27. Will provide quotations for libraries wishing to change dealers or consolidate direct subscriptions.
28. If a library is transferring its orders from another agent to Puvill, Puvill asks that the library cancel with their present supplier.

SUDAN

The Nile Bookshop
New Extension Street 41
P.O. Box 8036
Khartoum, Sudan

Telephone numbers: 43749
                            44189
Calls must be operator-assisted.

1.   Independent firm established in 1977.
2.   No.
3.   Will not do business with Israel.
4-
5.   No.
6.   Provides serials from countries worldwide.
7a. Types of materials handled:
        Periodicals
        Back issues
7b. No response.
8.   Will communicate with back issue dealers when supplying back issues for a client.
9.   Services provided:
        New order reports
10-
13. No response.

14. Issues a catalog.
15. Client will deal with different customer service representatives depending on the nature of the inquiry.
16. Will report back to the library on titles it cannot supply.
17. Rush orders accepted at no extra charge.
18. Service fee charged is a standard percentage.
19-
23. No response.
24. Multiple copies of invoices supplied.
25-
26. No.
27. Will provide quotations for libraries wishing to change dealers or to consolidate direct subscriptions.
28. No response.

SWEDEN

Akerbloms Universitetsbokhandel AB
P.O. Box 83
S-901 03 Umea, Sweden

Telephone number: (46) (90) 125770
Fax number: (46) (90) 120673

1. Independent firm established in 1843.
2-
5. No.
6. Provides serials and monographs from countries worldwide.
7a. Types of materials handled:
    Periodicals
    Monographic standing orders
    CD-ROM
    Back issues
    Government publications
    Replacements
    Yearbooks/annuals
    Serials with variant publishing

7b. Books (monographic firm orders).
8. Will communicate with back issue dealers
    when supplying back issues for a client.
9. Services provided:
        Automatic renewal til forbid
        New order reports
10. Journal consolidation available only upon
    demand at an additional charge.
11. Computerized services:
        Order and claim service
12-
14. No.
15. Client will deal with one customer
    service representative.
16. Will report back to the library on titles
    it cannot supply. Will try to obtain the
    materials for two years.
17. Rush orders accepted at no additional
    charge.
18. Service fee is a standard percentage.
19. Service/handling charges are included in
    the price on the invoice.
20. Firm will not separate charges from the
    price.
21. No.
22. Titles are alphabetized on invoices.
23. Purchase order numbers provided on
    invoices.
24. Multiple copies of invoices supplied
    (maximum 3).
25-
27. No.
28. If a library wishes to transfer its
    orders from another dealer, the firm asks
    that the library cancel. It will,
    however, notify the publisher that the
    client has now changed dealers.

NEDBOOK Scandinavia
Holandargatan 31
113 59 Stockholm, Sweden

Telephone number: (46) (8) 348-881
Fax number: (46) (8) 332-613
For additional information see NEDBOOK
International B.v. listing under
THE NETHERLANDS.

Swets Subscription Service
Box 30244
S-43403 Kungsbacka, Sweden

Telephone number: (46) (30) 028-314
For additional information see Swets
Subscription Service listing under
THE NETHERLANDS.

Tidskriftscentralen Subscription Services
Box 6086
102 32 Stockholm, Sweden

Telephone number: (46) (8) 30 15 00
Fax number: (46) (8) 30 13 35

1. Firm is operated by Nordiska Bokhandels
    Gruppen.
2-
3. No.
4. Company maintains memberships in library
    associations and is regularly represented
    at these meetings. (Associations were not
    specified)
5. Representatives actively participate in
    library association meetings in their
    country and/or area of the country they
    represent.
6. Provides serials and monographs from
    countries worldwide.

7a. Types of materials handled:
      Periodicals
      Monographic standing orders
      CD-ROM
      Back issues
      Government publications
      Loose-leaf services
      Sets
      Microforms
      Replacements
      Yearbooks/annuals
      Serials on videocassette
      Serials with variant publishing
7b. Books (monographic firm orders handled by another branch of the firm).
8. Will communicate with back issue dealers when supplying back issues for a client.
9. Services provided:
      Automatic renewal til forbid
      New order reports
      Claim reports
10. Journal consolidation available upon demand at an additional charge.
11. Computerized services:
      Online access to title file
12. Database availability: Clients have access to the title file through a PC.
13. No.
14. Issues quarterly newsletter which includes bibliographic information with a few lines of text.
15. Client may request to have an individual staff member assigned as its customer service representative.
16. Will report back to the library on titles it cannot supply.
17. Rush orders accepted at no added charge.
18. Service fee is a standard percentage "depending on various facts."
19. Service/handling charges are included in the price on the invoice.
20. Client may request that service/handling charges be listed separately on the invoice.
21. No.

22. Titles are entered on the invoice as requested by the client.
23. Purchase order numbers provided on invoices.
24. Multiple copies of invoices supplied.
25. No.
26. Prepayment options and terms are available depending on the purchasing amount.
27. Will provide quotations for libraries interested in changing dealers or in consolidating direct subscriptions.
28. Will assist a library wishing to transfer its orders to this company.

Wennergren-Williams International
Nordenflychtsvagen 74
Box 30004
S 104 25 Stockholm, Sweden

Telephone number: (46) (8) 1367000
Fax number: (46) (8) 6187182
Telex number: 19937

1. Firm was established in 1921; owned since September 1991 by The Faxon Company, Inc.
2. Its owner, Faxon, has offices worldwide.
3. Will not do business in countries where Faxon already has representatives.
4. Company maintains memberships in and is regularly represented at the meetings of the:
    A.S.A.
    ALPSP
    United Kingdom Serials Group
    EUSIDIC
    STM
    EIIA
    TLS (Technical Librarian Society in Sweden)
    SBS & SAB (two Swedish Librarian Societies)

5. Representatives actively participate in library association meetings in their country and areas of the country they represent.
6. Provides serials from countries worldwide.
7a. Types of materials handled:
    Periodicals
    Monographic standing orders
    Government publications
    Replacements
    Yearbooks/annuals
    Memberships
    Serials on videocassette
    Serials with variant publishing
    Single copies, sample copies
7b. Answer not clear.
8. Will communicate with back issue dealers when supplying back issues for a client.
9. Services provided:
    Automatic renewal til forbid
    New order reports
    Claim reports
10. Not available.
11. Computerized services:
    Online ordering and claiming and
        looking at the customer's own
        purchasing through the company
12. Database availability:
    Title file
    Order stock of purchased
        subscriptions
13. No.
14. Issues a quarterly newsletter. Issues various lists with: abstracts of new titles, ceased titles, name changes, and such information as change of frequency, delayed publications, and publications in economic trouble, etc.
15. Larger clients will have their own personal customer service representative assigned as well as a backup. Smaller clients deal with the first person who answers the phone.
16. Will always report back to the library on titles it cannot supply.

17. Rush orders accepted at no added charge.
18. No service fee charged.
19- Service/handling charges are included in
20. the price on the invoice and will not be listed separately upon request.
21. No.
22. Titles will be listed on the invoice as requested by the client: by ISSN, alphabetically, client's reference number, client's consignee, or other alternatives.
23. Purchase order numbers provided on the invoice.
24. Multiple copies of invoices supplied.
25. No.
26. Prepayment options and terms: Various models are available. The clients can request what suits them best. The interest (recommendations from Sweden's RIKSBANK) goes to the client's benefit ONLY.
27. No.
28. Prefer that libraries wishing to transfer titles to this company cancel with their present suppliers themselves. However, this comapny will assist the library with transferring the titles with the help of former invoices, lists, and even will provide its own staff to work at the library.

European Book Center
Books Import Export S.A.
Rte Henri Dunant 1
P.O. Box 4
1702 Fribourg, Switzerland

Telephone number: (41) (37) 28-31-43
Fax number: (41) (37) 28-26-29
Cable address: Bokcenter/Fribourg/Switzerland

1. Firm established on April 26, 1967, and is an independently owned company.
2-
3. No.
4. Company maintains memberships in and is regularly represented at the meetings of the:
    Swiss Booksellers Association
    Fribourg Booksellers Association
    Zurich Booksellers Association
5. Representatives actively participate in library association meetings in their country and/or area of the country they represent.
6. Provides serials and monographs from any European country.
7a. Types of materials provided:
    Periodicals
    Monographic standing orders
    CD-ROM
    Back issues
    Government publications
    Loose-leaf services
    Sets
    Microforms
    Replacements
    Yearbooks/annuals (client may request every second or third year)
    Memberships
    Serials on videocassette
    Serials with variant publishing
7b. Books (monographic firm orders).
8. Communicates with back issue dealers when supplying back issues for a client.

9. Services provided:
       Automatic renewal til forbid
       New order reports
       Claim reports
       Out-of-print searching
10. Journal consolidation available upon discussion with agent.
11. This question was unclear to the agents.
12. Response unclear.
13. Automation and interfacing with NOTIS are in the planning stages.
14. Will supply publisher's catalogs and information upon specific requests.
15. Clients are assigned one individual customer service representative.
16. Will report back to the library. "We follow strictly the wishes of individual libraries; different libraries have different internal policy and we follow the individual policy of every library."
17. Rush orders accepted at no extra charge.
18. Service fee: "If we earn a commission from the publisher, there is no service fee. If it is [a] very small fee which is not enough to cover expenses, then we add [a] small percentage which depends on the amount of the subscription. If publisher does not allow us commission, then we add our fee."
19. Service/handling fees included in the price on the invoice.
20. Client may request that service charges be listed separately on the invoice.
21. No.
22- Titles are listed by purchase order
23. number on the invoice or according to the wishes of the client.
24. Multiple copies of invoices supplied (limit four).
25. Invoices accompany the books.
26. Prepayment options and terms: Customers may prepay and every case is discussed individually according to library wishes and rules.

27. Will provide quotations for libraries wishing to consolidate orders or change vendors.
28. It will assist libraries by contacting their present dealers if they wish to switch vendors.

Buchhandlung Jaeggi AG
Freie Strasse 32
CH-4001 Basel, Switzerland

Telephone number: (41) (61) 261 52 00
Fax number: (41) (61) 261 52 05

1. Independent company established in 1822.
2-
5. No.
6. Provides serials from countries worldwide.
7a. Types of materials handled:
      Periodicals
      Monographic standing orders
      Back issues
      Government publications
      Loose-leaf services
      Sets
      Replacements
      Yearbooks/annuals (client may request every second or third year)
      Serials on videocassette
      Serials with variant publishing
7b. Would rather not handle book orders.
8. Contacts the editors when supplying back issues for a client.
9. Services provided:
      Automatic renewal til forbid
      New order reports
      Claim reports
      Out-of-print searching
10. Journal consolidation available on demand with additional shipping charges.
11. Computerized services:
      Bibliographies
      Lists of titles available

12. Not available.
13. No plans to interface.
14. No.
15. Client will deal with one person only in charge of the corresponding department.
16. Will report back within three months to the library on titles it cannot supply. Jaeggi will try to obtain material for about one to three months.
17. Rush orders accepted with an added charge for airmail postage.
18. No service fee.
19- Shipping charges are charged separately
20. about every three months.
21. No.
22. Titles are entered on the invoice in no special order.
23. Purchase order numbers provided on the invoice.
24. Multiple copies of invoices supplied (no limit).
25. Invoices can be generated on computer tape or transferred by other electronic means.
26. No.
27. Will provide quotations for a library interested in changing dealers or consolidating direct subscriptions.
28. If a library wishes to transfer its orders to Jaeggi, the library will not have to cancel with its present suppliers.

Staeheli's Bookshops Ltd.
77 Bederstrasse
8021 Zurich, Switzerland

Telephone number: (41) (1) 201-3302
Fax number: (41) (1) 202-5552
Cable address:: STAEHELIBOOKS

1. Independent company established in 1934.

2. Other offices:

>   Buchhandlung Staeheli & Co.
>   Am Marketplatz 20
>   7208 Spaichingen
>   Federal Republic of Germany

3. There are countries with which they will not do business but countries were not specified.
4-
5. No.
6. Provides serials and monographs from countries worldwide.
7a. Types of materials handled:
>   Periodicals
>   Monographic standing orders
>   Back issues
>   Government publications
>   Sets
>   Replacements
>   Yearbooks/annuals
>   Serials on videocassette
>   Serials with variant publishing
7b. Books (monographic firm orders).
8. Will communicate with back issue dealers when supplying back issues for a client.
9. Services provided:
>   Out-of-print searching
10. Journal consolidation is available only on demand with an extra charge.
11. None.
12. No response.
13-
14. No.
15. Client will deal with different specialists on specific subjects according to the origin of the subscription.
16. Will report back to the library on titles it cannot supply. It will try until it receives an answer from the publisher.
17. Rush orders accepted. There is only an extra charge if the firm has to pay more.

18. Service fee is not charged "if the publisher's discount is fair!!! which is unfortunately not very often." If there is no publisher discount, the firm charges according to the work and cost involved.
19. Service/handling charges may be either included in the price on the invoice or listed separately.
20. Client may request that service/handling charges be listed separately.
21. No.
22. Titles are listed on one invoice per title or according to customers' wishes.
23. Purchase order number provided on the invoice.
24. Multiple copies of invoice provided (no limit).
25-
26. No.
27. Normally does not provide quotations for libraries interested in changing dealers or consolidating direct subscriptions.
28. If a library wishes to transfer orders to this firm, it asks that the library cancel with its former dealer.

THAILAND

EBSCO Thailand, Ltd.
24/90 SO1 Tanpuyingpahon
Ngam Wong Warn Road
Bangkok 10900, Thailand

Telephone numbers: (66) (2) 511-0657
                    (66) (2) 513-1974
Fax number: (66) (2) 513-6733
For additional information see EBSCO Subscription Services, Inc. listing under UNITED STATES.

Nibondh & Company Ltd.
P.O. Box 402
40-42 Chareon Krung Road
Bangkok, Thailand

Telephone number: (66) (2) 221-2611
Fax number: (66) (2) 224-6889
Cable address: NIBONDH BANGKOK

1. Independent company established in 1920.
2-
4. No.
5. Representatives actively participate in
    library association meetings in their
    country and/or area of the country they
    represent.
6. Provides subscriptions from countries
    worldwide to its customers in Thailand;
    provides Thai subscriptions to our
    customers outside Thailand.
7a. Types of materials handled:
        Periodicals
        Monographic standing orders
        Back issues
        Government publications
        Sets
        Replacements
        Yearbooks/annuals (client may request
            every second or third year)
        Memberships
        Serials with variant publishing
7b. Books (monographic firm orders).
8. No. Nibondh goes directly to the
    publisher when supplying back issues for
    a client.
9. Services provided:
        Automatic renewal til forbid
        New order reports
        Claim reports
        Out-of-print searching
10. Journal consolidation is the standard
    practice.
11. None.
12-
14. No.

15. Client will deal with one customer service representative assigned to the account.
16. Will report back to the library on unavailable titles. Will keep the order on file for one year.
17. Rush orders accepted and there is an added charge (such as airmail).
18. Charges a fluctuating service fee dependent on the difficulty in obtaining material.
19. Service/handling charges are included in the price on the invoice.
20. Client may request that service/handling charges be listed separately on the invoice.
21. Never.
22- Titles are entered on the invoice by
23. purchase order number.
24. Multiple copies of invoices supplied (limit three).
25. No.
26. Prepayment options and terms: Prepayment is required of new clients.
27. Will provide a quotation for the library wishing to change vendors or to consolidate direct subscriptions.
28. No.

Martinus Nijhoff
GPO Box 2991
Bangkok 10501, Thailand

Telephone number: (66) (2) 247-1032
Fax number: (66) (2) 247-1033
For additional information see Martinus Nijhoff International B.v. listing under THE NETHERLANDS.

TURKEY

EBSCO Subscription Services
Mesutiyet Cad. 5/4
06640 Ankara, Turkey

Telephone number: (90) (4) 125-6894
Fax number: (90) (4) 125-2621
For additional information see EBSCO
Subscription Services, Inc. listing under
UNITED STATES.

UNITED KINGDOM

Alert Publications
11 Mount Road
Feltham, Middlesex TW13 6JG, England

For additional information see Hampton
Barnes, Inc. listing under UNITED STATES.

B. H. Blackwell Ltd.
Beaver House, P.O. Box 40
Hythe Bridge Street
Oxford, OX 1 2EU, England

Telephone number: (44) (865) 792792
Fax number: (44) (865) 791438
Telex number: 83118
Toll-free numbers:
    from Canada: (1) (800) 458-3707
    from U.S.A.: (1) (800) 458-3706

1. Firm was established in 1879 and is an
    independent, family-owned company.

2. Has offices in Germany, Australia, and
   the United States:

     B. H. Blackwell Ltd.
     Slomanhaus
     Baumwall 3
     D2000 Hamburg 11, Germany
     Telephone number: (49) (40) 372655

     B. H. Blackwell Ltd.
     17/22 Darley Road
     Manly, N.S.W., Australia 2095
     Telephone number: (61) (2) 977 8355

     Blackwell's Periodicals
     North American Help Desk
     c/o Blackwell North America
     1001 Fries Mill Road
     Blackwood, N.J. 08012, U.S.A.
     Telephone numbers:
        (USA)   (1) (800) 458-3706
        (Canada)(1) (800) 458-3707

3. No.
4. Firm maintains memberships in and is
   regulary represented at the meetings of
   the:
     North American Serials Interest Group
        (NASIG)
     United Kingdom Serials Group (UKSG)
     American Library Association
     Canadian Library Association
5. Representatives actively participate in
   library association meetings in their
   country and/or area of the country they
   represent.
6. Provides serials and monographs from
   countries worldwide.
7a. Types of materials handled:
     Periodicals
     Monographic standing orders
     CD-ROM
     Back issues
     Government publications
     Loose-leaf services
     Sets

7a. Types of materials handled (continued):
    Microforms
    Replacements
    Yearbooks/annuals (client may request
        every second or third year)
    Memberships
    Serials on videocassette
    Serials with variant publishing
    Grey literature
7b. Books (monographic firm orders).
8. Will communicate with publishers and
    other back issue vendors when supplying
    back issues for a client.
9. Services provided:
    Automatic renewal til forbid
    New order reports
    Claim reports
    Out-of-print searching
10. Journal consolidation/check-in service is
    available upon request for additional
    service and shipping charges.
11. Computerized services offered:
    Blackwell's CONNECT: Online connection
        to serials database for new
        orders, cancellations, claims,
        changes of address, and reviews of
        price, frequency, etc.
    ISIS: Serials management software for
        PC single user or multi-user,
        stand alone or networkable.
        Available in the United Kingdom
        and Europe.
    Three-Year Price Comparison: Financial
        planning tool available on
        diskette for loading into most
        spreadsheet and database
        management software.
12. Database available via Blackwell's
    CONNECT.
13. Interfaces with:
    NOTIS
    GEAC
    INNOVACQ
    CARL
    library in-house systems as
        required

14. Issues:
    "Blackwells's Annual Catalogue of
        Periodicals and Continuations,"
        published annually every April.
    "Customer Information Bulletin,"
        mailed every two weeks to each
        client, covering price, frequency
        changes, etc.
15. Each account is allocated one Library
    Liaison Officer who provides full
    customer service, including orders,
    cancellations, renewals, claims, and
    information upon request.
16. Will report back to the library on titles
    that cannot be supplied within six
    months.
17. Rush orders are accepted at no additional
    charge.
18. A service fee which is standard
    percentage is charged.
19- Service/handling charges may be listed
20. separately or included in the overall
    price depending upon customer's wishes.
21. For current subscriptions, shipping
    charges are included in basic price.
22. Titles may be invoiced alphabetically,
    by order number, by ISSN, or by fund
    code depending upon the customer's
    wishes.
23. Purchase order numbers provided on
    invoices.
24. Multiple copies of invoices (up to 3) are
    provided.
25. Invoices can be generated on computer
    tape or transferred by other electronic
    means.
26. Prepayment options and terms are
    available, details upon request.
    Prepayment discount generally reflects
    prevailing interest rates.
27. Will provide quotations for libraries
    wishing to consolidate direct orders or
    change vendors.

28. "Blackwell's will provide every practical assistance in effecting a smooth and error-free transfer; it must be recognized that the library is formally responsible for cancelling with previous supplier."

Collets Subscription Service
Denington Road
Wellingborough, Northants, NN8 2QT, United Kingdom

Telephone number: (44) 0933-224351
Fax number: (44) 0933-276402
Telex number: 317320 Collet G

1. Independent company established in 1934.
2-
3. No response.
4. Maintains memberships in and is regularly represented at meetings of the:
    Library Association of the United Kingdom
    ASLIB
    Association of Subscription Agents
5. Representatives actively participate in library association meetings in the United Kingdom, United States, and Europe.
6. Provides serials and monographs from countries worldwide with in-depth specialization in Russia and Eastern Europe.
7a. Types of materials handled:
    Periodicals
    Monographic standing orders
    Back issues
    Government publications
    Loose-leaf services
    Sets
    Microforms
    Replacements
    Yearbooks/annuals (clients may request every second or third year)

7a. Types of materials handled (continued):
    Memberships
    Serials with variant publishing
    Grey literature by subject areas
7b. Books (monographic firm orders provided by Collets Book Service).
8. Will communicate with back issue dealers and appropriate services when supplying back issues for a client.
9. Services provided:
    Automatic renewal til forbid
    New order reports
    Claim reports
    Information on new journals
10. Journal consolidation service is available on demand; special terms apply.
11. Computerized services are being planned for 1993.
12. Its database is not available to clients.
13. Interfaces with library automation systems are being planned for 1993.
14. Issues newsletter concerning new journals and journals published in the former Soviet Union and Eastern Europe.
15. Customer service representatives: Usually one member of a team is assigned to the account for the majority of inquiries.
16. Will report back to the library on titles that cannot be supplied. Each case is dealt with as to how long the firm will try to obtain the material before reporting back and will depend also on the clients' instructions.
17. Rush orders accepted at no added charge.
18. Service fee is charged for journal consolidation orders and is a standard fee.
19- Service/handling charges are listed
20. separately on the invoice.
21. Rarely pays all or part of the shipping charges.
22. Titles are listed alphabetically on the invoice but may be arranged according to client's preference.
23. Purchase orders appear on the invoice.

24. Multiple copies of the invoice supplied (limit three).
25. Generation of invoices on computer tape or transference by other electronic means is being planned for 1993.
26. Prepayment options and terms are available. Terms are usually a certain percentage per full month, geared to bank rates.
27. Will provide quotations for libraries wishing to consolidate direct subscriptions.
28. If a library wishes to place a major portion of its account with Collets, Collets "can cancel/take over from publisher direct, bypassing other agents."

Dawson Holdings PLC
Cannon House, Park Farm Road
Folkestone
Kent CT19 SEE, United Kingdom

Telephone number: (44) 303-850101
Fax number: (44) 303-850440
Telex number: 96392

1. Independent company established in 1809.
2. Firm has other offices in France, Spain, and the United States:

> Dawson France SA
> B.P. 40
> 91121 Palaiseau, Cedex France
> Telephone number: (33) (1) 69-09-01-22
>
> Dawson Iberica
> c/o Base, Aribau 282-284
> Piso 7-Oficina 3
> E 08006 Barcelona, Spain
> Telephone number: (34) (3) 4142000

Dawson Subscription Service Inc.
2 South Seminary
Mount Morris, IL 61054 U.S.A.
Telephone number: (1) (815) 734-4183

Quality Books Inc.
918 Sherwood Drive
Lake Bluff, IL 60044-2204 U.S.A.
Telephone number: (1) (708) 295-2010

3. No.
4. Firm maintains memberships in and is regulary represented at the meetings of the:
   Library Association
   Publishers Association
   Booksellers Association
   Association of Subscription Agents
5. Representatives actively participate in library association meetings in their country and/or area they represent.
6. Provides serials and monographs from countries worldwide.
7a. Types of materials handled:
   Periodicals
   Monographic standing orders
   CD-ROM
   Back issues
   Government publications
   Loose-leaf services
   Sets
   Microforms
   Replacements
   Yearbooks/annuals (client may request every second or third year)
   Memberships
   Serials on videocassette
   Serials with variant publishing
7b. Books (monographic firm orders) handled by:
   Dawson U.K. Ltd.
   Book Division
   Crane Close, Denington Road
   Wellingborough, Northants NN8 2QG, England

8. Firm holds the "largest stock of back issues of scientific, technical, and scholarly periodicals in Europe. If not in stock, [Dawson will] contact other dealers."
9. Services provided:
    Automatic renewal til forbid
    New order reports
    Claim reports
    Out-of-print searching
10. Journal consolidation service available via air freight service. Shipping charges (at cost) are charged.
11- Computerized services offered: Online
13. access to its 90,000 title database library management system, OASIS.
14. Issues the following publications:
    Back issues catalog
    Dawson Newsletter (quarterly)
    Guide to International Journals & Periodicals (annual)
    Library & Information News (monthly)
    Standing Orders & Continuations (biannual)
    "Guide" includes: title, subject, frequency, country of origin, price (U.K. and overseas)
15. Clients will deal with one customer service representative.
16. Will report back to the library on titles that it cannot supply. Will make three attempts to obtain materials before notifying the library.
17. Rush orders accepted at no added charge.
18. Service fee: Charge is dependent on publisher's discount. If a discount is less than 5%, the service fee is charged to compensate.
19. Service/handling charges are included in the price.
20. Client may request that service charges be listed separately.
21. Shipping charges: To some U.K. customers carriage is free on annual. Overseas clients are charged shipping charges.

22. Titles are entered in the order specified by the customer.
23. Purchase order number included on invoice.
24. Multiple copies (no limit) of invoices provided.
25. Invoices can be generated on computer tape or transferred by other electronic means.
26. Prepayment options and terms: Advantage Scheme : 1% discount for each forward month of payment before end of August.
27. Will provide quotations for libraries changing dealers or consolidating direct subscriptions.
28. Will assist the library switching vendors or consolidating orders by administering the change over by contacting the publishers direct.

EBSCO Subscription Services
5 Jamaica Wing
Scotts Sufferance Wharf
1 Mill Street
St. Saviours Docks
London SE1 2DF, England

Telephone number: (44) (71) 357-7516
Fax number: (44) (71) 357-7507
For additional information see the EBSCO Subscription Services listing under the UNITED STATES.

W. H. Everett & Son Ltd.
8 Hurlingham Business Park
Sulivan Road
London SW6 3DU, England

Telephone number: (44) (71) 731-8562
Fax number: (44) (71) 371-5870

1.   Independent firm established in 1793.

2-
3. No.
4. Company maintains memberships in and is
   regularly represented at the meetings of:
   CALL
   AALL
   United Kingdom Serials Group
   NAG
   American Library Association
5. Representatives actively participate in
   library association meetings in their
   country and in the area of the country
   they represent.
6. Provides serials and monographs from
   countries worldwide.
7a. Types of materials handled:
   Periodicals
   Monographic standing orders
   Back issues
   Government publications
   Loose-leaf services
   Sets
   Microforms
   Yearbooks/annuals (client may request
      every second or third year)
   Memberships
   Serials on videocassette
   Serials with variant publishing
7b. Books (monographic firm orders).
8. Will communicate with back issue dealers
   when supplying back issues for a client.
9. Services provided:
   Automatic renewal til forbid
   New order reports
   Claim reports
   Order checklists on demand
10. Journal consolidation is available on
    demand with additional service and
    shipping charges.
11. Computerized services: Its systems are
    fully automated.
12. No.
13. Interfacing available with NOTIS and GEAC
    library automation systems beginning with
    1993 renewals.

14. Provides subject-based lists upon request for clients.
15. Client will be assigned one customer service representative.
16. Will report back to the library on titles it cannot supply. Reports will be made within one week or one month depending upon publisher's location.
17. Rush orders accepted with no added charge (usually).
18. Service fee is charged. It is not a standard percentage but based on publisher discounts available to the company, the size of the list, average price per title, and ease of sourcing. Everett's "never uplifts the list price of a low or nil discount journal."
19- Service/handling may be listed separately
20. on the invoice or may be included in the price depending on the customer's choice.
21. No.
22. Titles appear on the invoice in alphabetical order but can be separated by fund, etc.
23. Purchase order numbers are included on the invoice.
24. Multiple copies of invoices provided (maximum two).
25. Invoices can be generated on computer tape or transferred by other electronic means.
26. Prepayment options and terms are available.
    a. Prepayment can be made at any time in the year prior to the normal renewal date.
    b. Discounts will be given for early payment based upon the amount prepaid.
    c. Discount rates will alter as the United Kingdom bank rate alters. Discounts are calculated at the annual rates on the number of complete months for which Everett's holds your funds prior to the first day of November, during which month Everett's will be paying the publishers on your behalf.

d. The net amount due on account of the invoice will be calculated and advised to the client in January. Client may choose to take the discount either as a credit for future purchases or else by way of cash payment to the library.
27. Will provide free quotations for libraries wishing to change dealers or to consolidate direct subscriptions.
28. A library wishing to transfer orders to Everett's should cancel with its present supplier. As the new agent, Everett's will advise all publishers individually that it is taking over the subscriptions and it will also quote the name of the previous supplier with instructions to the publisher not to duplicate.

Faxon U.K. Ltd.
Dormer House
Leamington Spa
CV32 5AA Warwickshire, United Kingdom

Telephone number: (44) (926) 450424
Fax number: (44) (926) 450616
For additional information see The Faxon Company, Inc. listing under the UNITED STATES.

Ickenham Book Services
Melthorne Court
49 High Road
Ickenham, Middlesex UB10 8LF, England

Telephone number: (44) (81) 756-1884
Fax number: (44) (81) 573-9726

1. Independent firm established in 1988.
2-
3. No.

4. Company maintains memberships in and is regularly represented at library association meetings. Did not specify which associations.
5. Representatives actively participate in library association meetings in their country and/or area of the country they represent.
6. Provides serials and monographs from mainly the United Kingdom, Ireland, and Europe.
7a. Types of materials handled:
    Periodicals
    Monographic standing orders
    Back issues
    Government publications
    Loose-leaf services
    Sets
    Microforms
    Replacements
    Yearbooks/annuals (client may request every second or third year)
    Memberships
    Serials on videocassette
    Serials with variant publishing
7b. Books (monographic firm orders).
8. Will communicate with back issue dealers when supplying back issues for a client.
9. Services provided:
    Automatic renewal til forbid
    New order reports
    Claim reports
    Out-of-print searching
10. Journal consolidation available.
11. Computerized services: Only in-house records are computerized.
12-
14. No.
15. Client will deal with one customer service representative.
16. Will report back to the library on titles it cannot supply. Will continue search for the title/issue as long as the customer wishes it to do so.
17. Rush orders accepted at no added charge.

18. No service fee charged on books. There is in some cases a small fee charged.
19- Service/handling charges are listed
20. separately on the invoice.
21. Will pay part of the shipping charges.
22. Titles will appear on the invoice in any arrangement requested by the customer.
23. Purchase orders supplied on the invoice.
24. Multiple copies of invoices provided (no limit).
25. Not at this time.
26. Prepayment options and terms are available. Contact the firm directly for details.
27. Will provide quotations for libraries interested in changing dealers or in consolidating direct subscriptions.
28. Will assist libraries wishing to transfer its orders to Ickenham on their instructions.

Nordic Subscription Service U.K. Ltd.
20 Green End
Whitchurch, Shropshire SY13 1AB, England

Telephone number: (44) (0948) 4334
Fax number: (44) (0948) 5667

1. Independent firm established in 1984.
2. Other offices:

   Nordic Subscription Service
   ROKHOJ6
   DK 8520 Lystrup, Denmark
   Telephone number: (45) (86) 223188

   Nordic Consultants Ltd.
   16 Rosevine Road
   London, SW20 8RB, England
   Telephone number: (44) (81) 946-7435

3-
5. No.

6. Provides serials from countries worldwide.
7a. Types of materials handled: Subscriptions only.
7b.-
8. No.
9. Services provided: New order reports.
10-
11. No response.
12-
14. No.
15. Client will deal with different individuals depending on the nature of the inquiry.
16. Will report back to the library within seven days on titles it cannot supply.
17. Rush orders accepted at no added charge.
18- No service fee charged/no handling
20. charges.
21. No.
22- Titles are entered on the invoice by
23. purchase order number.
24. Multiple copies of invoices provided (no limit).
25-
26. No.
27. Will provide quotations for libraries interested in changing dealers or in consolidating direct subscriptions.
28. Libraries wishing to transfer orders to Nordic must cancel with their present suppliers.

Stobart & Son Ltd.
International Subscription Agents
Hawley House, 1st Floor
5-7 High Street, Plaistow
London, E13 0AD, England

Telephone number: (44) (81) 503-4444
Fax number: (44) (81) 503-4840
Telex number: 896797G

1. Independent company established in 1927.

2-
5. No.
6. Provides serials and monographs from
   countries worldwide but are specialists
   in materials from the United Kingdom, the
   United States, Europe, and the British
   Commonwealth.
7a. Types of materials handled:
       Periodicals
       Monographic standing orders
       CD-ROM
       Back issues
       Government publishers
       Loose-leaf services
       Sets
       Microforms
       Replacements
       Yearbooks/annuals (client may request
           every second or third year)
       Memberships
       Serials on videocassette
       Serials with variant publishing
       Newspapers
7b. Books (monographic firm orders handled by
    its branch, Madeira Book Supply Company).
8. Will communicate with back issue dealers
   when supplying back issues for a client.
9. Services provided:
       Automatic renewal til forbid
       New order reports
       Claim reports
       New title reports
       Publisher publication schedules
       Status reports
10. Journal consolidation available on demand
    (called Consolidation Service). There is
    a value added service charge and freight.
    Shipping is additional at cost.
11. Computerized services offered:
       Invoicing
       Claiming
       Ordering
       Title information
12-
14. No.

15. Client will deal with one customer service representative.
16. Will report back to the library on titles it cannot supply. They use no time limits.
17. Rush orders accepted at no extra cost.
18. Service fee is charged and is a standard percentage determined by the size of the order, annual turnover, and mix of titles.
19. Service/handling charges are included in the selling price.
20. Client may request that service/handling charges be listed separately.
21. Will pay all or part of the shipping charges.
22. Titles usually appear in alphabetical order on the invoice but other options are available.
23. Purchase order numbers are provided on the invoice.
24. Multiple copies of invoices supplied (theoretically no limit as it has a computer reprint facility).
25. Not at present.
26. Prepayment options and terms are available. Firm offers a prepayment plan which gives a bonus credit to maximize the best use of budgeted funds. Contact the firm for more details.
27. Will provide quotations for libraries interested in changing dealers or in consolidating direct subscriptions.
28. Libraries wishing to switch its orders to Stobart must first cancel with their present suppliers. Stobart will assist with clerical assistance and support. Will notify the publisher of the change of agent.

Swets U.K. Ltd.
32 Blacklands Way
Abingdon Business Park
Abingdon, Oxfordshire OX14 1SX,
United Kingdom

Telephone number: (44) (02) 35-30809
For additional information see the Swets
Subscription Service listing under
THE NETHERLANDS.

Thornton's of Oxford
11 Broad Street
Oxford, OX1 3AR, England

Telephone number: (44) (0865) 242939
Fax number: (44) (0865)-204021
Cable address: THORNBOOK

1. Independent company established in 1835.
2. No.
3. No response.
4-
5. No.
6. Provides serials and monographs from
    countries worldwide.
7a. Types of materials handled:
        Periodicals
        Monographic standing orders
        Back issues
        Yearbooks/annuals (client may request
            every second or third year)
7b. Books (monographic firm orders).
8. Will communicate with back issue dealers
    when supplying back issues for a client.
9. Services provided:
        Automatic renewal til forbid
        New order reports
10. No.
11. Computerized services offered:
        Issues academic subject catalogs by
            computer
12-
13. No.

14. Issues fifteen catalogs per year.
15. Clients will deal with different individuals depending on the nature of the inquiry.
16. Will report back to the library on titles it cannot supply. Will try to obtain the material for one year.
17. Rush orders accepted at no added charge.
18. Service fee charged depends on the publisher's terms. Postal charges added.
19- Service/handling charges are included
20. in the price and will not be separated upon client request.
21. No.
22- Titles are entered on the invoice by
23. purchase order number.
24. Multiple copies of invoices provided (no limit).
25. No.
26. Prepayment options and terms: All subscriptions to journals are payable in advance. Yearbooks, etc. are supplied on credit.
27. Will provide quotations for libraries interested in changing dealers or in consolidating direct subscriptions.
28. Will assist libraries wishing to switch orders to Thornton's.

J. B. Tratsart Ltd.
154A Greenford Road
Harrow HA1 3QT
Middlesex, England

Telephone number: (44) (81) 422-8295

1. Independent company established in March 1948.
2-
5. No.
6. Provides serials from countries worldwide.

7a. Types of materials handled:
     Periodicals
     Monographics standing orders
     Back issues
     Government publications
     Loose-leaf services
     Yearbooks/annuals
     Serials with variant publishing
7b. No response.
8. No.
9. Services provided:
     Automatic renewal til forbid
     New order reports
     Claim reports
     Out-of-print searching
10. Few.
11. None.
12-
14. No.
15. Client will deal with different
    individuals depending upon the nature of
    the inquiry.
16. Will report back to the library on titles
    it cannot supply. Has no set time for
    reporting back.
17. Rush orders accepted at no added charge.
18-
21. No service fee.
22. Titles are entered on the invoice as
    desired by the customer.
23. Purchase order numbers supplied on
    invoices.
24. Multiple copies of invoices supplied.
25. No response.
26. No.
27. No response.
28. If a library wishes to switch its orders
    to Tratsart, Tratsart will assist them.

UBS Publishers' Distributors Ltd.
475 North Circular Road
Neasden, London NW2 7QG, England

Telephone number: (44) (81) 450-8667
Fax number: (44) (81) 452-6612 Attn.: UBS
For additional information see the UBS
Publishers' Distributors Ltd. listing under
INDIA.

Waterstone's International Mail Order
4, Milson Street
Bath, Avon BA1 1DA, United Kingdom

Telephone number: (44) (0225) 448595
Fax number: (44) (0225) 444732

1. Company is owned by W. H. Smith Group and
    was established in 1984.
2. Headquarters office:

> Waterstone's Booksellers
> Ixworth House
> 37 Ixworth Place
> London SW3 3QH, United Kingdom

3-
5. No.
6. Provides serials (annuals) and monographs
    from the United Kingdom, the United
    States, and selected European countries.
7a. Types of materials handled:
    Yearbooks/annuals (client may request
        every second or third year)
7b. Books (monographic firm orders)
    Specialties:
        Signed first editions (new,
        not used)
8. No.
9. Services provided: Depend on customer
    needs and possibilities.
10. No.
11. No response.
12. Negotiable.
13. No.

14. Issues catalogs in three formats:
    Bi-annual color general catalog
    General newsletter (4-5 times/year)
    Signed first editions catalog
        (every four months) and there
        is a subscription fee
15. Client will deal with different customer
    service representatives depending on the
    nature of the inquiry.
16. Will report back to the library on titles
    it cannot supply. Length of time varies
    with each case.
17. Rush orders NOT accepted.
18. Service fee is charged only when
    customers wish to use a highspeed courier
    such as FEDEX.
19. Service/handling charges are included in
    the price on the invoice.
20. Client may request that service/handling
    charges be listed separately.
21. Rarely.
22. Titles are entered on the invoice as
    required by the customer.
23. Purchase order number provided on the
    invoice if client requests.
24. Multiple copies of invoices provided (no
    limit).
25. Not at present.
26. Not applicable.
27. Will provide a quotation for a library
    interested in changing dealers or
    consolidating direct subscriptions.
28. Will assist a library that wishes to
    transfer orders to Waterstone's.

Hubert Wilson Ltd.
1-9 Broad Street
Margate, Kent CT9 1EW, England

Telephone number: (44) 0843-228873
Fax number: (44) 0843-291838
Cable address: WILBOOKS, MARGATE

1. Independent company established in 1956.

2-
5. No.
6. Provides serials and monographs from countries worldwide.
7a. Types of materials handled:
     Periodicals
     Monographic standing orders
     CD-ROM
     Back issues
     Government publications
     Loose-leaf services
     Sets
     Microforms
     Replacements
     Yearbooks/annuals (client may request every second or third year)
     Memberships
     Serials with variant publishing
7b. Books (monographic firm orders).
8. Will communicate with back issue dealers when supplying back issues for a client.
9. Services provided:
     Automatic renewal til forbid
     New order reports
     Claim reports
     Out-of-print searching
10. Journal consolidation is available on demand. Shipping costs from the company are charged, but the cost of publisher's shipping is saved.
11. Computerized services offered:
     Invoicing
     Reporting
     Claiming
     Quotations
     Lists of orders
12. Database is available to clients via hard copies.
13. May consider interfacing with library automation systems in the near future.
14. No.
15. Client will deal with one individual, the subscriptions manager, but access to the Managing Director is always available.

16. Will report back to the library on titles that it cannot supply. Will report back only after it has exhausted every possibility.
17. Rush orders accepted at no added charge.
18- No service fee. There is a handling
19. charge (when there is no discount from the publisher) included in the price.
20. Client may request that the handling fee be listed separately on the invoice.
21. No.
22. Titles are entered on the invoice as requested by the customer.
23. Purchase order numbers are provided on the invoice.
24. Multiple copies of invoices supplied (no limit).
25. Invoices are not available on computer tape but can be faxed.
26. Prepayment options and terms: For prepayment in July for the following year, Wilson gives a 2 1/2% discount.
27. Will provide quotations for libraries interested in changing dealers or in consolidating direct subscriptions.
28. Will assist libraries wishing to transfer orders to the company by liaison with previous suppliers and publishers.

UNITED STATES OF AMERICA

Academic Book Center
5600 N.E. Hassalo Street
Portland, OR 97213

Telephone number: (1) (503) 287-6657
Fax number: (1) (503) 284-8859
Toll-free number: (1) (800) 547-7704
Internet: ACBC@ATTMAIL.COM

1. Independent company established in 1976.

2-
3. No.
4. Company maintains memberships in and is regularly represented at the meetings of library associations (none specified).
5. Representatives actively participate in library association meetings in their country and/or area of the country they represent.
6. Provides serials and monographs from the United States and Canada only.
7a. Types of materials handled:
    Monographic standing orders
    Back issues (non-periodical only)
    Government publications
    Sets
    Replacements
    Yearbooks/annuals
    Serials with variant publishing
7b. Books (monographic firm orders) are handled by another branch of the company.
8. Will communicate with back issue dealers when supplying back issues for a client.
9. Services provided:
    Automatic til forbid
    New order reports
    Claim reports
    Approval plans
10. All standing order materials are sent from our company to the library. Academic does not dropship.
11. Computerized services:
    Various services
    BISAC electronic ordering, machine-readable invoicing and PC-based desktop files for non-STO services (i.e., Approval plans)
    Internet access
12. Database is available to clients in printed and PC-based form.
13. Interfaces with library automation systems: BISAC electronic ordering from a variety of systems.

14. No.
15. Client will deal with one individual assigned to the account.
16. Will report back to the library on titles it cannot supply. Will continue to attempt to supply until the order is declared "unobtainable" by the publisher (i.e., out-of-print).
17. Rush orders are not available for standing orders.
18. Service fee: Majority of volumes are supplied without service fee. A service fee is added only when there is little or no discount given to us by the publisher.
19- Service/handling charges may be listed
20. separately on the invoice or included in the price as requested by client.
21. Payment of the shipping charges by Academic is negotiable.
22. Titles are entered on the invoice as requested by customer.
23. Purchase order number is included in the invoice.
24. Multiple copies of invoices supplied: Standard is the original invoice with two copies; Academic may provide more, if necessary.
25. Invoices can be generated on computer tape for books on the approval plan; not yet available for standing orders.
26. Prepayment options and terms: Added discounts available for prepayments (i.e., deposit accounts). Contact the agent for details.
27. Will provide quotations for libraries interested in changing dealers or consolidating orders.
28. Academic Book Center will assist libraries wishing to transfer to it. Academic will prepare cancellation letters and for very large transfer may even provide staff assistance.

Accents Publications Service, Inc.
911 Silver Spring Avenue
Suite 202
Silver Spring, MD 20910-4620

Telephone number: (1) (301) 588-5496
Fax number: (1) (301) 588-5249
Telex number: 6503468108MCI UW

1. Independent company established in 1984.
2-
4. No.
5. Its representatives actively participate
    in library association meetings in their
    country and/or area of the country they
    represent.
6. Provides serials and monographs from
    countries worldwide.
7a. Types of materials handled:
        Periodicals
        Monographic standing orders
        CD-ROM
        Back issues
        Government publications
        Loose-leaf services
        Sets
        Microforms
        Replacements
        Yearbooks/annuals (client may request
            every second or third year)
7b. Books (monographic firm orders)
        Specialties:
        Government publications and
            information products
        Association and society
            publications
        Document retrieval
8. Company will communicate with back issue
    dealers when supplying back issues for a
    client.

9. Services provided:
    Automatic renewal til forbid
    Extensive reporting on: standing
        orders, subscriptions, firm orders,
        rush orders
10. Standing orders for continuations are
    shipped directly from their facilities.
    Subscriptions to periodicals are drop-
    shipped.
11. Computerized services offered:
    Accounting
    Reporting
    Ordering
12-
13. No.
14. Company issues catalogs and a monthly
    newsletter consisting of bibliographic
    information and abstracts.
15. At the client's request, the client may
    be assigned one customer service
    representative.
16. Will report on titles they cannot supply
    after exhausting all possibilities.
17. Rush orders accepted at an additional
    charge to client.
18- Service fees are based on a standard
19. pricing policy and are invoiced as part
    of the prices of publications.
20-
21. No.
22. Titles are invoiced in any order per
    client's request (alphabetical, order
    number, etc.).
23. Purchase order numbers appear on the
    invoice.
24. Will supply multiple copies of invoices.
25. No.
26. Prepayment options and terms: Client may
    maintain a deposit account which entitles
    the client to a 5% discount.

27. Will provide client with quotations from their present list if library is interested in changing dealers or consolidating subscriptions.
28. Will assist library in dealing with present suppliers if library wishes to transfer orders.

Adler's Foreign Books, Inc.
915 Foster Street
Evanston, IL 60201-3199

Telephone number: (1) (708) 866-6329
Fax number: (1) (708) 866-6287
Order fax: (1) (800) 433-9229
Telex: 25-6262 EURO PUB EVN

1. Owned by Midwest European Publications, Inc., and was established in 1940.
2-
4. No.
5. Its representatives actively participate in library association meetings in their country and/or area of the country they represent.
6. Provides serials from countries worldwide.
7a. Types of materials handled:
    Periodicals
    Monographic standing orders
    CD-ROM
    Back issues
    Government publications
    Loose-leaf services
    Sets
    Microforms
    Replacements
    Yearbooks/annuals (client may request every second or third year)
    Memberships
    Serials on videocassette

7a. Types of materials handled (continued):
    Serials with variant publishing
    (congresses, proceedings,
    symposia)
7b. No.
8. Communicates with back issue dealers when
    supplying back issues for a client.
9. Services provided:
    Automatic renewal til forbid
    New order reports
    Claim reports
10. Journal consolidation available.
11. Computerized services: Ordering,
    bookkeeping, and inventory.
12-
14. No.
15. Client will interact with different
    customer service representatives
    according to language of the
    subscription.
16. Will report back to a library on titles
    that cannot be supplied within six
    months.
17. Rush orders accepted at no added charge
    to client.
18- Service fee is a flat fee listed
20. separately on the invoice.
21. No.
22- Titles are listed on the invoice by
23. order number.
24. Supplies multiple copies of invoice up to
    three copies.
25-
26. No.
27. Will provide quotations for a library
    interested in changing dealers or
    consolidating direct subscriptions.
28. No.

African Imprint Library Services
Caribbean Imprint Library Services
410 W. Falmouth Hwy.
P.O. Box 350
West Falmouth, MA 02574

Telephone number: (1) (508) 540-5378
Fax number: (1) (508) 548-6801

1. Independent firm established in 1970.
2-
3. No.
4. Company maintains memberships in and is
   always represented at the meetings of:
   > African Studies Association
   > Caribbean Studies Association
   > S.A.L.A.L.M.
5. Representatives on occasion actively
   participate in library association
   meetings in their country and/or area of
   the country they represent.
6. Provides serials and monographs from all
   African countries and all Caribbean and
   Central American countries.
7a. Types of materials handled:
   > Periodicals
   > Monographic standing orders
   > Back issues
   > Government publications
   > Loose-leaf services
   > Sets
   > Microforms
   > Replacements
   > Yearbooks/annuals (client may request
   >   every second or third year)
   > Serials on videocassette
   > Serials with variant publishing
   > Newspapers
7b. Books (monographic firm orders).
8. Will communicate with back issue dealers
   when supplying back issues for a client.

9. Service provided:
   Automatic renewal til forbid
   New order reports
   Claim reports
   Out-of-print searching
10. Journal consolidation is standard practice.
11. Computerized services offered:
   Country and subject listings for clients
12. Database availability to clients:
   Country and subject listings
13. Interfacing with library automation systems is being planned.
14. Issues an annual newsletter which announces new and ceased periodicals.
15. Client will deal with different customer service representatives depending on the nature of the inquiry.
16. Will search until the order is cancelled. Will report back to the library if it learns that the title has ceased.
17. Rush orders accepted at no additional charge.
18. No service fee is charged, but its prices are higher than the publisher's prices.
19- Service/handling charges are included
20. in the price and will not be separated.
21. No.
22. Titles are listed alphabetically on the invoice by country of origin.
23. Purchase order numbers provided on the invoice.
24. Multiple copies of invoice supplied (no limit).
25. No.
26. Prepayment options and terms are available with 5% discount to those maintaining a credit balance.
27. Will provide quotations for those interested in changing dealers or in consolidating direct subscriptions.

261

28. Libraries wishing to transfer orders to this agent should first cancel with their present suppliers.

Jerry Alper, Inc.
271 Main Street
P.O. 218
Eastchester, NY 10707

Telephone number: (1) (914) 793-2100
Fax number: (1) (914) 793-7811
Telex number: (1) (710) 562-0119
Cable address: ALPERBOOKS

1. Independent company established in 1981.
2-
3. No.
4. Maintains memberships in and is regularly represented at the meetings of the:
   American Library Association
   IFLA
   ACRL
5. No.
6. Provides serials and monographs from countries worldwide.
7a. Types of materials handled:
   Periodicals
   Monographic standing orders
   Back issues
   Government publications
   Sets
   Microforms
   Replacements
   Yearbooks/annuals (client may request every second or third year)
   Serials with variant publishing
7b. Books (monographic firm orders).
8. Will communicate with back issue dealers when supplying back issues for a client.

9. Services provided:
   Automatic renewal til forbid
   Out-of-print searching
10. No response.
11. None.
12. Database availability to clients is through Serials Quest.
13. No.
14. Issues a catalog and corporate brochure. Bibliographic information in catalog includes: volumes, years, place of publication, binding, all published, last published, etc.
15. Client will deal with one customer service representative.
16. Will report back to the library within three to six months on titles it cannot supply.
17. Rush orders accepted at no added charge.
18. No service fee is charged but there is a handling charge.
19- Postage, handling, insurance costs are
20. listed separately on the invoice.
21. No.
22. Titles are listed alphabetically on the invoice.
23. Purchase order numbers are provided on the invoice.
24. Multiple copies of invoices supplied within a reasonable limit.
25. No.
26. Prepayment options and terms are available. Contact the company directly.
27. Will provide quotations for libraries interested in changing dealers or consolidating direct subscriptions.
28. If a library wishes to transfer its orders to Alper, it must cancel with its present suppliers.

Ambassador Book Service, Inc.
42 Chasner Street
Hempstead, NY 11550

Telephone number: (1) (516) 489-4011
Fax number: (1) (516) 489-5661
Toll-free number: (1) (800) 431-8913

1. Independent company established in 1973.
2. No.
3. Will not do business with Iraq, Libya, and Jordan.
4. Maintains memberships in and regularly attends the annual and midwinter meetings of the:
   American Library Association
   Special Libraries Association
5. Representatives actively participate in library association meetings in their country and/or area they represent.
6. Will provide monographic serials and monographs from around the world. Specializes in academic level publications, with emphasis on science and technology.
7a. Types of materials handled:
   Monographic standing orders
   Government publications
7b. Books (monographic firm orders are its main focus).
8. Not applicable.
9. Services provided:
   Out-of-print searching for
      monographs
10. Not applicable.
11. Computerized services offered:
   Electronic ordering
   Customized reporting
   Management reports
12. No.
13. Currently interfaces with:
   DRA, Dynix, Acq 350, WLN.
14. No.

15. Clients will deal with one customer service representative.
16. Reports back to libraries on titles they cannot supply when publisher confirms that the title is out-of-print.
17. Rush orders are accepted. There is an added charge for these as no discounts are extended to the client.
18. There is a service fee of $4.00 (minimum) on books only up to $40. List price, 10% service fee on books listing at $41 and higher.
19- Service charges are included in the
20. price but may be itemized if requested.
21. Shipping charges may be paid in part or in full depending upon the volume.
22. Invoices can be sorted as requested by the library.
23. Purchase order numbers always included.
24. Standard invoice is three parts and a packing slip. Additional copies will be supplied as requested.
25. Invoices can be generated on computer tape or transferred by other electronic means.
26. Prepayments will be placed in interest-bearing accounts at the prevailing rates.
27. Not applicable.
28. Company will assist libraries in cancelling monographic standing orders with former suppliers.

American Overseas Book Co., Inc.
550 Walnut Street
Norwood, NJ 07648

Telephone number: (1) (201) 767-7600
Fax number: (1) (201) 784-0263
Telex number: 882384

1. Independent company established in 1969.

2. Has an affiliate in England, but prefers to have all initial contacts made with the United States office.
3. No.
4. Maintains memberships in the:
     American Library Association
     Medical Library Association
     Special Libraries Association
   The company is regularly represented at these meetings depending on other corporate priorities.
5. Representatives will occasionally actively participate in library association meetings depending on the focus of the meeting.
6. Provides serials and monographs from countries worldwide.
7a. Types of materials handled:
     Periodicals
     Monographic standing orders
     CD-ROM
     Back issues
     Government publications
     Loose-leaf services
     Sets
     Microforms
     Replacements
     Yearbooks/annuals (client may request every second or third year)
     Memberships
     Serials on videocassette
     Serials with variant publishing
     Serials on audiocassette or other media.
7b. Books (monographic firm orders): If books are shipped directly from the publisher to the customer, they are treated as serials. If the books are processed through its book warehouse, they are treated as monographs.

8. Back issues: The company prefers to go direct to the publisher or use its own extra copy service. However, it does have standing agreements with a number of back issue dealers.
9. Services provided:
   Automatic renewal til forbid
   New order reports
   Claim reports
   Detailed order confirmation
   Multiple address (mini-network)
       control
10. Journal consolidation is available on demand. Cost ranges for $0-$25 per title, depending on the frequency of the publication, quantities of each title, claiming history with that publisher, regularity of publication, etc. Shipping within the United States is generally by United Parcel Service (UPS); for foreign locations it uses a freight forwarder, often one requested by the customer.
11. Computerized services:
   Online ordering
   Online claiming
   Lease of journal check-in software
       for local serials control
12. Its database is available to clients through microcomputer/modem access--IBM-compatible equipment.
13. It is currently discussing an interface with The Library Corporations's Bibliofile/Intelligent Catalog system.
14. Issues a monthly newsletter and catalog. The catalog cites title, ISSN, frequency, current volume(s) and price. Membership entitlements are listed at the end of the catalog. Instructions for using the company's services are included.

15. Each account is assigned a customer service representative. Some contracts also require a contract administrator to handle questions on procedures, paperwork, etc.
16. Libraries are notified in their Order Confirmation of "order direct" titles within ten days of their order request. Special orders for symposia or back issues may take two weeks to receive a response from available sources.
17. Rush orders are accepted at no extra charge.
18. Service fee: "Fees range from 0% to 4% on publisher list price. Alternately, we offer a flat fee per subscription, based on average cost of a subscription. Customers are welcome to request rates either on publisher list price or net cost to us."
19- Service fees are generally shown
20. separately on the invoice, but can be included in each line total if needed.
21. Shipping charges: "In most cases, percentages are offered on the basis of shipping direct from the publisher, with shipping included in the price."
22. Titles are usually arranged alphabetically on the invoice (most customers prefer this), but customers may request invoices by accounts, order numbers, etc.
23. Purchase order numbers are included on the invoice.
24. Multiple copies of the invoice are provided according to the number specified in the contract.
25. Invoice information can be transferred to a floppy disk or uploaded to the customer's computer or provided on computer tape.

26. Prepayment options/terms: Prepayment options are offered, including a sliding schedule of discounts, for quarterly prepayments.
27. Will supply quotations for libraries wishing to consolidate orders or switch vendors. "Since prices change so rapidly, however, the quotation may be limited to 30 days, for the cost of the subscriptions; the fee for service should remain the same unless the total dollar value changes significantly or the mix (technical/popular) changes."
28. Will assist libraries who are switching vendors or consolidating orders. "We will assist in the transition, particularly with titles that are not true subscriptions, i.e., annuals. We are especially experienced in dealing with the United States Government Printing Office. We also work with renewal notices and current labels to determine expiration dates."

Baker & Taylor International Ltd.
652 East Main Street
Bridgewater, NJ 08807

Telephone number: (1) (908) 218-0400
Fax number: (1) (908) 707-4387
Telex number: 7607824 BTBKS UC

1. Division of Baker & Taylor, Inc., established in 1828.
2. Offices in Australia, Japan, and the United Kingdom:

   Baker & Taylor International Ltd.
   550 Darling Street
   Rozelle, NSW 2039, Australia

Baker & Taylor International Ltd.
Phoenix Bldg., F5
4-3, Azabudai 1-chome
Minato-ku, Tokyo 106, Japan

Baker & Taylor International Ltd.
Northdale House
North Circular Road
London NW10 7UH, United Kingdom
3. No response.
4. Company maintains memberships in and is
   regularly represented at the meetings of
   the:
   American Library Association
   NESA (Near East/South Asia Council
      of Overseas Schools)
   ECIS (European Council of
      International Schools)
   IFLA
5. Some representatives actively participate
   in library association meetings in their
   country and/or area of the country they
   represent.
6. Provides serials and monographs from the
   United States, the United Kingdom, and
   Canada.
7a. Types of materials handled:
   Monographic standing orders
   CD-ROM
   Back issues
   Government publications
   Sets
   Replacements
   Yearbooks/annuals (client may request
      every second or third year)
   Serials with variant publishing
7b. Books (monographic firm orders). Baker
   and Taylor works with over 14,000 U.S.
   publishers. Series, serials, and sets are
   handled out of the Eastern Service
   Center. Other international orders are
   handled out of its Midwestern Service
   Center.

8. For monographic standing orders Baker &
   Taylor deals with out-of-print book
   dealers.
9. Services provided:
   Automatic renewal til forbid
   New order reports
   Claim reports
   Out-of-print searching
10. Not applicable.
11. Computerized services: B & T Link: World
    Edition, a CD-ROM database which consists
    of serials, series, and sets. The CD-ROM
    database contains three modules:
    ordering, the title source on CD-ROM, and
    inventory.
12. Database is available through
    subscription.
13. Interfaces with library automation
    systems:
    ACQFAST
    Bib-Base/Acq. CARL System
    DRA
    DYNIX
    Galaxy
    Super CAT
    Advance
    INLEX
    INNOVACQ
    NONESUCH Acquisitions
    PALS
    LAMP
14. Issues catalogs:
    CSQ (Continuation Service
       Quarterly)
    School Selection Guide K through 9
       and 7 through 12
    Directions: a monthly journal for
       academic and research libraries
    Also provides Continuations Service
       General Core Collection, listing
       every other year and listings of
       selected series subject
       bibliographies

15. Sales managers maintain overall relations with each customer. In addition, customers will have a dedicated customer service representative and a credit representative.
16. Will report back to a library immediately if a title is not on our Continuations Service database. Baker & Taylor will conduct several searches to obtain the title. The search procedure takes two to four weeks.
17. Rush orders accepted with an added charge.
18. No.
19-
20. Not applicable.
21. Payment of shipping charges are negotiated with each library based on the library's specific needs.
22. Titles are entered on the invoice as specified by the customer.
23. Purchase order numbers are provided on the invoice.
24. Multiple copies of invoices supplied.
25. Invoice generation on computer tape or other electronic means is currently under development.
26. No.
27. Will provide quotations for libraries interested in changing vendors or consolidating direct subscriptions.
28. Baker & Taylor will handle cancellations for a library wishing to transfer its orders to it.

Ballen Booksellers International
125 Ricefield Lane
Hauppauge, NY 11788

Telephone number: (1) (516) 543-5600
Fax number: (1) (516) 864-5850
Telex number: 9103800079
Toll-free number: (1) (800) 645-5237

1. Independent company established in October 1969.
2. Other offices are located in Germany (European Office); Taiwan (Far East Office);and Israel (Middle East office).
3. No.
4. Ballen maintains memberships in and is represented at all major meetings of the:
   American Library Association
   Medical Library Association
   Special Library Association
   Many regional groups
5. Representatives actively participate in library association meetings in their country and/or area of the country they represent.
6. Provides serials and monographs from countries worldwide.
7a. Types of materials handled:
   Monographic standing orders
   Sets
   Yearbooks/annuals (client may request every second or third year)
   Serials with variant publishing
7b. Books (monographic firm orders).
8. No.
9. Services provided:
   Automatic renewal til forbid
   New order reports
   Claim reports
   Approval plans
10. All materials are collected at the agency and batch-shipped to the library. Ballen does not routinely drop ship.

11. Computerized services:
       Online ordering
       Online claiming
       Online cancellation
       Invoice tapes
       Access to our MARC record database
    All online access is done through its
    BallenNet system which requires a PC and
    a modem. All communication is done via
    toll-free WATS lines. Software is
    provided at no cost to the client.
12. Database availability: Database is
    available to clients via the online
    BallenNet system which allows clients to
    browse through Ballen's series database
    as well as review history on each
    standing order. The client can place new
    orders, enter claims, make changes (to
    purchase order number or quantity), and
    enter special instructions. BallenNet is
    provided at no cost to Ballen's clients.
13. Interfaces with library automation
    systems:
       GEAC
       NOTIS
    Ballen is able to interface with local
    library systems by means of transmission
    of an ASCII file.
14. A printout of Ballen's serial database is
    available upon request.
15. Clients will deal with one customer
    service representative.
16. If Ballen cannot supply a new title, the
    client is notified at once. If, over
    time, we have been unsuccessful in
    obtaining a title, we advise the client
    as to the specifics of the problem. A
    decision is made with the client as to
    how far to take a search. There is no
    cut-off time.

17. Rush orders accepted at no added charge for the rush service. There may be a charge for special shipping to the client if the client specifies overnight shipping.
18-
20. No service fees apply.
21. Ballen pays all or part of the shipping charges.
22. Titles may be entered in any way requested by the client. Titles are normally invoiced alphabetically by series title.
23. Purchase order numbers are provided on the invoice.
24. Multiple copies of invoices provided (no limit).
25. Invoices can be generated on computer tape.
26. Prepayment options and terms: Ballen does not require prepayment due to the nature of the material it supplies. If a client wishes to prepay, Ballen will establish an escrow account on which interest is paid to the client.
27. Ballen will provide a quotations list for libraries interested in changing vendors or consolidating standing orders. The quotation will be an estimate of the cost for the following year as prices vary greatly from year to year and from volume to volume.
28. Will process cancellations for the library wishing to transfer its orders to Ballen. Cancellation letters are prepared on library letterhead using an authorized signature. Confirmation of the cancellation is requested from the present supplier.

Beijing Book Company, Inc.
701 E. Linden Avenue
Linden, NJ 07036-2495

Telephone number: (1) (908) 862-0909
Fax number: (1) (908) 862-4201
Telex number: 844753

1. Owned by China National Publications
   Import & Export Corp. and established in
   1991.
2-
3. No.
4. Maintains no library memberships at this
   time but is regularly represented at the
   meetings of many. (None specified).
5. Representatives actively participate in
   library association meetings only in the
   United States.
6. Provides serials and monographs only from
   the United States.
7a. Types of materials handled:
        Periodicals
        Monographic standing orders
        CD-ROM
        Back issues
        Government publications
        Loose-leaf services
        Sets
        Microforms
        Replacements
        Yearbooks/annuals (client may request
           every second or third year)
        Memberships
        Serials on videocassette
        Serials with variant publishing
        Some equipment related to
           microproductions and music
           products
7b. Books (monographic firm orders).
8. Communicates with back issue dealers when
   supplying back issues for a client.

9. Services provided:
      Automatic renewal til forbid
      New order reports
      Claim reports
      Out-of-print searching
10. Journal consolidation is the standard practice.
11. Computerized services: The company has been computerized with AST Computer System SCO Unix.
12. No.
13. Interfacing with library automation systems is not available now but may be in the future.
14. Its catalogs are compiled by its headquarters which also issues its "Directory of Foreign Newspapers and Periodicals," which includes 27,000 titles of newspapers and periodicals published around the world.
15. No response.
16. Will report back to the library on titles it cannot supply. Will try to obtain the title for two months before notifying the library.
17. Rush orders accepted without added charge.
18. Service charge is based on a standard percentage.
19- Service/handling charges are listed
20. separately on the invoice.
21. Shipping charges are partially or fully paid by the agent.
22. Titles for periodicals are entered on the invoice by Beijing's subscription order numbers.
23. Purchase order numbers are provided on the invoice.
24. Will supply multiple copies of invoices if required.
25. No.
26. Prepayment options and terms: Clients are not requested to prepay.
27. Will provide quotations for libraries interested in changing vendors or in consolidating direct subscriptions.

28. Will assist libraries wishing to transfer orders to them by making it unnecessary for the clients to cancel with their suppliers.

Bernan/Unipub
4611-F Assembly Drive
Lanham, MD 20706

Telephone number: (1) (301) 459-7666
Fax number: (1) (301) 459-0056
Toll-free number: (1) (800) 247-4888

1. Bernan/Unipub is a division of the Kraus Organization which has headquarters in New York.
2. No.
3. No response.
4. Regularly attends the meetings of the:
    American Library Association
    Special Libraries Association
    American Booksellers Association
    American Association of Law
        Libraries
5. Representatives actively participate in library association meetings in their country and/or area of the country they represent.
6. Provides serials and monographs from countries worldwide because it handles publications of the United Nations, European Communities, the World Bank, etc.
7a. Types of materials handled:
    Periodicals
    Monographic standing orders
    CD-ROM
    Government publications
    Sets
    Yearbooks/annuals
    Serials with variant publishing
7b. Books (monographic firm orders).
8. Communicates with back issue dealers when supplying back issues for a client.

9. Services provided:
    Automatic renewal til forbid
    Claim reports
    Out-of-print searching
10. Journal consolidation available only upon demand and there are additional service charges and shipping charges.
11. Response unclear.
12-
13. No.
14. Issues a monthly newsletter and annual catalog. These provide information on the agencies it represents, its price policy, the kinds of services offered as well as information on the books it distributes.
15. Client will deal with different customer service representatives depending upon the nature of the inquiry.
16. Will report back to the library on titles it cannot supply.
17. Rush orders accepted at no added charge.
18. No service fee is charged.
19- Shipping and handling charges are listed
20. separately on the invoice.
21. No.
22. Titles are entered on the invoice in no specific order.
23. Purchase order numbers are provided on the invoice.
24. Multiple copies of invoices supplied (maximum three).
25. No.
26. Prepayment options and terms are available. Contact agent for details.
27. Will provide quotations for libraries interested in consolidating direct subscriptions or in changing vendors.
28. If a library wishes to transfer orders to Bernan/Unipub, it must cancel with its present suppliers.

Black Magazine Agency
Box 1018
Logansport, IN 46947

Telephone number: 219-753-2429
Fax number: 219-753-5480
Toll-free number: 800-782-9787

1. Independent company established in 1937.
2-
5. No.
6. Provides serials from countries
    worldwide.
7a. Types of materials handled:
       Periodicals
7b. No.
8. Will try to obtain back issues from
    publisher first before communicating with
    a back issue dealer.
9. Services provided:
       Claim reports
10. No.
11-
13. No response.
14. Issues a "condensed" price list sent at
    renewal time; a large computerized
    listing is sent upon request.
15. Client will deal with one customer
    service representative assigned to the
    account.
16. Will report back to the library on titles
    it cannot supply. Will offer a refund if
    service from a publisher cannot be worked
    out satisfactorily for the library.
17. Rush orders accepted at no added charge.
18- Service fee is not charged. Percentage of
19. discount is based on the magazine list.
    No handling charges are charged unless
    previously agreed upon by both parties.
20. Client may request that service charges
    be listed separatley on the invoice.
21. Will pay all or part of the shipping
    charges.
22. Titles are entered alphabetically on the
    invoice.

23. Purchase order numbers are provided on the invoice.
24. Multiple copies of the invoice supplied (no limit).
25-
26. No.
27. Will provide quotations for libraries interested in changing vendors or in consolidating back orders.
28. If a library wishes to transfer orders to this agent, it must first cancel with its present supplier.

Blackwell North America, Inc.
6024 S.W. Jean Road, Bldg. G
Lake Oswego, OR 97035

Blackwell North America, Inc.
1000 Fries Mill Road
Blackwood, NJ 08012

Telephone numbers:
  Oregon office: 503-684-1140
  N.J. office: 609-629-0700
Toll-free numbers:
  Oregon office: 1-800-547-6426
  N.J. office: 1-800-257-7341
Fax number:
  Oregon office: 503-639-2481

1. Owned by Blackwell's, England; established in 1975.
2. Other offices:

> Blackwell (Pacific)
> Contact: Philip Bull
> Telephone number: (02) 977-8355

> B. H. Blackwell Ltd.
> Oxford, England
> Telephone number: (44) 865-792792

> Blackwell's
> Hamburg, Germany
> Contact: Bettina Brandis

3. Will not do business with countries specified with restrictions by the Dept. of Commerce and State Department of the U.S.
4. Company maintains memberships in library associations and is regularly represented at these meetings (none specified).
5. Representatives actively participate in library association meetings in their country and/or area of the country they represent.
6. Provides monographic serials and monographs from countries worldwide with emphasis in the United States, Canada, and United Kingdom if distributed in the United States.
7a. Types of materials handled:
Monographic standing orders
Government publications
Sets
Yearbooks/annuals
Serials with variant publishing
7b. Books (monographic firm orders).
8. Not applicable.
9. Services provided:
Automatic renewal til forbid
New order reports
Claim reports
Out-of-print searching
10. Not applicable.
11. Computerized services offered:
Management reports
12. Database availability to clients:
Through its NTO service
13. Library automation system interfaces:

ACQ 350	BibBase
CARL	CLSI
Data Research	DYNIX
GEAC	INLEX
INNOVATIVE	LCS
NOTIS	OCLC
INTERNET	

14. Newsletter available through NTO and PC-NTAS and is issued twice a year with general information.

15. Client will deal with one individual assigned to the account.
16. Will report back to the library on titles it cannot handle. Orders will be kept open for one year.
17. Rush orders accepted with an added charge.
18. No.
19-
20. Not applicable.
21. Pays all or part of the shipping charges.
22. Titles are arranged per customer instruction.
23. Purchase order numbers provided on the invoice.
24. Multiple copies of invoices supplied.
25. Invoices can be generated on computer tape or transferred by other electronic means.
26. Prepayment options and terms are available; please contact Customer Service Department for details.
27. Will provide quotations for a library that is interested in changing dealers or in consolidating direct standing orders.
28. Will assist a library that wishes to transfer its account to Blackwell North America, Inc.

**Blackwell's Periodicals
North American Help Desk
c/o Blackwell North America
1001 Fries Mill Road
Blackwood, NJ 08012**

Telephone numbers:
    (within U.S.A.): 1-800-458-3706
    (from Canada):   1-800-458-3707
For additional information see the
B. H. Blackwell Ltd. listing under the
UNITED KINGDOM.

BookMart
253 South William St.
Newburgh, NY 12550

Telephone number: (914) 562-8532
Fax number: (914) 297-2483

1. Independent company established in 1962.
2-
5. No.
6. Provides serials and monographs from countries worldwide.
7a. Types of materials handled:
        Periodicals
        Monographic standing orders
        Back issues
        Government publications
        Yearbooks/annuals (client may request every second or third year)
        Serials on videocassette
        Serials with variant publishing
7b. Books (monographic firm orders).
8. Will communicate with back issue dealers when supplying back issues for a client.
9. Services provided:
        Automatic renewal til forbid
        New order reports
10. Journal consolidation is available on demand as a special service that is provided at an additional cost.
11. None.
12-
14. No.
15. Client will deal with one assigned customer service representative.
16. Will report back to the library within thirty days on titles that it cannot supply.
17. Rush orders accepted. There is sometimes an additional charge.
18. Service fee is charged and is a percentage based on the size of the order.

19- Service/handling charges may be listed
20. separately on the invoice or may be
included in the price depending on
customer preference.
21. Does not pay all or part of the shipping
charges if shipping from its own
facility.
22. Titles are listed alphabetically on the
invoice.
23. Purchase order numbers are supplied on
the invoice.
24. Multiple copies of invoices supplied (no
limit).
25. No.
26. Prepayment options and terms: Prepayment
is requested but will discuss exceptions.
27. Will provide quotations for libraries
interested in changing vendors or in
consolidating direct subscriptions.
28. Will assist a library in any way it can
if that library wishes to transfer orders
to BookMart.

Books from Mexico
Post Office Box 9
Mount Shasta, CA 96067-0009

Telephone number: (916) 926-6202
Fax number: (916) 926-6609

1. Independent company established in 1982.
2. Other office:
    Books from Mexico
    Apartado Postal 22-037
    Delegacion Tlalpan
    14000 Mexico, D.F. Mexico
    Telephone number: 011-525-655-2937
    Fax number: 011-525-573-2914
3. No response.

4. Company maintains memberships in and is regularly represented at the annual meetings of the:
   Arizona State Library Association
   SALALM: Seminar for the Acquisition
      of Latin American Library Materials
5. Representatives actively participate in the FORO BINACIONAL DE BIBLIOTECAS, a Mexican and United States library organization.
6. Provides serials and monographs from Mexico only.
7a. Types of materials handled:
   Periodicals
   Monographic standing order
   Back issues
   Government publications
   Replacements
   Yearbooks/annuals (client may request every second or third year)
   Serials with variant publishing
7b. Books (monographic firm orders).
8. The firm is a back issue dealer.
9. Services provided:
   Automatic renewal til forbid
   Out-of-print searching
   Notifications of: discontinued series, changes in numbering scheme for numbered serials, and title changes, etc.
   Approval plans
10. Journal consolidation is standard practice.
11. No response.
12. Database availability: Provides a list of publications handled on a subscription basis.
13. No present plans to interface with U.S. automated systems.
14. Issues a monthly catalog listing approximately 120 new monographic titles published in Mexico. Each entry contains up to four subject and form tags and extensive bibliographic information: author, title, place, publisher, pages, size, and critical apparatus: price, plus

cogent annotations on contents, scope, and nature of publication. Provides a list of publications it handles on subscription basis to any interested party.

15. Client will deal with one customer service representative.

16. Will report back within six months to a library on titles it cannot supply. If a title is subsequently acquired, it will send a quote to the library before sending.

17. Rush orders accepted. Special rush order fee is $10.00 plus air express charges from Mexico to the destination.

18. Separate service fee is not charged as its charges are represented in prices quoted.

19. Service/handling charges are generally included in the price.

20. Client may request that service/handling charges be listed separately on the invoice.

21. Shipping charges are stated separately on invoices for monographic publications and are included in the subscription price.

22. Titles are entered on the invoice as per customer instruction. Titles may be arranged by order number, title, the agents's unique identification number, etc.

23. Purchase order numbers are always included on the invoice.

24. Multiple copies of invoices supplied.

25. No.

26. Prepayment options and terms: Generous discounts off the prices of books and serials are given when customers prepay approval plan yearly amount. Books from Mexico will send details upon request.

27. Will provide quotations for libraries interested in changing vendors or in consolidating direct subscriptions.

28. Will assist libraries transferring orders to it by not duplicating publications currently received from another dealer. It operates from lists provided by the customer and also accepts returns of duplicate materials. Books from Mexico specializes in an orderly transition from other sources.

Brodart Company
500 Arch Street
Williamsport, PA 17701

Telephone number: 717-326-2461
Fax number: 717-326-1479
Toll-free number: 1-800-233-8467

1. Independent company established in 1941.
2. Other offices:

> Brodart Ltd.
> 109 Roy Blvd.
> Braneida Industrial Park
> Brantford, Ontario N3T 5N3, Canada

3. Will not do business with countries in a war zone.
4. Maintains memberships in and is regularly represented at meetings of library associations. None specified.
5. Representatives actively participate in library association meetings in their country and/or area of the country they represent.
6. Provides monographic serials and monographs from countries worldwide.
7a. Types of materials handled:
    Monographic standing orders
    Back issues
    Government publications
    Loose-leaf services
    Sets
    Yearbooks/annuals (client may request every second or third year)
    Serials with variant publishing

7a. Types of materials handled (continued):
    Serials on videocassette
        (depending on the title)
    Medical, technical, reference
        materials
    Travel guides
7b. Books (monographic firm orders).
8. Communicates directly with the publishers
    of any materials it supplies.
9. Services provided:
    Automatic renewal til forbid
    New order reports
    Claim reports
    Yearly updates on all new title
        listings
10. Not applicable.
11. None.
12. Database availability to customers:
    Nothing is available through
    Continuations, but Brodart offers a
    complete title listing.
13. Not applicable.
14. Issues a monthly status report with total
    customer history found on this report.
15. Client will generally deal with the
    Continuations Coordinator for any and all
    problems.
16. Will report back to the library on titles
    it cannot supply after doing full
    research.
17. Rush orders accepted at no added charge.
18. Service fee is a flat fee of $1.00 per
    title. This may be overridden under
    special bid or contract situations.
19- Service/handling charges are included
20. automatically in the price of the book
    on the invoice and will not be listed
    separately.
21. Will pay free freight on some bids.
22. Titles appear in alphabetical order on
    the invoice.
23. Purchase order numbers appear on
    invoices.
24. Multiple copies (standard is three) are
    provided but more will be sent if
    requested (no limit).

25. No.
26. Prepayment options and terms: Customers may have a deposit account with invoices being deducted as shipments are made.
27. Will provide its monthly status report for libraries interested in changing vendors.
28. Brodart will cancel all orders with present jobbers and distributors for libraries wishing to transfer orders to Brodart.

Broude Brothers Ltd.
141 White Oaks Road
Williamstown, MA 01267

Telephone number & toll-free number:
          800-525-8559
Fax number: 413-458-8131
Cable address: Broude, Williamstown, MA

1. Independent company established in 1929.
2. Other offices:

      Broude Europa
      Postfach 1327
      D-8470 Nabburg, Germany
      Telephone number: (9606) 7252
          Specializes in European music publications.

3. No.
4. Maintains membership in and exhibits at the annual meeting of the:
   Music Library Association
5. Representatives actively participate in library association meetings in their country and/or area of the country they represent.
6. Provides serials from countries worldwide. Broude Brothers are specialists in materials related to music, dance, and the theatre.

7a. Types of materials handled:
Periodicals
Monographic standing orders
Back issues
Serials with variant publishing
7b. Books (monographic firm orders).
8. Will communicate with back issue dealers when supplying back issues for a client.
9. Services provided:
Automatic renewal til forbid
Claim reports
10. No.
11. Computerized services: Broude Brothers operates from computerized databases of publications available and of customers.
12. Database availability to clients: Available in form of comprehensive catalogs issued from time to time, and in the form of checklists containing recent publications issued at more frequent intervals.
13. Interfacing with library automation systems: Broude Brothers is considering the possibility.
14. Issues comprehensive catalogs (the majority of entries in these listings are back-list items) every several years; issues checklists containing new or recent publications several times per year; issues checklists devoted to specific categories (e.g., thematic indexes) several times per year.
15. Clients will deal with any of two or three people (depending upon the department involved); complete files—both hard-copy and electronic—enable us to trace transactions for at least ten years back, and all personnel at the office are therefore current with the client's status. Continuation files trace transactions from inception of order.
16. Will report back to the library on titles it cannot supply.
17. Rush orders accepted. Rush charges such as Next-Day UPS must be passed along.

18. Service fee: Broude Brothers does not normally impose service charges; however, it must impose such charges when a publisher does not grant it a sufficient discount. Charges will then cover Broude's cost.

19- Service charges are listed separately on
20. the invoice.

21. Shipping charges: Broude Brothers' prices are F.O.B. Williamstown.

22. Titles are entered on the invoice in various ways depending on circumstances. Back items in a numbered series are usually entered by number, etc.

23. Purchase order numbers are provided on the invoice.

24. Multiple copies of invoices (normally three) are provided; will provide more, if needed.

25. No.

26. Prepayment options and terms: Broude Brothers is usually prepared to make reasonable arrangements for payment, early or deferred, as circumstances warrant.

27. If a library is interested in changing dealers Broude Brothers will review clients' holdings against its database showing currently available volumes; it will normally send a client a list of currently available volumes for the client to check against his holdings.

28. If a library wishes to transfer its orders to Broude Brothers, it is suggested that it is best for the library to cancel with its present suppliers in order to avoid potential problems.

J. S. Canner and Company, Inc.
10 Charles Street
Needham Heights, MA 02194

Telephone number: (617) 449-9103
Fax number: (617) 449-1767

1. Division of Plenum Publishing
    Corporation, established in 1938.
2-
4. No.
5. No response.
6. Provides predominantly United States and
    Western European serial publications.
7a. Types of materials handled:
    Periodicals
    Back issues
    Sets
    Replacements
    Microfilm of journals published by
        the Plenum Publishing Corporation
7b. No.
8. Will communicate with back issue dealers
    when supplying back issues for a client.
9. Services provided:
    Out-of-print searching
10-
15. No response.
16. Will hold an order open for approximately
    60 days and then report to the library on
    unavailability.
17. No response.
18. No.
19-
22. No response.
23. Purchase orders provided on the invoice.
24. Will supply multiple copies of invoice
    (no limit).
25. No.
26. Prepayment may be made but the company
    does not require it.
27-
28. No response.

293

Caribbean Imprint Library Services
410 W. Falmouth Highway
P.O. Box 350
West Falmouth, MA 02574

Telephone number: (508) 540-5378
Fax number: (508) 548-6801
See listing for the African Imprint Library
Services under UNITED STATES.

Cheng & Tsui Company, Inc.
25 West Street
Boston, MA 02111

Telephone number: (617) 426-6074
Fax number: (617) 426-3669

1. Independent company established in 1975.
2-
5. No.
6. Provides monographic serials and
   monographs primarily from China,
   Taiwan, Hong Kong, Japan, and Australia
   but it does supply from other countries
   as well. Materials supplied relate to
   East Asian studies.
7a. Types of materials handled:
    Yearbooks/annuals
7b. Books (monographic firm orders).
8. No.
9. Services provided:
   Claim reports
10. No.
11. None.
12-
13. No.
14. Issues annual catalog providing title,
    author, publisher, ISBN, pages, date of
    publication, price, index/bibliography.
15. Client will not have a specified customer
    service representative.
16. Will report back to client on orders it
    cannot supply.

17. Rush orders accepted. There is a $4.00 charge for same-day shipping.
18- Service/handling charges are listed
20. separately on the invoice.
21. All or part of the shipping charges are paid by the company only in special circumstances.
22- Titles on invoice are arranged by
23. purchase order numbers.
24. Two copies of the invoice are supplied, but it will supply extras if requested.
25. No.
26. Prepayment options and terms: Prepayment is allowed but there are no special terms or discounts.
27-
28. Not applicable.

China Publications Service
P.O. Box 49614
Chicago, IL 60649

Fax number: 312-288-8570

1.   Independent firm established in 1982.
2-
3.   No.
4.   Maintains membership in and regularly exhibits and attends the meetings of the: Association for Asian Studies (representing China National Publishing Industry Trading Corporation (Beijing, China), Documentation Centre, People's University of China (Beijing, China)).
5.   Its representatives actively participate in library association meetings in their country and/or area of the country they represent.
6.   Provides serials and monographs from China.

7a. Types of materials handled:
    Periodicals
    Monographic standing orders
    Microforms
    Yearbook/annuals
7b. Books (monographic firm orders).
8. Back issues: Chinese publishers do not supply back issues, except for some in U.S. stock or some at their exclusive agents.
9. Services provided:
    Automatic renewal til forbid
    Out-of-print searching for
        monographs
10. Journal consolidation: Periodicals are sent directly by its agent in China; monographs and microforms are sent from the Chicago office.
11. None.
12-
13. No.
14. Issues annually and occasionally "Recent Publications from the People's Republic of China" and issues irregularly "New Booklists" by subject disciplines.
15. Client will deal with different customer service representatives.
16. Will report back to the library on titles it cannot supply. Time of reply depends upon answers received from its agents in China.
17. Rush orders accepted at no extra charge. Book will be supplied immediately if in stock; orders from China take an average of 3 months by airmail and 6 months or more by seamail. Periodicals are sent directly to the customer from China.
18. Service fee: There are no postage and handling charges for publications of the Documentation Centre, Beijing, China (China Publications Service is its exclusive international agent); for other items there is a 10% charge for postage and handling.
19- Service/handling charges are listed
20. separately on the invoice.

21. See answer under 18.
22- Titles are listed by purchase order
23. number or in alphabetical order for
    large quantity of titles.
24. Multiple copies of invoice provided
    (triplicate for libraries).
25. No.
26. Prepayment options and terms: Prepayment
    for periodicals as required in China.
    Monographs are billed on delivery.
27. Will provide quotations (if prices are
    available) for libraries wishing to
    change dealers or consolidate direct
    subscriptions.
28. It suggests that libraries cancel with
    their present suppliers before
    transferring their orders to China
    Publications Service but China
    Publications Service will do so if the
    library authorizes them.

China Publishing & Trading Inc. (N.Y.)
56-11 219th Street
Bayside, NY 11364

Telephone number: (718) 224-0463
Fax number: (718) 229-6003
For additional information see China National
Publishing Industry Trading Corporation
listing under PEOPLE'S REPUBLIC OF CHINA.

Cox Subscriptions Inc.
411 Marcia Drive
Goldsboro, NC 27530

Telephone number: (919) 735-1001
Fax number: (919) 734-3332
Toll-free number: 800-553-8088

1. Independent company established in
    January 1975.

2-
3. No.
4. Maintains memberships in and is regularly represented at library association meetings (none specified).
5. Its representatives actively participate in library association meetings in their country and/or area of the country they represent.
6. Provides serials from countries worldwide.
7a. Types of materials handled:
    Periodicals
    Back issues
    Government publications
    Loose-leaf services
    Sets
    Replacements
    Yearbook/annuals
    Memberships
    Serials with variant publishing
7b. No response.
8. Will communicate with back issue dealers when supplying back issues for a client. It also maintains a missing copy back of many periodicals.
9. Services provided:
    Automatic renewal til forbid
    New order reports
    Claim reports
    Out-of-print searching
10. Response unclear.
11. No response.
12. No.
13. Response unclear.
14. Issues an annual catalog in January for all clients. Catalog contains 2,500 titles of the 200,000 titles it can supply.
15. Client will deal with different customer service representatives depending on the nature of the inquiry.
16. Will report back to the library on titles it cannot supply.
17. Rush orders accepted at no extra charge.

18-
19. No.
20. Client may request that service charges be listed separately.
21. Pays all of the shipping charges.
22. Titles are entered alphabetically on the invoice.
23. Purchase order numbers provided on the invoice.
24. Multiple copies of invoices provided (no limit).
25. Invoices can be generated on computer tape or by other electronic means (which was not specified).
26. Prepayment options and terms are available with an additional discount for prepayment. Contact agent for details.
27. Will provide quotations for libraries interested in changing vendors or in consolidating direct subscriptions.
28. Will assist libraries who wish to transfer their orders to Cox by providing [to publishers] the expiration dates with the former vendors.

Dawson Subscription Service Inc.
2 South Seminary
Mount Morris, IL 61054

Telephone number: (815) 734-4183
For additional information see Dawson Holdings PLC listing under the UNITED KINGDOM.

E.B.S. Inc. Book Service
290 Broadway
Lynbrook, NY 11563

Telephone number: (516) 593-1195
Fax number: (516)-596-2911
Toll-free number: 1-800-899-0290

1. Independent company established in 1949.
2. No.
3. Will not do business with India.
4. Company maintains memberships in and is
    regularly represented at meetings of the:
    American Library Association
    Special Libraries Association
    New York Library Association
5. Company has major attendance at the
    Frankfurt Book Fair.
6. Specializes in American publications and
    generalized worldwide publications
    (monographic serials and monographs).
7a. Types of materials handled:
    Monographic standing orders
    CD-ROM
    Government publications
    Serials with variant publishing
    Yearbooks/annuals
7b. Books (monographic firm orders).
8. No response.
9. Services provided:
    Automatic renewal til forbid
    New order reports
    Claim reports
    Handles series with change of
        publishers each year/each
        volume
10. Not applicable.
11. Computerized services offered to clients:
    PC-based software
12. Not applicable.
13. Company is working on future interfaces
    with NOTIS, GEAC, and DYNIX library
    automated systems.
14. Issues a monthly journal, Academic
    Library Book Review.

15. Customers are usually assigned one customer service representative.
16. Will report back to the library on materials that cannot be supplied.
17. Rush orders accepted. Extra charges on rush orders depend on the difficulty of obtaining the item.
18. Service fee depends on the mix of orders received. Call or write the company for more information.
19. Service/handling charges may be listed separately on the invoice or included in the price of the item.
20. A client may request separately listed service/handling charges.
21. Shipping charges: Call or write the company for details.
22. There are 22 ways to sort items on their invoice.
23. Purchase order numbers are included on invoice.
24. Multiple copies of invoices provided within limits.
25. Invoices can be generated on computer tape or transferred by other electronic means.
26. Prepaid invoices receive discount terms as do deposit accounts.
27. Will provide quotations for libraries wishing to consolidate direct subscriptions or change vendors.
28. Their staff will process the cancellation paperwork for libraries cancelling with their present suppliers and transferring orders to them.

EBSCO Subscription Services
P.O. Box 1943
Birmingham, AL 35201-1943

Telephone number: (205) 991-6600
Fax number: (205) 991-1479
Telex number: 78-2663

1. Division of EBSCO Industries, Inc., established in 1943.
2. Has 27 offices worldwide. Listed below are the complete addresses of 9 regional offices serving various parts of the United States.

Southeast U.S.A.
(Includes: Alabama, Florida, Georgia, Kentucky, Mississippi, South Carolina, Tennessee, Puerto Rico, Virgin Islands)
EBSCO Subscription Services
P.O. Box 2543
Birmingham, AL 35202-2543
Telephone number: (205) 991-1211
Toll-free number: (800) 633-4604
Fax number: (205) 995-1613

Midwest U.S.A.
(Includes: Illinois, Indiana, Iowa, Michigan, Minnesota, Missouri, Ohio, Wisconsin)
EBSCO Subscription Services
1140 Silver Lake Road
Cary, IL 60013-1685
Telephone number: (708) 639-2899
Toll-free number: (800) 323-6501
Fax number: (800) 828-6648

South Central U.S.A.
(Includes: Arkansas, Louisiana, Oklahoma, Texas, Central America)
EBSCO Subscription Services
5350 Alpha Road
Dallas, TX 75240-7341
Telephone number: (214) 387-2426
Fax number: (214) 991-2175

Mountain/Plains U.S.A.

(Includes: Colorado, Kansas, Montana, Nebraska, North and South Dakota, Utah, Wyoming)

    EBSCO Subscription Services
    2801 Youngfield St., Suite 120
    Golden, CO 80401-2264
    Telephone number: (303) 237-1753
    Toll-free number: (800) 888-7018
    Fax number: (303) 237-1752

Southwest U.S.A.

(Includes Arizona, California--San Luis Obispo, Kern, and San Bernadino counties and everything south, Nevada, New Mexico)

    EBSCO Subscription Services
    P.O. Box 92901
    Los Angeles, CA 90009-2901
    Telephone number: (310) 536-9709
    Toll-free number: (800) 888-7018
    Fax number: (310) 643-7415

New England/Northeast U.S.A.

(Connecticut, Maine, Massachusetts, New Hampshire, Rhode Island, South New Jersey, Southeastern Pennsylvania, Vermont)

    EBSCO Subscription Services
    1163E Shrewsbury Ave.
    Shrewsbury, NJ 07702-4321
    Telephone number: (908) 542-8600
    Toll-free number: (800) 526-2337
        (New Jersey, call collect)
    Fax number: (908) 544-9777

Northwest U.S.A./Pacific Islands
(Alaska,California-north of San Luis
Obispo, Kern, and San Bernadino
counties, Hawaii, Idaho, Oregon,
Washington, U.S. Territories in the
Pacific)
    EBSCO Subscription Services
    2 Waters Park Drive, Suite 211
    San Mateo, CA 94403-1149
    Telephone number: (415) 572-1505
    Toll-free number: (800) 288-7393
    Fax number: (415) 572-0117

Mid-Atlantic U.S.A.
(Delaware, Maryland, North Carolina,
Virginia, District of Columbia, West
Virginia)
    EBSCO Subscription Services
    6800 Versar Center, Suite 131
    Springfield, VA 22151-4148
    Telephone number: (703) 750-2589
    Toll-free number: (800) 368-3290
    Fax number: (703) 750-2442

New York / Tri-State Area U.S.A.
(Includes New York, North New Jersey,
Pennsylvania--except the Southeastern
section)
    EBSCO Subscription Services
    17-19 Washington Street
    Tenafly, NJ 07670-2084
    Telephone number: (201) 569-2500
    Telephone number (N.Y.):(212) 695-3715
    Fax number: (201) 569-0586

Foreign offices are listed under the entries:

    Australia (EBSCO Australia
       Subscription Service)
    New Zealand (EBSCO NZ Ltd.)
    Brazil (Libris-EBSCO Ltda.)
    Canada - two offices:
       CANEBSCO Subscription Services,
         Ltd.
       Les Services d'abonnement CANEBSCO
         LTEE

France (La Cauchoiserie)
Germany (EBSCO Subscription Services)
Hong Kong/China (ESS Overseas, Inc.)
Italy (EBSCO Italia S.r.l.)
Korea (ESS Overseas, Inc.)
The Netherlands (EBSCO Subscription
    Services: serves Western European
      nations except Italy, France,
      Germany, Spain and Turkey)
Spain (EBSCO Subscription Services)
Taiwan (ESS Overseas, Inc.: also
    serves Indonesia, Malaysia,
    Philippines and Singapore)
Thailand (EBSCO Thailand, Ltd.)
Turkey (EBSCO Subscription Services)
United Kingdom (EBSCO Subscription
    Services)

3. No.

4. ESCO maintains memberships in and is
    regularly represented at the meetings of
    the:
    American Library Association
    Special Libraries Association
    Medical Libraries Association
    Public Library Association
    Association of College & Research
      Libraries
    North American Serials Interest Group
    AALL
    AASL
    Plus most regional, state, and local
    associations.

5. EBSCO's representatives actively
    participate in library association
    meetings in their country and the area of
    the country they represent.

6. Provides materials from countries
    worldwide.

7a. Types of materials handled:
    Periodicals
    Monographic standing orders
    CD-ROM
    Back issues
    Government publications
    Sets
    Replacements

7a. Types of materials handled (continued):
     Yearbooks/annuals (client may request
         every second or third year)
     Memberships
     Serials on videocassette
     Serials with variant publishing
7b. No.
8. Will communicate, as needed, with back
    issue dealers when supplying back issues
    for a client. EBSCO maintains
    relationships with Kraus Reprint and
    Kraus Periodicals and with Jaeger for
    missed issues, back sets, and reprints.
9. Services provided:
     Automatic renewal til forbid
     New order reports
     Claim reports
10. Journal consolidation is available only
    on demand. EBSCO has a special program
    called Journal Express Transport Service,
    which offers several check-in, claim, and
    shipping options at various set fees
    depending on services rendered.
11. Computerized services:
     EBSCONET[R] online subscription service
         for online ordering, claiming,
         electronic mail, bibliographic
         searching of the database, missing
         issues, availability checks, order
         file review
     Electronic invoices available
         through magnetic tape, floppy
         diskette, and online/EDI
     Online ordering and claiming through
         automated library system interfaces
         (over 40)
     EBSCO/RETRO[TM] (retrospective
         conversion service)
     EBCcan[TM] (keyless data input system)
     Access to the CARL system and UNCOVER
         database through EBSCONET
12. Database is available to clients through
    the EBSCONET[R] online subscription
    service's EBSCO/SEARCH[R], which allows
    keyword searching.

13. Interfaces with other library automation
    systems:
        IMPACT (Auto-Graphics, Inc.)
        CARL (CARL Systems, Inc.)
        CARLYLE (Carlyle Systems, Inc.)
        LibraryWorks (CASPR, Inc.)
        DATALIB (Centel-Sigma Data Svcs.
            Corp.)
        CHECKMATE II (CLASS)
        CLSI LIBS 100plus (CLSI, Inc.)
        Columbia Lib. Sys., Ocelot
            (Columbia Computing Services, Ltd.)
        BibloTech (Comstow Information
            Services)
        STAR (Cuadra Associates, Inc.)
        DATA RESEARCH (Data Research
            Associates, Inc.)
        CARD DATALOG (Manager and
            Professional) (Data Trek,
            Inc.)
        DYNIX, Marquis (Dynix, Inc.)
        GEAC, GLIS, ADVANCE (Geac Computers
            International, Inc.)
        LIS (Lib. Info. Sys.) (Georgetown
            University)
        DOBIS/LIBIS (IBM Corporation)
        Information Navigator (IME Systems,
            Inc.)
        TECHLIB plus (Information
            Dimensions, Inc.)
        INLEX/3000, THE ASSISTANT (Inlex,
            Inc.)
        INMAGIC (Inmagic, Inc.)
        INNOPAC, INNOVACQ (Innovative
            Interfaces, Inc.)
        EC (Eee-See) (IPC Software)
        MILS (Loma Linda University)
        PALS (Mankato State
            University/Unisys)
        MANDARIN (Media Flex, Inc.)
        ARIN (NASA)
        NOTIS, KeyNOTIS (NOTIS Systems,
            Inc.)
        Online Union Catalog (OCLC)
        BIBLIO-LINK, PRO-CITE (Personal
            Bibliographic Software)

SERIAL CONTROL SYSTEM (Professional
        Software)
UNICORN (Sirsi Corporation)
MultiLIS (Sobeco Group Inc.)
Sydney Library System
        (International Library Systems)
ULISYS (JES Consulting)
VTLS-89, MARCUS, Micro-VTLS
        (Virginia Tech Library System)
WLN (Western Library Network)
14. Publications issued:
        A quarterly newsletter entitled "At
            Your Service..."
        Six annual serials catalogs for
            various types of libraries
        Semi-annual CD-ROM catalog
        Bi-monthly listing of serials changes
    Catalog listings contain such
    ordering/bibliographic information as:
    frequency, country of origin, publisher,
    price for new and renewal orders, and
    some descriptive listings.
15. Each client is assigned to one specific
    customer service representative who
    belongs to a team of customer service
    representatives familiar with the
    library's account and order requirements.
16. Will report back to the library. All
    customers are advised on unavailable
    titles through EBSCO's network of
    regional offices which contact customers
    directly. EBSCO will try to obtain
    materials for three months.
17. Rush orders accepted at no extra charge.
18. Service fee: Whether a service fee is
    charged and the amount or percentage of
    it depend on a number of criteria such
    as the mix of titles ordered.
19- Service/handling charges will be listed
20. separately or will be included in the
    price according to the client's wishes.
21. Does not pay all or part of the shipping
    charges if it is a standard part of
    obtaining the issues.
22. Titles are entered on the invoice in
    alphabetical/title number order.

23. Purchase order numbers appear on the invoice.
24. Multiple copies of invoices are provided (no limit).
25. Invoices can be electronically generated through magnetic tape, floppy diskette, and online/EDI.
26. Prepayment options and terms are available on a schedule based on the time the prepayment invoices are paid. The prepayment schedule is developed annually with prepayment credit depending on current interest rates, etc.
27. Will provide quotations for libraries interested in consolidating direct subscriptions or changing vendors.
28. For a library transferring its orders to EBSCO, EBSCO will provide assistance in any number of ways that might be requested by the library during the transition period.

East View Publications
11215 North 28th Place
Minneapolis, MN 55441

Telephone number: (612)-550-0961
Fax number: (612)-559-2931
Toll-free number (USA) 800-477-1005

1. Independent company established in 1989.
2. One branch office in Russia:
        Contact: Mr. Usachev
        Telephone number: (7-095) 114-31-66
3. No.
4. Is planning to apply for membership in library associations.
5. Participated at the 1991 IFLA meeting in Moscow.
6. Will supply serials and monographs from all countries that formerly comprised the U.S.S.R.

7a. Types of materials handled:
     Periodicals
     Monographic standing orders
     Back issues
     Government publications
     Sets
     Microforms
     Replacements
     Yearbooks/annuals (client may request
          every second or third year)
     Serials with variant publishing
          (congresses, proceedings,
          symposia)
7b. Books (monographic firm orders).
8. Is the only back issue dealer for Russian
    publications.
9. Services provided:
     Automatic renewal til forbid
     New order reports
     Claim reports
     Out-of-print searching
     Performs searches for formerly
          classified Russian-language
          materials
     Provides dissertations and
          dissertation abstracts
     Provides materials from selected
          archives in Russia
10. Journal consolidation is the standard
    practice.
11. Computerized services: Will offer
    computerized title ordering for
    Russian language books.
12. Database is not yet available to clients.
13. No.
14. Issues bimonthly catalogs. Information
    includes: title, author, ISSN/ISBN,
    publisher, date and place of publication,
    page numbers, and brief annotations.
15. Client will deal with different
    individuals depending on the nature of
    their inquiry.
16. Will report back to the library on titles
    that cannot be supplied. Depending on the
    material, they will try to obtain
    material for up to one year.

17. Rush orders are accepted at an extra charge.
18. Charges a service fee only on special searches.
19- Service/handling charges are listed
20. separately on the invoice.
21. Will pay all or part of the shipping charges.
22- Titles entered on the invoice by purchase
23. order number.
24. Will supply multiple copies of invoices as specified by client.
25. Invoices can be sent via fax/modem.
26. Prepayment options and terms: Prepaid microform orders have no postage or handling charges. First-time individuals (not organizations) must prepay all orders, including subscriptions.
27. Will provide a library that is interested in changing dealers or consolidating with quotations from their present list.
28. Will assist a library wishing to switch a major portion or all of their account to the company. Will contact the library's present supplier.

Educational Music Service
13 Elkay Drive
Chester, NY 10918

Telephone number: (914) 469-5790
Fax number: (914) 469-5817

1. Independent company established in 1979.
2-
5. No.
6. Provides music materials (serials, sheet music and monographs) from countries worldwide.

7a. Types of materials handled:
     Subscriptions
     Standing orders/continuations
     Sheet music
7b. Books (monographic firm orders).
8. No.
9. No response.
10. No.
11. No online services at present.
12-
14. No.
15. Client will deal with different customer service representatives depending on the nature of the inquiry.
16. Will report back to the library after six months on titles it cannot obtain.
17. Rush orders accepted. There may be an added charge, depending upon the speed required.
18- Handling charges ($1.50 per shipment)
19. are included with the postage on the invoice.
20. No.
21. Does not pay all or part of the shipping charges, except in correcting errors.
22- Titles are listed on the invoice in
23. random order with the composer, title, and component and purchase order number.
24. Multiple copies of invoices provided (maximum three).
25. No.
26. No prepayment options and terms available except for certain special offers.
27. Will provide quotations for libraries interested in changing vendors or consolidating direct subscriptions.
28. Libraries wishing to transfer orders to this company must cancel directly with their present supplier.

The Faxon Company
15 Southwest Park
Westwood, MA 02090-1584

Telephone number:	(617) 329-3350
Fax number:	800-999-3594
Telex number:	496-00398
Toll-free number:	800-766-0039
Cable address:	FAXON WOOD

1. Privately held, independently owned company established in 1881.
2. Faxon has 36 offices located in 19 countries. Listed below are the addresses of its United States offices:

Academic Information Services:
Westwood, MA address
   Toll-free number: (1)(800) 283-2966
   Fax number: (1)(800) 344-5605

Business Information Services:
Westwood, MA address
   Toll-free number: (1)(800) 283-2966
   Fax number: (1)(800) 648-2059

Medical Information Services:
Westwood, MA address
   Toll-free number: (1)(800) 999-3594
   Fax number: (1)(800) 648-2059

Federal Information Services:
The Faxon Company, Inc.
450 Spring Park Place
Suite 100
Herndon, VA 22070
   Telephone number: (1)(703) 471-5055
   Toll-free number: (1)(800) 966-5880
   Fax number: (1)(703) 481-0806

Public & School Library Division
Turner Subscriptions, Inc.
116 East Sixteenth Street
New York, NY 10003
      Telephone number: (1)(212) 254-4454
      Toll-free number: (1)(800) 847-4201
      Fax number: (1)(212) 529-8954

Asia/Pacific Client Service Center:
Westwood, MA address
      Telephone number: (1)(617) 329-3350
      Fax number: (1)(617) 329-9556
      Telex: 187900005
      Cable address: FAXON WOOD

Division America Latina:
Westwood, MA address
      Telephone number: (1)(617) 329-3350
      Fax number: (1)(617) 329-9556
      Telex number: 187900005
      Cable address: FAXON WOOD

Foreign offices are found under the listings:

      Australia (Faxon Australia)
      Brazil (Faxon Brasil)
      Canada (Faxon Canada, Ltd.)
      Chile (Faxon Cono Sur)
      Colombia (Faxon Colombia)
      France (Faxon France SA)
      Germany (Kunst und Wissen)
      India (Informatics (India) Pvt. Ltd.)
      Japan (Faxon Asia Pacific Company Ltd.)
      Japan (Nihon Faxon Co., Ltd.)
      Korea (Faxon Korea)
      The Netherlands (Faxon Europe)
      Russia/Commonwealth of Independent States
         (Faxon International Moscow/ICSTI)
      Singapore (Faxon Singapore)
      Sweden (Wennergren Williams Information
         Services AB)
      Taiwan (Faxon Taiwan)
      United Kingdom & Ireland (Faxon U.K.,
         Ltd.)

3. Faxon complies with the U.S. Dept. of
   Commerce's regulations regarding nations
   to which U.S. goods and services cannot
   be exported. The specific nations that
   are excluded change periodically and
   currently include North Korea, Cambodia,
   and Libya. Additionally, Faxon has in
   place a company policy prohibiting the
   sale of goods or services to agencies of
   the South African government which are
   affiliated with the support of the
   apartheid movement.
4. Faxon as a company and many of its
   employees as professionals are members of
   the:
   > American Library Association
   > Association of College and Research
   >   Libraries
   > IFLA
   > Medical Library Association
   > North American Serials Interest Group
   > SISAC
   > Special Libraries Association
   > Over 60 state, regional, and
   >   international library and
   >   information associations. Faxon
   >   actively participates as a
   >   contributing member and an involved
   >   participant as much as it involves
   >   itself as a vendor to the library
   >   community.
5. Faxon participates in over 30
   state/regional library association
   meetings in North America. Additionally,
   Faxon employees actively attend library
   and information association meetings in
   over thirty other nations.
6. Provides serials and monographs from over
   45,000 publishers located in 153 nations
   around the world.
7a. Types of materials handled:
   > Periodicals
   > Monographic standing orders
   > CD-ROM
   > Back issues
   > Government publications

7a. Types of materials handled (continued):
   Loose-leaf services
   Sets
   Microforms
   Replacements
   Yearbooks/annuals (client may request
      every second or third year)
   Memberships
   Serials on videocassette
   Serials with variant publishing
   On-demand article delivery
7b. Books (monographic firm orders). Faxon
   processes standing and firm orders
   through its Fulfillment Centers located
   in Ann Arbor, Michigan, USA and in
   Amsterdam, The Netherlands.
8. Back issues are provided from a wide
   variety of legitimate sources of which
   back issue dealers are one such source.
9. Services provided:
   Automatic renewal til forbid
   New order reports
   Claim reports
   Out-of-print searching
   Other: Faxon provides literally
      hundreds of informational and
      subscription processing services on
      behalf of its clients. These
      services range from planning
      information to software and
      database systems that can be
      accessed online and installed
      onsite.
10. Journal consolidation available upon
   demand. All journals processed through
   Faxon's Fulfillment Centers are processed
   by Faxon and, if necessary, automatically
   claimed. The company's All-in-One service
   accommodates both serials and
   continuations. With Faxon's exclusive
   Patterns™ services offering, claiming
   will be dramatically reduced due to the
   computer-based and title-specific
   predictive checking in that Patterns
   permits.

11. Computerized services: Faxon Manager is a comprehensive service to aid in serials and collection management. The core service enables predictive check-in, claiming, public access to an online serials public access catalog (S-PAC™), and management reporting. Software modules include sophisticated printer and route slip maintenance, the tracking of issues through every phase of binding and reshelving, and UnionLinx™, extracts and shares holdings data with other Union List members. Ordering, renewal, and invoicing functions aid in collection development, budgeting and financial transactions. Faxon Manager plays a pivotal role in Faxon's future service development plans; it is constantly evolving and will be continually enriched.

The MicroLinx software system, designed for IBM personal computers, provides for streamlined management of journal collections. Supplied as program disks with complete documentation, MicroLinx serves as a check-in system, an information organizer, and a report generator. Title information can be automatically loaded into the system from the Faxon title file or the MARC file. Other computer-based Faxon services include: DataLinx^R, InfoServ^R, PubLinx^R, SerialsQuest, BookQuest, SMARTS, FI$CAL, All-in-One™, Faxon Finder, and Faxon Xpress.

12. Database availability to clients: Faxon maintains machine-readable files containing bibliographic and publisher information on more than 260,000 titles, information on 45,000 publishers, and subscription transactions for more than 30,000 libraries and information centers around the world. Faxon is also capable of generating serials holdings records in the USMARC format from its serials control services.

13. Interfaces with library automation
    systems: Faxon supports automated
    interfaces with NOTIS, III, GEAC,
    DATATREK, and a variety of international
    systems for purposes of invoice
    processing. There is also full EDI X.12
    electronic interface support with NOTIS
    and MSUS/PALS.
14. Issues a quarterly information
    newsletter.
    Additional information is supplied via:
        Faxon Guide to Serials (annual/print
            or microfiche)—contains
            alphabetical listing of publisher
            and price of most active domestic
            and foreign serials titles
        Faxon Health Information Catalog
            (annual/print)—provides
            information on over 5,000 titles in
            the fields of medicine and health
            sciences
        Faxon Business Information Catalog
            (annual/print)—includes
            publisher and price information on
            thousands of business-related and
            high technology titles
        Faxon Guide to CD-ROM (annual/print)—
            offers complete product and
            ordering information on over 400
            CD-ROM titles. Listings include:
            title, publisher, frequency,
            hardware requirements, price and
            product description
        The Faxon Report (quarterly)—
            newsletter for Faxon clients
            containing Faxon news as well as
            articles of general interest on
            relevant topics such as CD-ROM,
            Networking, Internet, etc.
        Faxon Planning Report (annual)—
            contains the latest information on
            publisher activities, average
            prices of new titles, planned price
            increases, and new directions in
            publishing. Information is also
            analyzed by library type for

318

clients wishing to compare their
library to others in a variety of
ways.

15. Each client is supported by a specific
Faxon Client Service Representative who
is assigned to assist the client.
Additionally, those clients who elect to
employ Faxon's electronic services are
further supported and assisted through a
team of professionals providing training,
usage assistance, and systems support.

16. Faxon will notify the library immediately
upon determining that a requested title
is unavailable. Depending upon the reason
for the lack of availability, Faxon will
seek the title through the title's new
publisher (if so instructed by the
client), utilize the BookQuest/
SerialsQuest services (at the
client's request) to seek out-of-print
titles and back issues, and/or, if so
desired, pursue obtaining the needed
articles through Faxon's document
delivery service.

17. Rush orders accepted at no added charge.

18. Service fee: Faxon provides many
software, database, and networking
facilities in addition to an extensive
number of differing professional services
and a large selection of subscription
management services. The client's invoice
is made up of each of these, depending
upon what has been chosen.

19. Service/handling fees are typically shown
separately on the invoice.

20. Client may elect to differentiate any and
all charges by fund, user/patron
department, and, as appropriate, by
specific Faxon offering. Client may have
service charges listed separately on the
invoice.

21. Shipping and handling charges,
international value added taxes, duties,
sales taxes, if any, etc. vary on an
order and client-specific basis.

22. Titles are entered on the invoice as specified by the client. Typically, titles are arranged alphabetically by title but they can also be organized by publisher, subject, ISSN number, etc.
23. Purchase order numbers are provided on the invoice.
24. Multiple copies of invoices: Electronically transmitted invoices permit the client to make as many copies as needed. A reasonable number of paper invoices are also readily accommodated.
25. Invoice generation: Faxon employs worldwide standards for compliant EDI transfer of information including invoices. Data transmission employing SISAC conforming record formats via X.25 and dial-up communications services can be accommodated. Additionally, magnetic tape and PC diskette formats are also available.
26. Prepayment options and terms: Each year Faxon offers its clients a prepayment incentive program. While the specific details vary year to year, the prepayment option typically begins in April, concludes in August, and provides an interest credit schedule that is based on market conditions.
27. Faxon will provide a professsionally prepared quotation for a library wishing to change agents or consolidate direct subscriptions. This quotation includes subscription management services, software and database offerings, as well as professional services.
28. If a library wishes to transfer its orders to Faxon, Faxon will assist them by notifying publishers that orders are being transferred. If applicable, the library's letterhead can be used.

Reginald F. Fennell Subscription Service, Inc.
1002 West Michigan Avenue
Jackson, MI 49202

Telephone number: (517) 782-3132
Fax number: (517) 782-1109

1. Independent company established in 1910.
2-
5. No.
6. Supplies serials from countries worldwide.
7a. Types of materials handled:
    Periodicals
    Back issues
    Government publications
    Loose-leaf services
    Sets
    Microforms
    Yearbooks/annuals
    Memberships
    Serials with variant publishing
7b. No.
8. Will communicate directly with the publisher when supplying back issues for a client.
9. Services provided:
    Claim reports
10. Journal consolidation service available upon request at no additional service charge over the whole order. Additional service charge on "individual titles with no agent operating margin."
11. None.
12. Response unclear.
13. Not applicable.
14. No.
15. Client is assigned one individual customer service representative.
16. Will report back to library on titles they cannot supply.
17. Rush orders accepted at no extra charge.

18. Service fee is not a standard percentage nor a flat fee but is determined in another manner. There is no service fee on the majority of orders.
19. Service/handling charges are included in the price.
20-
21. No.
22- Titles are listed alphabetically on
23. invoices with purchase order numbers included.
24. Multiple copies of invoices provided (no limit).
25-
26. No.
27. Will provide quotations for libraries wishing to consolidate orders or change vendors.
28. If a library wishes to transfer subscriptions to Fennell, the company suggests that the library not cancel but let prior year subscriptions expire.

Franklin Book Company, Inc.
7804 Montgomery Avenue
Elkins Park, PA 19117

Telephone number: (215) 635-5252
Fax number: (215) 635-6155
Toll-free number: 1-800-323-2665

1. Independent, privately held corporation established in 1969.
2. While Franklin Book Company does not have foreign offices, it does maintain foreign banking arrangements to ease payment of foreign publishers.
3. No.
4. Maintains membership in and is regularly represented at the meetings of the:
    American Library Association
    Special Libraries Association

322

5. Representatives actively participate in library association meetings in their country and/or area of the country they represent.
6. Provides monographic serials and monographs from countries worldwide.
7a. Types of materials handled:
    Monographic standing orders
    Government publications
    Sets
    Replacements
    Yearbooks/annuals (client may request every second or third year)
    Serials on videocassette
    Serials with variant publishing
7b. Books (monographic firm orders).
8. No.
9. Services provided:
    Automatic renewal til forbid
    New order reports
    Claim reports
    Others as requested by customers
10. Not applicable.
11. Computerized services offered: Customers may place orders and claims, view order status, send and/or receive electronic mail, account for funds expended during the current fiscal year, review the last two years' invoices, and review historical standing order data from the inception of the order with Franklin to the present through BOOKEASE, Franklin's automated library support tool.
12. Database availability to clients: Customers may call Franklin's business office to request the BOOKEASE TUTORIAL GUIDE and register two of the three required passwords for access to BOOKEASE. A computer terminal or PC with a Hayes-compatible modem, minimum 1200 baud, is required. Some suggested telecommunications software would include: Crosstalk v.3.6 or higher, SmartcomII v. 2 or higher, and ProComm v.2.4 or higher.

13. Franklin will interface all data processing systems as customers require.
14. No.
15. Client will have one individual assigned to its account. Customers may be requested to direct written or telephone inquiries to that person. Standing order inquiries are referred to a primary person. In most cases, regular order inquiries can be handled by any member of the customer service department.
16. Will regularly report back to the library on the availability of standing and regular orders. Franklin keeps back orders open until either supplied by the publisher or officially declared by the publisher as abandoned or out-of-print.
17. Rush orders accepted and are placed as drop shipments, unless the drop shipments are prohibited by the publisher or the customer. There is a $6.00 per publisher rush charge in addition to any special shipping which may have been approved by the customer.
18. Service/Handling Charges:
      Service/Pass through Charges:
      a. RUSH CHARGE - $6.00/publisher;
      b. RUSH SHIPPING - pass through at cost
      c. PRE-BINDING - pass through at cost (currently $4.25/item)
    On short or no discount items, the smaller of a percentage or flat fee will be added into the price of the book to assure a minimum profit.
19. Rush charges and shipping are shown as such on the invoice. Pre-binding may be shown or added into the cost of the item as established in the customer profile.
20. Client may request that service charges be listed separately on the invoice.
21. Will pay all or part of the shipping charges.
22. Titles are entered on the invoice as determined by the customer. Customer may choose alphabetical arrangement by author

or title, or numerical order by purchase order number. Customer may also choose to have standing orders invoiced with regular orders or separately.

23. Purchase order numbers appear on the invoice. If no purchase order numbers are used by the client, the order date appears in its place.
24. Multiple copies of invoices provided (no limit).
25. Invoices can be generated on computer tape or transferred by other electronic means.
26. Prepayment options and terms: Several plans are available dependent upon the needs and desires of the individual customers.

> Deposit Account: Customer may establish a deposit account. Transmittal invoices accompany shipments.

> Proforma Invoicing: Customer may request invoicing prior to the availability of specific materials. Transmittal invoices accompany shipments. When all items have been shipped, the statement is balanced and Franklin either bills for the underpayment or refunds the overpayment.

27. Not applicable.
28. If a library wishes to change from its present agent to Franklin, Franklin will assist with the cancellation of all or a major portion of its entire account. The method would be chosen by Franklin and the customer. The library could include the former vendor(s) on the listing of the titles being ordered in addition to the last volume received. Franklin could then produce the cancellation notices on the library's or Franklin's stationery for signature by the authorized agent of the library.

French & European Publications, Inc.
115 Fifth Avenue
New York, NY 10003

Telephone number: (212) 673-7400
Fax number: (212) 475-7658
Cable address: FRANCOPUB NEW YORK

1. Independent company established in 1928.
2-
5. No.
6. Provides serials from France.
7a. Types of materials handled:
      Periodicals
7b.-
8. No.
9. Services provided:
      Automatic renewal til forbid
10. No.
11. None.
12-
14. No.
15. Client will deal directly with
    Emanuel Molho, president.
16. Will report back within two months to the
    library on titles that it cannot supply.
17. Rush orders accepted at no added charge.
18. No service charges.
19-
20. Not applicable.
21. No.
22. Titles are listed on the invoice in no
    particular order.
23. Purchase order numbers will be supplied
    on the invoice if desired by customer.
24. Multiple copies of invoices provided (no
    limit).
25. No.
26. Prepayment options and terms: All
    subscriptions must be paid in advance.
27. Will provide quotations for libraries
    interested in changing dealers or
    consolidating direct subscriptions.

28. Libraries wishing to transfer its orders
    to French & European Publications, Inc.
    must first cancel with their present
    suppliers.

Theodore Front Musical Literature, Inc.
16122 Cohasset Street
Van Nuys, CA 91406

Telephone number: (818) 994-1902
Fax number: (818) 994-0419

1. Independent company established in 1961.
2-
3. No.
4. Company maintains memberships in and is
    regularly represented at the meeting of
    the:
        Music Library Association
        Canadian Library Association
        IAML
5. Representatives actively participate in
    library association meeting in their
    country and/or area of the country they
    represent.
6. Supplies serials from countries
    worldwide.
7a. Types of materials handled:
        Periodicals
        Monographic standing orders
        Back issues
        Replacements
        Monumenta
        Musicological editions
        Complete works/collected editions
        Music and book series
        Serials with variant publishing
        Sheet music
        Recordings and videos
7b. Books (monographic firm orders).
8. Will sometimes communicate with back
    issue dealers when supplying back issues
    for a client.

9. Services provided:
   Automatic renewal til forbid
   Claim reports
   Out-of-print searching
10. Journals consolidation is the standard practice.
11. Computerized services:
    Billing
    Claims
    New issue quote slip announcements
    E-mail
12-
13. No.
14. Catalogs are issued four times a year; special sale or special interest flyers are also issued periodically. Full bibliographic information is provided.
15. Clients will interact with different customer service agents depending on the nature of the inquiry.
16. Will report back to the library on unavailable titles generally after several attempts have been made to find the material.
17. Rush orders are accepted and there is an extra charge.
18. No service fee is charged.
19-
20. Not applicable.
21. Will pay all or part of the shipping charges.
22- Titles are entered on the invoice by
23. order number or alphabetically if order numbers are not available.
24. Multiple copies of invoices supplied (no limit).
25. No, not at the moment.
26. Prepayment options and terms available. Contact the company for details.
27. Will provide quotations for libraries consolidating direct orders or changing vendors.
28. Assistance is and has been provided in helping libraries cancel with their present suppliers when switching orders.

Gerard Hamon, Inc.
525 Fenimore Road
P.O. Box 758
Mamaroneck, NY 10543

Telephone number: (914) 381-4649
Fax number: (914) 381-2607
Toll-free number: (800) 333-4971

1. Independent company established in 1986.
2-
3. No.
4-
5. No response.
6. Provides serials and monographs primarily
    from French publishers but can acquire
    Spanish and German books.
7a. Types of materials handled:
        Periodicals
        Monographic standing orders
7b. Books (monographic firm orders).
8. No.
9-
13. No response.
14. Issues a yearly catalog.
15-
16. No response.
17. Rush orders accepted at no added charge.
18-
22. No response.
23. Purchase order numbers provided on
    invoice.
24. Multiple copies of invoices provided.
25. No.
26-
28. No response.

Hampton Barnes, Inc.
302 Main Street
Bennington, VT 05201

Telephone number: (802) 442-4022
Fax number: (802) 447-3430

1. Independently incorporated company
    established in 1984.
2. Other offices:

        Alert Publications
        11 Mount Road
        Feltham
        Middlesex, TW13 6JG , United Kingdom
3-
5. No.
6. Provides serials from countries
    worldwide.
7a. Types of materials handled:
        Periodicals
        Monographic standing orders
        Government publications
        Yearbooks/annuals
7b. No.
8-
10. No response.
11. None.
12. No response.
13-
14. No.
15. Client will deal with one customer
    service representative assigned to the
    account.
16. Will report back to the library on titles
    it cannot supply after exhausting all
    possibilities.
17. Rush orders accepted. There is sometimes
    an added charge.
18. No service fee.
19. Service/handling charges are included in
    the price.
20. Client may request that service/handling
    charges be listed separately on the
    invoice.
21. Pays all of the shipping charges.

22- Titles are listed on the invoice
23. according to purchase order number.
24. Multiple copies of invoices provided (no limit).
25-
26. No.
27. Will provide quotations for libraries interested in changing dealers or consolidating direct subscriptions.
28. If a library wishes to transfer orders from another vendor, it must cancel with the present supplier.

Haventa Ltd.
51 Union Street
Brunswick, ME 04011

```
Telephone number: (207) 729-1826
Fax number:       (207) 729-8609
Telex number:           503839
Cable address:          HAVENTA
```

1. Independent company established in 1978.
2-
3. No.
4. Company maintains memberships in and is regularly represented at the meetings of the:
    American Library Association
    A.B.A.
    AIBDA
    Distripress Ocuril
5. Representatives actively participate in library association meetings in their country and/or areas of the country they represent.
6. Provides serials and monographs from countries worldwide.
7a. Types of materials handled:
    Periodicals
    Monographic standing orders
    CD-ROM
    Back issues
    Government publications

7a. Types of materials handled (continued):
     Loose-leaf services
     Sets
     Microforms
     Replacements
     Yearbooks/annuals (client may request
          every second or third year)
     Memberships
     Serials on videocassette
     Serials with variant publishing
7b. Books (monographic firm orders).
8. Will communicate, on occasion, with back
    issue dealers when supplying back issues
    for a client.
9. Services provided:
     Automatic renewal til forbid
     New order reports
     Claim reports
     Out-of-print searching
10. Journal consolidation service is
    available on demand. The consolidation
    fee is $8.00 - $10.00 per publication
    annually plus postage.
11. Computerized services:
     Searches   Invoices
     Reports   Claims
     Slip-lists   Accounts
12. Database is available to clients by
    catalog or specialized list.
13. No.
14. Issues lists on demand plus a catalog.
15. Client will deal with one customer
    service representative assigned to the
    account.
16. Will report back to the library on titles
    it cannot supply. Will try to obtain a
    title until it gets an answer.
17. Rush orders accepted at no added charge.
18. Service fee is a percentage of the price
    less publisher discounts.
19. Service/handling charges are included in
    the price on the invoice.
20. No.
21. Will pay all or part of the shipping
    charges.

22. Titles are entered on the invoice according to the client's wishes.
23. Not applicable.
24. Multiple copies of invoices supplied (no limit).
25. Invoices can be generated on computer tape or transferred by other electronic means.
26. Prepayment options and terms are available as a percentage discount for cash with order. Percentage is determined by volume.
27. Will provide quotations for libraries interested in changing dealer or consolidating direct subscriptions.
28. Haventa will assist libraries wishing to transfer orders to it from another vendor by contacting the publishers.

International Press Publications, Inc.
P.O. Box 1064
Amherst, NY 14226-1064

For additional information see the International Press Publications, Inc. listing under CANADA.

International Service Company
333 Fourth Avenue
Indialantic, FL

Telephone number: (407) 724-1443
Fax number: (407) 724-1443
Cable address: INATSERVE

1. Independent company established in 1958.
2. Has overseas branches.
3. None.
4-
5. Not applicable.
6. Provides serials and monographs from countries worldwide.

7a. Types of materials handled:
        Periodicals
        Monographic standing orders
        CD-ROM
        Back issues
        Government publications
        Loose-leaf services
        Sets
        Microforms
        Replacements
        Yearbooks/annuals (clients may request
            every second or third year)
        Memberships
        Serials on videocassette
        Serials with variant publishing
7b. Books (monographic firm orders).
8. Will communicate with back issue dealers
    when supplying back issues for a client.
9. Services provided:
        Automatic renewal til forbid
        New order reports
        Claim reports
        Out-of-print searching
    The company is able to tailor its
    services to fit specific requests
    and welcomes all inquiries.
10. Journal consolidation is the standard
    practice.
11. Not available during 1992/1993.
12. Not available.
13. Not available during 1992/1993.
14. Issues special newsletters on a service
    basis for specific requests.
15. Clients will deal with one customer
    service representative assigned to the
    account.
16. Will report back to the library on titles
    it cannot supply. Will try to obtain the
    material for as long as the library
    specifies.
17. Rush orders accepted. There is no added
    charge unless the library requests
    International Service Co. to use special
    facilities incurring extra charges.
18. Service fee varies from 5% through 20%
    depending on the type of order.

19- Service/handling charges are listed
20. separately on the invoice.
21. Will pay all or part of the shipping
    charges if the order is prepaid and in
    large quantity.
22- Titles are entered on the invoice by
23. purchase order number.
24. Multiple copies of invoices provided (no
    limit).
25. Normally not.
26. Prepayment options and terms exist which
    are determined by the type of orders
    placed, the quantity, etc.
27. Does not normally provide quotations for
    libraries interested in changing dealers
    or in consolidating subscriptions.
28. If library wishes to transfer its orders
    to International Service Company, the
    library must cancel with its present
    supplier. If the library requests the
    company's assistance it will assist, if
    possible.

Alfred Jaeger, Inc.
66 Austin Blvd.
P.O. Box 9009
Commack, NY 11728-9009

Telephone number: (516) 543-1500
Fax number: (516) 543-1537
Telex number: 230 968-189
Toll-free number: 1-800-969-JAGR

1. Independent company established in 1958.
2-
3. No.
4. Maintains memberships in and is regularly
   represented at the meetings of the:
        American Library Association
        Medical Library Association
        Special Libraries Association
        North American Serials Interest Group

5. Representatives actively participate in library association meetings in their country and/or area of the country they represent.
6. Provides primarily English-language serials.
7a. Types of materials handled:
    Periodicals
    Back issues
    Sets
    Microforms
    Replacements
    Yearbooks/annuals
    Serials with variant publishing
    Back volumes of continuations
8. Will communicate with back issue dealers when supplying back issues for a client.
9. Services provided:
    Claim reports
    Out-of-print searching
10. Journal consolidation is standard practice to assure correct shipments and to protect against losses.
11. Database availability to clients is via Faxon's Linx "Courier" for electronic mail exchange of information.
12. Catalog now available on Serials/Quest—a computer matching concept.
13. Interfaces with library automation systems not currently available.
14. Issues an annual back volume catalog containing titles, volumes, years, binding, and prices.
15. Client will deal with various customer service representatives.
16. Will report back to the library on titles/issues it cannot supply. Time of searching for the title will depend on the ordering profile and also if the inquiry is an actual order or a quotation request.
17. Rush orders accepted with possible added charges if airmail or Federal Express is involved.
18. Service fee varies.

19. Service/handling charges are included in the price.
20. Not applicable for back volume market.
21. Will pay all of the shipping charges when it purchases journals from a library.
22. Titles are entered on the invoice alphabetically per order number if multiple titles are orders on the same number.
23. Purchase order numbers provided on the invoice.
24. Multiple copies of invoices provided (maximum 5).
25. Invoices cannot be generated on computer tape or transferred by other electronic means.
26. Prepayment options and terms may be available—contact the company for details.
27. Not applicable.
28. Libraries must cancel directly with their present suppliers before transferring their orders to Jaeger. This situation rarely arises with regard to back volumes.

Jerusalem Books Ltd.
1190 Ridge Road
Highland Park, IL 60035

Telephone number: (708) 831-3293
Fax number: (708) 831-3293
For additional information see Jerusalem Books Ltd. listing under ISRAEL.

Victor Kamkin Inc.
4956 Boiling Brook Parkway
Rockville, MD 20852

Telephone number: (301) 881-5973
Fax number: (301) 881-1637

1. Independent company established in 1953.
2. No.
3. Will not do business in Russia and The Commonwealth of Independent States.
4-
5. No.
6. Provides serials and monographs from Russia and The Commonwealth of Independent States only.
7a. Types of materials handled:
    Periodicals
    Monographic standing orders
    Yearbooks/annuals
    Serials with variant publishing
7b. Books (monographic firm orders).
8. No.
9. Services provided:
    Automatic renewal til forbid
    Claim reports
10. Journal consolidation is standard practice.
11. No response.
12-
13. No.
14. Issues a monthly catalog of new books published in Russia and the Commonwealth of Independent States and an annual periodical catalog of titles published in Russia and the Commonwealth of Independent States.
15. Client will deal with different customer service representatives depending on the nature of the inquiry.
16. Will report back to the library on titles it cannot supply.
17. Rush orders accepted with the added charge for actual postage charges.
18. Service fee is $1.50 per order.

19- Service/handling charges are listed
20. separately on the invoice.
21. Will pay all or part of the shipping
    charges.
22- Titles are entered on the invoice by
23. purchase order number.
24. Multiple copies of invoices supplied
    (maximum two).
25. No.
26. Prepayment options and terms are
    available and prepayment can be by check
    or Visa, MasterCard or American Express.
    Contact Kamkin for details.
27. Will provide quotations for libraries
    interested in changing vendors or
    consolidating direct subscriptions.
28. If a library wishes to transfer its
    orders to Kamkin, the library must cancel
    with its present supplier(s).

Kinokuniya Book Stores of America Co., Ltd.
1581 Webster Street
San Francisco, CA 94115

Telephone number: (415) 567-7625
Fax number: (415) 567-4109

1. Owned by Kinokuniya Company Ltd., Tokyo,
    Japan and was established in 1968.
2. Other offices:

       Kinokuniya Pub. Service
       93-97 Regent St.
       London, W1R 7TG, England

       Kinokuniya Bookstore
       15 Beach Road #05-07
       Singapore

       Kinokuniya Bookstore
       Taipei, Taiwan

3-
4. No.

5. Representatives actively participate in library association meetings in their country and/or area of the country they represent.
6. Provides serials only from Japan.
7a. Types of materials handled:
    Periodicals
    Yearbooks/annuals
    Serials with variant publishing
7b. No.
8. Will communicate with back issue dealers when supplying back issues for a client.
9. Services provided:
    New order reports
    Claim reports
10. Journal consolidation is the standard practice.
11. None.
12-
14. No.
15. Client will deal with different customer service representatives depending on the nature of the inquiry.
16. Will report back in less than 45 days to the library on titles it cannot supply.
17. Rush orders are accepted with an added charge.
18. No service fee.
19. Service/handling charges are included in the price on the invoice.
20. No.
21. Titles are entered on the invoice in no specific order.
22. No response.
23. Purchase order numbers are provided on the invoice.
24. Multiple copies of invoices provided (no limit).
25-
26. No.
27. No response.
28. Response unclear.

Kraus Periodicals Company
Route 100
Millwood, NY 10546

Telephone number: (914) 762-2200
Fax number: (914) 762-1195
Telex number: 6818112KRKP
Toll-free number: 1-800-223-8323

1. Division of the Kraus Organization and
    was established in 1947.
2-
4. No.
5. Representatives actively participate in
    library association meetings in their
    country and/or area of the country they
    represent.
6. Provides serials from countries
    worldwide.
7a. No response.
7b. Books (monographic firm orders should be
    sent to Kraus International Publications
    at the same address. See next entry.)
8-
11. No responses.
12. No.
13. Presently interfaces with EBSCONET.
14. No.
15. Client will deal with one assigned
    customer service representative.
16. Will report back within six months to the
    library on titles it cannot supply.
17. Rush orders accepted at no added charge.
18-
26. No responses.
27. Will provide quotations for libraries
    interested in changing dealers or
    consolidating direct subscriptions.
28. No.

Kraus Reprint/Kraus International Publications
Route 100
Millwood, NY 10546

Telephone number: (914) 762-2200
Fax number: (914) 762-1195
Telex number: 6818112KRKP
Toll-free number: 1-800-223-8323

1. Division of the Kraus Organization.
2-
5. No.
6. Provides serials and monographs from
    countries worldwide.
7a. Types of materials handled:
    Periodicals
    Back issues
    Government publications
    Microform standing orders
7b. Books (monographic firm orders).
8. Will communicate with back issue dealers
    when supplying back issues for a client.
9. Services provided:
    Automatic renewal til forbid
    Claim reports
    Records back orders
10. Not applicable.
11. None.
12. Not applicable.
13. No.
14. Has general catalogs and subject catalogs
    available: list authors, titles, volumes,
    years covered, publication date, place of
    publication, price and type of binding.
15. In written and phone contacts, clients
    will deal with different customer service
    representatives as they are available.
16. Agent reports back to the library on
    books they cannot supply immediately and
    give the availability date. Order is
    recorded in backorder file.
17. Rush orders accepted at no extra charge.
18. No service charges.
19- Shipping and handling charges are
20. always listed separately on the invoice.

21. No.
22. Titles appear on invoices in no particular order.
23. Purchase numbers appear on invoices.
24. Multiple copies of invoices provided (no limit).
25. No.
26. Prepayment is required for individuals and most dealers. Libraries are not required to pay in advance but may do so at their request. No special terms are available.
27. Will supply quotations for libraries interested in consolidating direct orders or changing vendors.
28. Libraries wishing to transfer orders to the firm must cancel orders with their former suppliers.

Latin American Book Source, Inc.
48 Las Flores Drive
Chula Vista, CA 91910

Telephone number: (619) 426-1226
Fax number: (619) 426-0212

1. Independent firm established in May 1989.
2-
3. No.
4. Maintains memberships in and is regularly represented at the meetings of library associations (none specified).
5. Representatives actively participate in library association meetings in their country and/or area of the country they represent.
6. Provides serials and monographs from all Latin American countries primarily with Mexico, Spain, Argentina, Venezuela, and Colombia.

7a. Types of materials provided:
        Periodicals
        Monographic standing orders
        Back issues
        Government publications
7b. Books (monographic firm orders).
8. Will communicate with back issue dealers
    when supplying back issues for a client.
9. Services provided:
        Automatic renewal til forbid
        New order reports
        Claim reports
10. Journal consolidation available upon
    demand.
11. No response.
12. Database is available to clients via
    its catalogs.
13. No.
14. Plans to begin to issue a quarterly
    newsletter and separate periodical
    catalog in 1992. Issues an annual
    catalog of books.
15. Client will deal with two customer
    service representatives: one for
    accounting and the other for
    book/periodical information.
16. Will report back within six to eight
    months to the library on titles it cannot
    supply. Will continue the search if
    client requests.
17. Rush orders accepted only from Mexico
    with no added charges unless alternate
    (DHL) means of transportation are agreed
    upon.
18. Service fee is charged.
19- Service/handling charges are listed
20. separately on the invoice.
21. No.
22- Titles are entered on the invoice by
23. purchase order number.
24. Multiple copies of invoices are supplied
    (no limit).
25. No.

26. Prepayment options and terms: All periodical subscriptions are on a prepaid basis with a minimum of three months. Options vary in the book department and depend greatly upon the company's knowledge of the customer. Contact the company for details.
27. Will provide quotations for libraries interested in changing dealers or consolidating direct subscriptions.
28. Libraries wishing to transfer order to the company must first cancel with their supplier(s) or transfer their subscriptions gradually to the company.

The Latin American Book Store
and Libros Sur
204 N. Geneva Street
Ithaca, NY 14850

Telephone number: (607) 273-2418
Fax number: (607) 273-6003

1. Independent companies. Latin American Book Store was established in 1983 and Libros Sur was established in 1990.
2. Have other offices in Buenos Aires, Argentina (Libros Sur). The mailing and business address is that listed above.
3. Within Latin America the company will deal with all Latin American countries but do not do business with the English-speaking Caribbean.
4. Maintains membership in SALALM and is regularly represented at the meetings. The firms are also members of LASA (Latin American Studies Association).
5. Representatives do not at this time actively participate in library association meetings in their country and/or area of the country they represent, but do actively participate in the SALALM meetings.

6. Provides serials and monographs from Latin America and Spain only. Specific attention through Libros Sur to Argentine publications.
7a. Types of materials handled:
    Periodicals
    Monographic standing orders
    Serials with variant publishing
7b. Books (monographic firm orders).
8. No response.
9. Services provided:
    Claim reports
    Out-of-print searching
    Balance accounts
    Financial statements
10. No response.
11. Computerized services: The database is on Macintosh and the companies are fully computerized for administrative operations.
12. Database is not officially available to clients.
13. Companies do not currently interface with library automation systems.
14. Companies issue bimonthly bibliographic lists of current titles from Latin America, Argentina, and Spain.
15. Clients will deal with one customer service representative.
16. Issue periodic reports to libraries on titles that are out of print, etc. They will search for a year for out-of-print materials and then request that the library confirm the need for further searching.
17. Rush orders accepted at no added charge.
18. Service charge covers shipping and handling which is a standard percentage.
19- Service/handling charges are listed
20. separately on the invoice.
21. The companies pay for importation of material to the United States.
22- Titles usually appear on the invoice
23. according to purchase order number. If there are no purchase order numbers, titles appear alphabetically.

24. Multiple copies of invoices are supplied, normally two, but more may be supplied if requested.
25. Invoices cannot be generated on computer tape or transferred by other electronic means at this time.
26. Prepayment options and terms: The companies offer prepayment for selection plans which carry a 15% discount price. They also accept prepayment for libraries wanting to secure funds. They offer financial statements on all prepaid accounts.
27. Not applicable.
28. For a library wishing to transfer its orders to either of these companies, the companies will assist in setting up a transition period according to outstanding orders and new materials that will avoid problems with duplication of titles, etc.

Libros Centroamericanos
P.O. Box 2203
Redlands, CA 92373

Telephone number: (714) 798-1342
Fax number: (714) 335-9945

1. Independent firm established in 1982.
2. No response.
3. No.
4. Maintains membership in and is regularly represented at the meetings of:
     SALALM
5. Representatives actively participate at the meetings of SALALM.
6. Provides serials amd monographs from Central America: Guatemala, Belize, El Salvador, Honduras, Nicaragua, Costa Rica, and Panama.

7a. Types of materials handled:
      Periodicals
      Monographic standing orders
      Back issues
      Government publications
      Loose-leaf services
      Sets
      Yearbooks/annuals (client may request
        every second or third year)
      Serials with variant publishing
7b. Books (monographic firm orders).
8. Will communicate with back issue dealers when supplying back issues for a client.
9. Services provided:
      Automatic renewal til forbid
      New order reports
      Claim reports
      Out-of-print searching
10. Journal consolidation available.
11. None.
12. Database is available through annual catalogs.
13. No response.
14. Issues monthly booklists and an annual catalog.
15. Client will deal with the one individual handling this business.
16. Will report back to the library on titles it cannot supply after about six months. The company prefers not to receive claims prior to six months.
17. Rush orders accepted at no extra charge.
18. No response.
19- Service/handling charges are included in
20. the price.
21. No.
22. Titles may be entered on the invoice by purchase order number, author/title.
23. Purchase order numbers provided on the invoice.
24. Multiple copies of invoices supplied (maximum three).
25. No.

26. Prepayment options and terms are available. If an institution wishes to prepay, Libros Centroamericanos will pay the postage and send an accounting with every shipment.
27. Will provide a quotation for libraries interested in changing dealers or consolidating direct subscriptions.
28. If a library wishes to transfer its orders to Libros Centroamericanos, the library must cancel with its present supplier(s).

Libros de Espana y America
Book Distributors
170-23 83rd Avenue
Jamaica Hills, NY 11432

Telephone number: (718) 291-9891
Fax number: (718) 291-9830

1. Independent firm established in 1977.
2-
5. No.
6. Provides serials and monographs from countries worldwide.
7a. Types of materials handled:
    Periodicals
    Monographic standing orders
    CD-ROM
    Back issues
    Government publications
    Loose-leaf services
    Sets
    Microforms
    Yearbooks/annuals (client may request every second or third year)
    Serials on videocassette
    Serials with variant publishing
7b. Books (monographic firm orders).
8. Will communicate with back issue dealers when supplying back issues for a client.

9. Services provided:
    Automatic renewal til forbid
    Out-of-print searching
10. Journal consolidation available upon
    demand from the library. Prices will be
    quoted for each subscription.
11. Computerized services:
    Reports
    Account statements
    Proforma invoicing
    Price quotations
12-
14. No.
15. Client will deal with different
    individuals depending upon the nature of
    the inquiry.
16. Will report back to the library on titles
    it cannot supply. Will try to obtain
    back issues for up to one year before
    notifying the library of unavailability.
17. Rush orders accepted with an added
    charge.
18. No service fees. Prices are quoted for
    each.
19. Service/handling fees are listed
    separately on the invoice.
20. No response.
21. All shipping charges are paid in advance.
22. Titles are listed on the invoice
    alphabeticallly.
23. Purchase order numbers provided on
    invoices.
24. Multiple copies of invoices supplied
    within limits.
25. No.
26. Prepayment options available.
27. Will provide quotations for libraries
    wishing to change dealers or
    consolidating direct subscriptions.
28. Will assist a library in any way if
    it wishes to transfer its orders from
    another agent.

Libros Latinos
P.O. Box 1103
Redlands, CA 92373

Telephone number: (714) 793-8423
Fax number: (714) 335-9945

1. Independent company established in 1973.
2-
3. No.
4. Maintains membership in and is regularly
    represented at the meetings of:
        ARLIS (Art & Research Libraries
            International Society)
        SALALM
5. Representatives actively participate at
    meetings of SALALM.
6. Provides serials and monographs from
    Latin America, Spain, and Portugal.
7a. Types of materials handled:
        Periodicals
        Monographic standing orders
        Back issues
        Government publications
        Loose-leaf services
        Sets
        Replacements
        Yearbooks/annuals (client may request
            every second or third year)
        Serials with variant publishing
7b. Books (monographic firm orders).
8. Will communicate with back issue dealers
    when supplying back issues for a client.
9. Services provided:
        Automatic renewal til forbid
        New order reports
        Claim reports
        Out-of-print searching
10. Journal consolidation available on demand
    at no additional charge.
11. None.
12. Database is available through its
    catalogs.
13. No response.

14. Issues many lists and catalogs by country/area or theme each with three or four lines of bibliographic information.
15. Client will deal with different individuals.
16. Will report back to the library after about six months on titles it cannot supply. Prefers not to receive claims prior to this time.
17. Rush orders accepted at no added charge.
18. No response.
19. Service/handling charges are included in the price.
20. Service/handling charges will not be separated on the invoice even though requested by client.
21. No.
22. Titles are entered on the invoice by purchase order number, author/title.
23. Purchase order numbers included on the invoice.
24. Multiple copies of invoices supplied (limit three).
25. No.
26. Prepayment options and terms are available. If an institution wants to prepay, the company pays the postage and sends an accounting with every shipment.
27. Will provide quotations for libraries interested in changing dealers or in consolidating direct subscriptions.
28. If a library wishes to transfer its orders to Libros Latinos, it must first cancel with its present supplier(s).

Libros Sur
204 N. Geneva Street
Ithaca, NY 14850

Telephone number: (607) 273-2418
Fax number: (607) 273-6003
For additional information see The Latin American Book Store entry under UNITED STATES OF AMERICA.

PEx (Publications Exchange, Inc.)
8306 Mills Drive, Suite 241
Miami, FL 33183

Telephone number: (305) 256-0162
Fax number: (305) 252-1813

1. Independent firm established in 1989.
2. Other offices:
    PEx corresponds with:

        World Services Publications
        Calle 24 No. 332, esq. a 21
        Vedado 10400
        C. Habana, Cuba
        Telephone number: 33-3002
            (All telephone calls must be
                operator-assisted)
        Fax number: 33-3066

3. No response.
4. Presently does not maintain any library
    association memberships.
5. Representatives actively participate in
    library association meetings in their
    country and/or area of the country they
    represent.
6. Provides serials and monographs from
    Cuba.
7a. Types of materials handled:
        Periodicals
        Monographic standing orders
        Back issues
        Government publications
        Yearbooks/annuals
        Recorded music (CDs, cassettes)
        Recorded videos
7b. Books (monographic firm orders).
8. Will communicate with back issue dealers
    when supplying back issues for a client.
9. Services provided:
        Automatic renewal til forbid
        Out-of-print searching
10. Journal consolidation is standard
    practice at no extra charge.
11. No computerized services for the moment.

12. Database is not available to clients at present.
13. No library automation system interfaces at present.
14. Issues:
> Annual Cuban Serials flyer: lists most common titles; detailed list available.
> Annual Cuban Books Catalog: lists new titles with summary and backtitle list.
> New Releases Flyer: quarterly
> Other catalogs available:
> Cuban videos
> Recorded music
15. Clients will deal with one individual customer service representative.
16. Will report back to the library on titles it cannot supply. It generally attempts to obtain items during 90 days.
17. Rush orders accepted at no extra charge.
18. No service fee.
19- Service/handling charges are listed
20. separately on the invoice.
21. No.
22- Titles are listed on the invoice by
23. purchase order numbers.
24. Multiple copies of invoices supplied.
25. Invoices can be generated on computer disk, if desired, for an extra charge.
26. Prepayment options and terms: Prepayment is required for new customers.
27. Will provide quotations for libraries interested in changing dealers or consolidating direct subscriptions.
28. If a library wishes to place a major portion of its account with this firm, PEx will assist by mediating with Ediciones Cubanas.

Albert J. Phiebig
P.O. Box 352
White Plains, NY 10602-0352

Telephone number: (914) 948-0138
Fax number: (914) 948-0784

1. Independent company established in 1947.
2. No.
3. Will not do business in countries restricted by U.S. government regulations.
4. Maintains membership in the Westchester Library Association.
5. No.
6. Provides serials and monographs from countries worldwide.
7a. Types of materials handled:
    Periodicals
    Monographic standing orders
    Back issues
    Government publications
    Loose-leaf services
    Sets
    Microforms
    Replacements
    Yearbooks/annuals (clients may request every second or third year)
    Memberships
    Serials with variant publishing
7b. Books (monographic firm orders).
8. Communicates with back issue dealers when supplying back issues for a client.
9. Services provided:
    Automatic renewal til forbid
    New order reports
    Claim reports
    Out-of-print searching
10. Journal consolidation is available.
11. None.
12-
14. No.
15. Client will deal with either one or more customer service representatives (varies).

16. Will report to library on titles that cannot be supplied. Will search for a title until countermanded but suggest a deadline of a year for out-of-print material.
17. Rush orders accepted at no extra charge.
18. Service fees depend on the cost to the agent. Wherever the agent has to effect payment to suppliers in foreign currency, the dealer has to cover the bank charges.
19- Service/handling charges are listed on
20. the invoice per customer instructions. They may be listed separately if so desired.
21. No.
22- Agent prefers to bill different orders
23. separately but titles can be alphabetized on the invoice. Purchase order numbers are included.
24. Agent normally supplies three copies; for shipments from White Plains the agent mails two copies separately and encloses the third with the shipment.
25-
26. No.
27. Will provide quotations for libraries wishing to consolidate direct orders or change vendors.
28. Prefers that libraries switching their account to this agent cancel directly with their present agent(s).

Popular Subscription Service
P.O. Box 1566
Terre Haute, IN 47808-1566

Telephone number: (812) 466-1258
Fax number: (812) 466-9443
Toll-free number: 1-800-426-5038

1. Independent company established in 1961.
2-
5. No.

6. Provides serials from countries worldwide.
7a. Types of materials handled:
        Periodicals
        Monographic standing orders
        Government publications
        Loose-leaf services
        Yearbooks/annuals
        Memberships
        Serials with variant publishing
7b. No.
8. No response.
9. Services provided:
        Automatic renewal til forbid
        Claim reports
10. No.
11. Computerized services:
        Computerized printouts of titles with names of clients receiving them
12-
13. No.
14. Issues an annual catalog which is a partial listing of titles available on subscription.
15. Clients will primarily deal with one customer service representative.
16. Will report back to the library on titles it cannot supply. There is no specific time frame. Agent will research immediately and advise the library at the time the invoice is issued.
17. Rush orders accepted at no added charge.
18. No service fee.
19-
21. Not applicable.
22. Titles appear on the invoice in alphabetical order.
23. Purchase order numbers provided on the invoice.
24. Multiple copies of invoices provided (no limit).
25. No.
26. Prepayment options and terms: Will accept prepayment but has no special offers or terms.

27. Will provide quotations for libraries interested in changing agents or consolidating direct subscriptions.
28. Libraries wishing to transfer orders to it must first cancel with their present supplier(s).

Theodore Presser Company
Presser Place
Bryn Mawr, PA 19010

Telephone number: (215) 525-3636
Fax number: (215) 527-7841

1. Independent company established in 1783.
2-
3. No.
4. Maintains membership in and representatives actively participate at the meetings of the Music Library Association.
5. No.
6. Provides music and monographs from countries worldwide.
7a. Types of materials handled:
        Monographic standing orders
        Music
7b. Books (monographic firm orders):
        Handled by The Theodore Presser Music Store
8-
11. Not applicable.
12-
13. No.
14. Issues on a free subscription basis:
        A catalog which features composer (author), title, instrumentation, stock number and price
        Quarterly newsletter, Educational Memo
        Semi-annual newsletter, Composer & Performance Notes
15. Clients will deal with different customer service representatives.

16. Will report back to the library on titles that it cannot supply. If a publication is not in stock or in print, it notifies the library immediately. If the library wishes to back order the item, Presser's retail division will back order and send when available. This may be between 4-6 weeks or up to a year, depending on the situation.
17. Rush orders accepted at no added charge if shipping is to be the regular way. There will be an added charge for special transit.
18. No service fee.
19- Handling charges are listed separately
20. on the invoice.
21. No.
22. Titles are listed on the invoice dependent upon how the order was submitted.
23. Purchase order numbers provided on the invoice.
24. Multiple copies of invoices provided (no limit).
25. No.
26. Prepayment options and terms:
    No special terms available
    Prepayment by check or money order
        in U.S. funds is accepted; if
        prepaying, shipping and handling
        should be included
27. Quotations supplied on a case-to-case basis. Quotes are given at list price.
28. No.

Readmore, Inc.
22 Cortlandt Street
New York, NY 10007

Telephone number: (212)-349-5540
Fax number: (212)-233-0746
Toll-free number: 1-800-221-3306

1. Owned by B. H. Blackwell (Oxford) and
    established in 1950.
2-
3. No.
4. Maintains memberships in the major
    library organizations and attends over 40
    shows per year.
5. Representatives actively participate in
    library association meetings in their
    country and regional shows where
    appropriate.
6. Provides serials from countries
    worldwide.
7a. Types of materials handled:
        Periodicals
        Monographic standing orders
        CD-ROM
        Back issues
        Government publications
        Loose-leaf services
        Sets
        Microforms
        Replacements
        Yearbooks/annuals
        Memberships
        Serials on videocassette
        Serials with variant publishing
7b. Book orders are placed with its sister
    company, Blackwell North America, which
    handles monographic orders.
8. Will communicate with back issue dealers
    when supplying back issues for a client.
9. Services provided:
        Automatic renewal til forbid
        New order reports
        Claim reports
        Out-of-print searching
        Full range of services

360

10. Journal consolidation available upon demand with fees and shipping charges which are in addition to the basic service charge.
11. Computerized services:
    Online access to our system
    Microbased serials processing
      system
12. Database availability: ROSS is available to our clients through an 800 number, Telenet, and Internet. There is a $295 charge for the communications software.
13. Interfaces currently with library automation systems: NOTIS, GEAC, Innovacq, DRA, DataTrek, Information Dimensions, and others. Readmore is committed to interface with any system that is commonly sold in its markets.
14. Issues a bimonthly newsletter and annual catalog. The bibliographic detail is promotional in nature and the data are not a MARC record.
15. Clients will be assigned one account representative.
16. Will report back to the library on titles it cannot supply. The time varies with the type of material and place of publication.
17. Rush orders accepted at no extra charge. All electronic orders are dispatched within 24 hours.
18. Service fee is a percentage which varies with the mix of titles.
19- Service charge appears at the end of the
20. invoice as a separate item.
21. Most subscription prices include the shipping costs which are bundled into the price of the journal.
22. Titles are entered as requested by the client.
23. Purchase order numbers are provided on the invoice.
24. Multiple copies of invoices supplied (no limit).

25. Invoices can be produced on tape or diskette, or transmitted electronically as a file.
26. Prepayment copies and terms are available. Terms vary by date and reflect the current market rates.
27. Will provide quotations for libraries interested in changing vendors or consolidating direct subscriptions.
28. If a library wishes to transfer its orders to Readmore, a transfer strategy is developed with each client. The transfer process will vary with each client depending on the volume of the orders, country of publication, etc.

Research Periodicals and Book Services, Inc.
11231 Richmond Avenue, Suite D106
Houston, TX 77082

Telephone number (713) 556-0061
Fax number: (713) 556-1406
Telex number: 510-600-0921   (PERIODICAL)
Toll-free number: 800-521-0061

1. Independent company established July 1985.
2-
5. No.
6. Provides serials and monographs from worldwide sources, but specializes in English-language journals, abstracts, and reviews.
7a. Types of materials handled:
    Periodicals
    Monographic standing orders
    CD-ROM
    Back issues
    Sets
    Microforms
    Replacements
    Yearbooks/annuals
    Serials on videocassette
    Serials with variant publishing

362

7b. Book orders are handled by another
    division of the company, RBS.
8. Will communicate with back issue dealers
    when supplying back issues for a client.
9. No response.
10. Journal consolidation available on demand
    with an additional charge.
11. Computerized services:
    Invoicing
    Order status reports
    Reminders
12-
14. No response.
15. Clients will deal directly with the
    subscription division of the company.
16. Will report back to the library on titles
    it cannot supply.
17. Rush orders not accepted.
18. Service charge depends on the types of
    publications and type of service.
19- Service/handling charges are listed
20. separately on the invoice.
21. No.
22. Titles are listed alphabetically on the
    invoice.
23. Purchase order numbers provided on the
    invoice.
24-
25. No response.
26. Prepayment options and terms:
    Prepayment required for subscriptions
    Prepayment for back volumes depends
        upon relationship with the client
27. Will provide a quotation for a library
    interested in changing dealers or
    consolidating direct subscriptions.
28. No response.

Norman Ross Publishing Inc.
330 West 58th Street
New York, NY 10019

Telephone number: (212) 222-4475
Fax number: (212) 765-2393
Telex number: 237334 CPC UR
Toll-free number: 800-648-8850
E-mail address: NROSS@PANDORA.SF.CA.US
        (can be accessed from BITNET and
        INTERNET)

1. Independent company established in 1972.
2-
3. No.
4. Maintains membership in and is regularly
   represented at the meetings of the:
       American Library Association
5. No response.
6. Provides serials/monographs on microform
   from countries worldwide.
7a. Types of materials handled:
       Microform formats of:
           Periodicals
           Back issues
           Government publications
           Serials with variant publishing
7b. Books on microform (monographic firm
    orders).
8. Will communicate with back issue
   dealers when supplying microform back
   issues for a client.
9. Services provided for microform orders:
       Automatic renewal til forbid
       New order reports
       Claim reports
       Out-of-print searching
10. Journal consolidation:
       All back files and claimed items
           come through its office.
       All standing order items are sent
           direct from the producer.
11. None.
12-
13. No.
14. Issues periodic catalogs.

15. Clients will usually deal with the same customer service representative.
16. Will report back to the library on items it cannot supply. Will search for the item until the firm has a final answer which can take two minutes to a month or more.
17. Rush orders accepted. There is an added charge ONLY under special circumstances.
18. No service fee.
19- Handling charges listed separately on
20. the invoice.
21. Pays all or part of the shipping charges.
22. Titles are entered on the invoice as requested per customer.
23. Purchase order numbers provided on the invoice.
24. Multiple copies of invoices provided (no limit).
25. Invoices can be generated on computer tape or transferred by other electronic means.
26. Prepayment options and terms:
     Save 5% postage and handling if
         orders are prepaid
27. Will provide quotations for a library interested in changing agents or consolidating direct subscriptions.
28. If a library wishes to transfer it orders to Norman Ross the library need not cancel with its present suppliers as the company will assist the library as needed.

Russian Press Service
1805 Crain Street
Evanston, IL 60202

Telephone number: (708) 491-9851
Fax number: (708) 467-1393

1. Independent company established in July 1991.

2. Other office in Russia (no address given).
3. No response.
4. The company is regularly represented at meetings of Slavic bibliographers.
5. No response.
6. Provides serials and monographs from Russia.
7a. Types of materials handled:
       Periodicals
       Monographic standing orders
       Back issues
       Government publications
7b. Books (monographic firm orders).
8. No.
9. Services provided:
       Automatic renewal til forbid
       Claim reports
       Out-of-print searching
10. Journal consolidation is standard practice at no extra charge.
11. Not yet computerized.
12-
13. No.
14. Issues a booklist which includes standard bibliographic data.
15. No response.
16. Will report back to the library on titles it cannot supply; timing of notification depends on the title.
17. Rush orders accepted at no extra charge.
18. No service fee charged.
19. Handling charges are included in the price.
20. Client may request that service/handling charges be listed separately.
21. Pays all of the shipping charges.
22- Titles are entered on the invoice by
23. purchase order number.
24. Multiple copies of invoices supplied.
25. Invoices are not yet able to be generated on computer tape or other electronic means.

26. Prepayment options and terms: Russian Press Service responds to proposals and will accept anything reasonable. Contact the company directly for details.
27. Will provide quotations for libraries interested in changing dealers or consolidating direct subscriptions.
28. If a library wishes to transfer its orders to Russian Press Service, the library must cancel with present suppliers.

Speedimpex U.S.A., Inc.
45-45 39th Street
Long Island City, NY 11104

Telephone number: (718) 392-7477
Fax number: (718) 361-0815

1. Independent firm established in 1962.
2. Two branch offices:

> Speedimpex
> 155 Deerhide Crescent, Unit 5
> Toronto, Ontario M9M 2Z2, Canada
>
> Speedimpex
> 9875 L'Esplanade
> Montreal, Quebec H3L 2X2, Canada

3. No response.
4-
5. No.
6- Supplies subscriptions to magazines and
7. newspapers from countries worldwide. Supplies books from Italy and Spain. Supplies art books from Italy and France.
8. No response.
9. Services provided:
   Automatic renewal til forbid
10. No response.
11. Computerized services:
    Catalogs and updated subscriptions
        listings

12-
13. No response.
14. Issues catalogs.
15. Each client is assigned its own account representative.
16. Will report back to client on titles they cannot supply.
17. Accepts rush orders at no additional charge to client.
18. No service fee.
19- Service/handling charges are listed
20. separately on the invoice.
21. Client pays all shipping charges.
22. Titles entered on invoice by title, author's name, publisher.
23. Purchase order numbers appear on invoices.
24. Will supply multiple copies of the invoice as specified by client.
25. Can generate invoices on computer tape or transfer them by other electronic means.
26. Prepayment options and terms are available. Customers can prepay or pay within a 30- to 90-day period, depending upon the agreement.
27-
28. No response.

Universal Serials & Book Exchange
2969 West 25th Street
Cleveland, OH 44113

Telephone number: (216) 241-6960
Fax number: (216) 241-6966
Telex number: 298256

1. Independent company established in 1948.
2-
5. No.
6. Provides serials and monographs from all Latin alphabet countries.

7a. Types of materials handled:
    Back issues
    Volumes
    Sets
    Runs
7b. Books are handled by another branch of
    the company which will supply monographs
    from most U.S. and European publishers.
8. Will communicate with other back issue
    dealers when supplying back issues for a
    client.
9. No response.
10. Not applicable.
11. None.
12-
13. No.
14. Issues a catalog of titles twice a year.
15. Client will deal with different
    individuals depending on the nature of
    the inquiry.
16. Will report back on titles it cannot
    supply within 90 days of receipt of
    order.
17. Rush orders accepted with an added charge
    to client.
18. Service fee is a flat fee of $7 per
    bibliographic number.
19- Service fee is listed separately on the
20. invoice.
21. No.
22. Titles are listed on the invoice by
    count.
23. Purchase orders appear on the invoice.
24. Will supply multiple copies of invoices
    (within reason).
25. No.
26. Prepayment options and terms: Members may
    prepay with a minimum of $500.
27-
28. Not applicable.

W. R. Watson & Staff
1181 Euclid Avenue
Berkeley, CA 94708

Telephone number: (510) 524-6156
Fax number: (510) 527-2626

1. Independent company established in 1929.
2-
3. No.
4. Company maintains memberships in library associations (none specified).
5. No.
6. Provides serials from Great Britain, France, Germany, and Italy.
7a. Types of materials handled:
    Periodicals
    Monographic standing orders
    Back issues
    Government publications
    Memberships
7b-
8. No.
9. Services provided:
    Automatic renewal til forbid
    New order reports
10. No.
11. Computerized services:
    Lists of current subscriptions and
        expiration dates
12-
14. No.
15. Clients will deal with one customer service representative.
16. Will report back to the library on titles it cannot supply as soon as the company has definite information.
17. Rush orders accepted at no added charge.
18. Service fee is charged and the amount depends on the list of titles. A fee is charged on all net/net items.
19- Service/handling charges are listed
20. separately on the invoice.
21. No.
22. Titles are entered alphabetically on the invoice.

23. Purchase order numbers provided on the
    invoice.
24-
25. No.
26. Prepayment options and terms: Some
    discount offered for prepayment.
27. Will provide quotations for libraries
    interested in changing vendors or in
    consolidating direct subscriptions.
28. If a library wishes to transfer
    its orders to this firm, W. R. Watson
    and staff will help with the changeover,
    each case being different.

Roy Young Bookseller
145 Palisade Street
Dobbs Ferry, NY 10522

Telephone number: (914) 693-6116
Fax number: (914) 693-6275

1. Independent company established in 1980.
2-
3. No.
4. Company maintains memberships in library
    associations and is regularly represented
    at the meetings (none specified).
5. Representatives actively participate in
    library association meetings in their
    country and/or area of the country they
    represent.
6. Provides serials and monographs from
    countries worldwide.
7a. Types of materials handled:
        Periodicals
        Back issues
7b. Books (monographic firm orders).
8. Will communicate with back issue dealers
    when supplying back issues for a client.
9-
11. No response.
12-
13. No.
14. Issues a catalog.

15. Clients will deal with one customer service representative.
16. Will report back to the library within two weeks on titles it cannot supply.
17. Rush orders accepted at no added charge.
18. No service fee.
19. No.
20. Not applicable.
21. No.
22. Titles are entered on the invoice as requested by the client.
23. Purchase order provided on the invoice.
24. Multiple copies of invoices supplied.
25. Invoices can be generated on computer tape or transferred by other electronic means.
26. No.
27-
28. No response.

URUGUAY

Barreiro y Ramos S.A.
25 de mayo, Esq. J.C. Gomez
Casilla de Correo no. 15
C.P. 11000 Montevideo, Uruguay

Telephone number: (598) (2) 95 01 50
Fax number: (598) (2) 96 23 58

1. Independent company established in 1871.
2. No.
3. No response.
4-
5. No.
6. Provides serials and monographs from countries worldwide.
7a. Types of materials handled:
        Periodicals
7b. Books (monographic firm orders).
8. No.

9. Services provided:
   Automatic renewal til forbid
   New order reports
   Claim reports
10. No.
11. None.
12-
13. No.
14. Irregularly issues a national list of books.
15. Clients will deal with one customer service representative.
16. Will report back to the library within one week on titles it cannot supply.
17. Rush orders accepted with an added charge if overseas airmail service is used.
18. No service fee.
19-
20. Postal charges are invoiced separately.
21. Will pay part of the shipping charges.
22- Titles are entered on the invoice by
23. purchase order number.
24. Multiple copies of invoices supplied, usually two or three.
25. Not yet.
26. Prepayment options and terms: Prepayment is required for all except regular customers.
27. Will provide quotations for libraries interested in changing dealers or in consolidating direct subscriptions.
28. No.

Libreria Linardi y Risso
Juan Carlos Gomez 1435
Montevideo 11.000, Uruguay

Telephone number: (598) (2) 95 71 29
Fax number: (598) (2) 95 74 31
Telex number: 32 31025UY

1. Independent company established in 1944.
2-
3. No.

4. Maintains memberships in and is regularly
   represented at the the meetings of the:
   A.B.A. (Antiquarian Booksellers
      Association)
   SALALM (Seminar on the Acquisition
      of Latin American Library
      Materials)
5. Representatives actively participate in
   library association meetings in their
   country and/or area of the country they
   represent.
6. Provides serials and monographs from
   Latin America.
7a. Types of materials handled:
   Periodicals
   Monographic standing orders
   Back issues
   Government publications
   Loose-leaf services
   Sets
   Replacements
   Yearbooks/annuals (client may request
      every second or third year)
   Memberships
   Serials with variant publishing
7b. Books (monographic firm orders).
8. No.
9. Services provided:
   Automatic til forbid
   New order reports
   Claim reports
   Out-of-print searching
10. Journal consolidation available at no
    extra charge.
11. None.
12-
13. No.
14. Issues catalogs, bulletins, and lists.
    Information provided: author, title,
    edition, year, pages, illustrations, and
    a commentary about each item offered.
15. Clients will deal with one customer
    service representative.

16. Will report back to the library on titles it cannot supply. The company will keep searching for the material for years if the library agrees.
17. Rush orders accepted at no added charge.
18- The company charges "Gastos de envio y
20. seguro" which are listed separately in the same invoice.
21. No response.
22. Titles are listed alphabetically by author on the invoice.
23. Purchase order number provided on the invoice.
24. Multiple copies of invoices supplied (no limit).
25-
26. No.
27. Will provide quotations for libraries interested in changing dealers or in consolidating direct subscriptions.
28. If a library wishes to transfer orders to the firm it must first cancel with its present supplier(s).

VENEZUELA

Ahrensburg Book Sellers
Apartado 395
Caracas 1010-A Venezuela

Telephone numbers: (58) (2) 987-1607
(58) (2) 922372

1. Independent company established in 1910.
2-
5. No.
6. Provides serials and monographs only from Venezuela.

7a. Types of materials handled:
Periodicals
Monographic standing orders
Back issues
Government publications
Sets
Microforms
Replacements
Yearbooks/annuals
Serials with variant publishing
7b. Books (monographic firm orders).
8. Will communicate with back issue dealers when supplying back issues for a client.
9. Services provided:
Automatic renewal til forbid
New order reports
Claim reports
Out-of-print searching
10. Journal consolidation is standard practice. Whenever possible, Ahrensburg replaces items lost in the mail at no extra charge.
11. No response.
12. Database is available through its catalog of in-print and periodical/serial publications.
13. No response.
14. Issues a catalog of in-print and periodical/serial publications. Information includes: author/editor; title; publisher; date of publication; number of edition; price; number of pages; and type of cover.
15. Client will deal with one customer service representative.
16. Will report back to the library on titles it cannot supply. Ahrensburg will keep the order on file.
17. Rush orders accepted at no added charge. The only orders the company does not accept are those that are automatically cancelled after a certain date. This is due to the poor quality of mail service in Venezuela.
18. There is no handling fee for newspapers but a flat fee is charged for each book.

19- Service/handling charges are listed
20. separately on the invoice.
21. Firm pays all shipping fees and then
    charges them to the client in the
    invoice.
22. Response unclear.
23. Purchase order number provided on the
    invoice.
24. Multiple copies of invoices provided
    (limit three). Invoices are sent for each
    package (except for newspapers and
    magazines). Normal packages contain one
    to three books (less than 2 kilos in
    weight).
25. No.
26. Prepayment options and terms: Clients pay
    after books are received, except in the
    case of yearly subscriptions when the
    invoice is sent in the middle of the
    year.
27. Will provide a quotation (if available
    and possible) for libraries interested in
    changing dealers or consolidating direct
    subscriptions.
28. If a library wishes to transfer orders to
    Ahrensburg, Ahrensburg will assist them
    in whatever is requested.

Venezuelan Book Service (VBS)
POBA International #463
P.O. Box 02-5255
Miami, FL 33102-5255, USA

Telephone number: (58) (2) 6613591
Fax number: (58) (2) 6618407

1. Independent company established in
    November 1983.
2. Its offices and warehouse are in Caracas;
    however, it has a mail address in the
    United States, as a private mail service

for better service to its clients worldwide. The Venezuelan addresses are:

VBS
Calle Madariaga
Qta. Lago
Los Chaguaramos
Caracas, Venezuela

VBS
Apartado Postal 47963
Caracas 1041-A, Venezuela

3. Will do business with any country which can make commercial transactions in U.S. dollars.
4. Maintains membership in and is regularly represented at the meetings of:
   SALALM
   ACURIL
   Also, is in regular contact with the Biblioteca Nacional (Red de Bibliotecas).
5. Its representatives actively participate in library association meetings in their country and/or area of the country they represent.
6. Provides serials and monographs from Venezuela.
7a. Types of materials handled:
   Periodicals
   Monographic standing orders
   Back issues
   Government publications
   Sets
   Replacements
   Yearbooks/annuals
   Serials with variant publishing
   Maps
   Directories
7b. Books (monographic firm orders).
8. When supplying back issues for a client, VBS tries to obtain them directly from

the publisher unless publisher no longer exists or the publication is out of print. Then back issue dealers may be contacted.
9. Services provided:
    Automatic renewal til forbid
    Claim reports
    Out-of-print searching
10. No.
11. Computerized services are being planned for 1993.
12-
13. Not applicable.
14. Issues a monthly BOLETIN (by areas of interest) which provides author, title, year of publication, and price. Publishes the semiannual magazine or catalog: LIBROS DE VENEZUELA which provides: title, author, publisher, translator (if any), copyright, size in centimenters, pagination, and an abstract of the new books or serials published, and comments.
15. Clients will deal with one customer service representative.
16. Will report back to the library on titles it cannot supply. VBS will only report back when it is very sure the title cannot be supplied. This usually takes four to six months.
17. Rush orders accepted at no extra charge because airmail is the regular mode of shipping for all items. The only exception is when journals are sent UPS or by a similar service.
18. The service fee charged is a standard percentage. There are different standard percentages for different kinds of materials, depending on the factors such as: the difficulty in finding and/or collecting them, domestic delivery costs (when the publisher is not in Caracas), and many others.
19. Service/handling charges are included in the price. Only shipping charges are listed separately.

20. If a client requests that service and handling charges be listed separately, VBS would be open to studying the possibility though it would be complicated.
21. Will pay part of the shipping charges when the client has special arrangements: standing orders, blanket orders, or in some special offer some type of books.
22. Titles are entered on the invoice by the client's purchase order number.
23. Purchase order numbers are always listed on the invoice.
24. Multiple copies of invoices provided (usually not more than five though sometimes there are exceptions).
25. Invoices are sometimes, for special instances, faxed.
26. Prepayment options and terms:
    Prepayment options by pro-forma invoice (valid for 30 days) have a 10% discount.
    To build a Venezuelan collection in several or specific areas, some libraries, according to their budgets, deposit to the VBS account or send a check for a determined amount. Then VBS selects and sends the materials for a period of three to six months. In these cases VBS pays part of the shipping charges. There is no added charge for the selection service.
27. Will provide quotations for libraries interested in changing dealers or consolidating direct subscriptions.
28. Not applicable.

VIETNAM

Xunhasaba
Export & Import Company of Books, Periodicals, Cultural Commodities
32 Hai Ba Trung-Ha
Hanoi, Vietnam

```
Telephone number:        2.52313
Fax number:            844.252860
Telex number:      411532 VNRT-VT
Cable address:         XUNHASABA
```

1. Independent company (state enterprise)
    established on April 18, 1957.
2-
5. No.
6. Provides serials and monographs from
    Vietnam and countries worldwide.
7a. Types of materials handled:
        Periodicals
        Monographic standing orders
        Back issues
        Government publications
        Replacements
        Yearbooks/annuals
        Serials with variant publishing
        Cultural commodities
7b. Books (monographic firm orders).
8. Will communicate with back issues dealers
    when supplying back issues for a client.
9. Services provided:
        Automatic renewal til forbid
        New order reports
        Claim reports
        Out-of-print searching
10. Journal consolidation is available only
    on demand with an additional service
    charge and additional shipping charges.
11. None.
12-
13. Not applicable.
14. No.
15. No response.
16. Will report back to the library within a
    month on titles it cannot supply.

17. Rush orders accepted at no extra charge.
18. There is a service charge.
19. Service/handling charges are included in the price.
20. Client may request that service/handling charges be listed separately.
21. Xunhasaba pays all of the shipping charges.
22- Titles are entered on the invoice by
23. purchase order number.
24. Multiple copies of invoices provided (no limit).
25. No.
26. Prepayment options and terms are available. Contact Xunhasaba directly.
27. Will provide quotations for libraries interested in changing dealers or consolidating direct subscriptions.
28. If a library wishes to transfer orders to Xunhasaba, the library must cancel with its present suppliers.

ZIMBABWE

The Literature Bureau
P.O. Box 837
Causeway
Harare, Zimbabwe

Telephone number: (263) (4) 726929
Cable address: LITERATURE BUREAU

1. It is a government department.
2-
5. No.
6. Provides publications of the government of Zimbabwe.
7a. No response.
7b-
8. No.
9-
10. Not applicable.

11. None.
12. Not applicable.
13. No.
14. Issues a monthly newsletter and catalog of all publications.
15. Clients will deal with different individuals depending upon the nature of the inquiry.
16. No.
17. Rush orders NOT accepted.
18. No service fee.
19. No.
20. Not applicable.
21. Pays all of the shipping charges.
22. Titles are entered on the invoice alphabetically and sectionally.
23. No.
24. Supplies two copies of invoices.
25. Not applicable.
26. Prepayment options and terms: Prepayments are encouraged but a 30-day account is offered.
27. Will provide quotations for libraries interested in changing dealers or consolidating direct subscriptions.
28. No.

GEOGRAPHICAL INDEX

This index lists the agents that supply materials from specific countries, regions, and continents as indicated by the agent on the survey. For additional agents consult the category WORLDWIDE, which appears in this index.

( ) Indicates the country under which this agent is listed.

AFRICA
Africa Book Services (EA) Ltd. (Kenya), 149
Faxon Europe, B.v. (The Netherlands), 169
African Imprint Library Services/ Caribbean Imprint Library Services (U.S.A.), 260

AFRICA (French-speaking countries)
Aux Amateurs de Livres International (France), 60
Jean Touzot Libraire-Editeur (France), 68

ARAB COUNTRIES
Sulaiman's Bookshop (Lebanon), 156

ARGENTINA
Fernando Garcia Cambeiro (Argentina), 1
Juan Manuel de Castro (Argentina), 4
Lange & Springer (Argentina), 5
Alberto Peremiansky (Argentina), 5
Faxon Cono Sur (Chile), 41
Servicio de Extension de Cultura Chilena, SEREC (Chile), 42
Latin American Book Source, Inc. (U.S.A.), 343
Libros Sur (U.S.A.), 345, 352

BELGIUM (continued)
Jean Touzot Libraire-Editeur (France), 68

BELIZE
Libros Centroamericanos (U.S.A.), 347

BHUTAN
K. K. Roy (Private) Ltd. (India), 115
International Standards Books & Periodicals (P) Ltd. (Nepal), 167

BOLIVIA
Fernando Garcia Cambeiro (Argentina), 1
Editorial Inca (Bolivia), 27
Faxon Cono Sur (Chile), 41
Servicio de Extension de Cultura Chilena, SEREC (Chile), 42

BOTSWANA
The Educational Book Service (Pty), Ltd. (Botswana), 29

BRAZIL
Fernando Garcia Cambeiro (Argentina), 1
Susan Bach Ltda. (Brazil), 31
Faxon Brasil (Brazil), 34
Libris-EBSCO Ltda. (Brazil), 33

BRITISH COMMONWEALTH
Stobart & Son Ltd. (United Kingdom), 244

BULGARIA
Martinus Nijhoff Eastern Europe (Bulgaria), 34
Slavic Verlag Dr. A. Kovac (Germany), 89

BURMA; _see_ Myamar

CANADA

Brodart Ltd. (Canada), 34
CANEBSCO Subscription Services, Ltd.
(Canada), 35
Faxon Canada, Ltd. (Canada), 35
International Press Publications Inc.
(Canada), 35
Aux Amateurs de Livres International
(France), 60
Jean Touzot Libraire-Editeur (France),
68
International Standards Books and
Periodicals (P) Ltd. (Nepal), 167
Academic Book Center (U.S.A.), 253
Baker & Taylor International Ltd.
(U.S.A.), 269
Blackwell North America, Inc.
(U.S.A.), 281

CANADA - QUEBEC

Les Services d'abonnement CANEBSCO LTEE
(Canada-Quebec), 39

CARIBBEAN

Caribbean Imprint Library Services
(U.S.A.), 260, 294

CENTRAL AMERICA

Caribbean Imprint Library Services
(U.S.A.), 260, 294
Libros Centroamericanos (U.S.A.), 347

CHILE

Fernando Garcia Cambeiro (Argentina), 1
H. Berenguer L. Publicaciones (Chile),
39
Faxon Cono Sur (Chile), 41
Servicio de Extension de Cultura
Chilena, SEREC (Chile), 42

CHINA

International Press Publications Inc.
(Canada), 35

CHINA (continued)
International Standards Books &
Periodicals (P) Ltd. (Nepal), 167

PEOPLE'S REPUBLIC OF CHINA
China National Publishing Industry
Trading Corporation (People's
Republic of China), 44
Chinese Materials Center (Republic of
China), 46
ESS Overseas Inc. (Hong Kong), 99
Cheng & Tsui Company, Inc. (U.S.A.), 294
China Publications Service (U.S.A.), 295
China Publishing & Trading Inc. (N.Y.)
(U.S.A.), 297

REPUBLIC OF CHINA (TAIWAN)
Chinese Materials Center (Republic of
China), 46
ESS Overseas, Inc. (Republic of China),
48
Faxon Taiwan (Republic of China), 49
Cheng & Tsui Company, Inc. (U.S.A.), 294

COLOMBIA
Fernando Garcia Cambeiro (Argentina), 1
Editorial Inca (Bolivia), 27
Faxon Colombia (Colombia), 49

COMMONWEALTH OF INDEPENDENT STATES; see
Russia and the Commonwealth of
Independent States

COSTA RICA
Fernando Garcia Cambeiro (Argentina), 1
Mario R. Argueta (Honduras), 94
Libros Centroamericanos (U.S.A.), 347

CUBA
PEx (Publications Exchange, Inc.)
(U.S.A.), 353

EUROPE (continued)
Waterstone's International Mail Order
(United Kingdom), 250

EUROPE, EASTERN
Kubon & Sagner (Germany), 79
Collets Subscription Service
(United Kingdom), 233

EUROPE, SOUTHEASTERN
Kubon & Sagner (except Austria, Germany
and Greece), (Germany), 79
Slavic Verlag Dr. A. Kovac (Germany), 89

EUROPE, WESTERN
EBSCO Subscription Services - Western
Europe (except: France, Italy,
Germany, Spain, Turkey)
(The Netherlands), 168
NEDBOOK International B.v.
(The Netherlands), 169
J. S. Canner and Company, Inc.
(U.S.A.), 293

EUROPEAN COMMUNITIES
Bernan/Unipub (U.S.A.), 278

FINLAND
Akateeminen Kirjakauppa (Finland), 58

FRANCE
Aux Amateurs de Livres International
(France), 60
C.P.E.D.E.R.F. (France), 62
La Cauchoiserie (France), 64
Dawson France S.A. (France), 64
Faxon France S.A. (France), 64
Librairie Luginbuhl (France), 65
Societe Internationale de Diffusion et
d'Edition S.I.D.E. (France), 66
Swets Europeriodiques S.A. (France), 68
Jean Touzot Libraire-Editeur (France),
68

FRANCE (continued)

French & European Publications, Inc.
(U.S.A.), 326
Gerard Hamon, Inc. (U.S.A.), 329
Speedimpex U.S.A., Inc. (U.S.A.), 367
W. R. Watson & Staff (U.S.A.), 370

GAMBIA

Jim Heffernan (Gambia), 70

FEDERAL REPUBLIC OF GERMANY

Antiquariat V. A. Heck (Austria), 18
B. H. Blackwell Ltd. (Germany), 72
Broude Europa (Germany), 72
EBSCO Subscription Services - Germany
(Germany), 72
Otto Harrassowitz (Germany), 73
Kunst und Wissen (Germany), 82
Lange & Springer Wissenschaftliche
Buchhandlung (Germany), 82
Neuwerk-Buch-und-Musikalienhandlung GmbH
(Germany), 84
Sautter & Lackmann Fachbuchhandlung
(Germany), 86
Schmidt Periodicals GmbH (Germany), 87
Slavic Verlag Dr. A. Kovac (Germany), 89
Buchhandlung Staeheli & Co. (Germany),
91
Stern-Verlag Janssen & Company
(Germany), 91
Swets & Zeitlinger GmbH (Germany), 94
International Standards Books and
Periodicals (P) Ltd. (Nepal), 167
Pakistan Law House (Pakistan), 189
Gerard Hamon, Inc. (U.S.A.), 329
W. R. Watson & Staff (U.S.A.), 370

GUATEMALA

Fernando Garcia Cambeiro (Argentina), 1
Mario R. Argueta (Honduras), 94
Libros Centroamericanos (U.S.A.), 347

393

INDIA (continued)

INDONESIA

IRELAND

ISRAEL

ITALY

JAPAN
K. Krishnamurthy, Books & Periodicals
(India), 111
Faxon Asia Pacific Company, Ltd.
(Japan), 147
Nankodo Company, Ltd. (Japan), 147
Nihon Faxon Co., Ltd. (Japan), 149
Nihon Swets Inc. (Japan), 149
Cheng & Tsui Company, Inc. (U.S.A.), 294
Kinokuniya Book Stores of America Co.,
Ltd. (U.S.A.), 339

KENYA
Africa Book Services (EA) Ltd.
(Kenya), 149
Book Sales (K) Ltd. (Kenya), 151

KOREA
ESS Overseas, Inc. (Korea), 152
Faxon Korea (Korea), 152
Universal Publications Agency, Ltd.
(Korea), 153
Will Journal Inc. (Korea), 155

LATIN ALPHABET COUNTRIES
Universal Serials & Book Exchange
(U.S.A.), 368

LATIN AMERICA
Fernando Garcia Cambeiro (Argentina), 1
Alberto Peremiansky (Argentina), 5
Puvill Libros (Spain), 211
Latin American Book Source, Inc.
(U.S.A.), 343
The Latin American Book Store and Libros
Sur (U.S.A.), 345
Libros Latinos (U.S.A.), 351
Libreria Linardi y Risso (Uruguay), 373

LEBANON
Sulaiman's Bookshop (Lebanon), 156

MALAYSIA
ESS Overseas, Inc.
(Republic of China), 48
Academic Library Services (M), Sdn. Bhd.
(Malaysia), 158
Parry's Book Center SDN. BHD.
(Malaysia), 158

MALDIVES
K. K. Roy (Private) Ltd. (India), 115

MALTA
Casalini Libri (Italy), 139

MEXICO
Fernando Garcia Cambeiro (Argentina), 1
DIRSA (Mexico), 161
Mexican Academic Clearing House/MACH
(Mexico), 163
Puvill Mexico Division (Mexico), 164
Puvill Libros (Spain), 211
Books from Mexico (U.S.A.), 285
Latin American Book Source, Inc.
(U.S.A.), 343

MIDDLE EAST
al-Arab Bookshop (Egypt), 57
Faxon Europe, B.v. (The Netherlands),
169

MONGOLIA
Apollo Book Company Ltd. (Hong Kong), 96

MOROCCO
Librairie Internationale (Morocco), 165

MYAMAR (formerly Burma)
K. K. Roy (Private) Ltd. (India), 115

NEPAL
Asia Books & Periodicals Co. (India),
101
Prints India (India), 113

NORWAY
Erik Qvist Bokhandel A/S (Norway), 184

PAKISTAN
International Standards Books &
  Periodicals (P) Ltd. (Nepal), 167
Mizra Book Agency (Pakistan), 186
NGM Communication (Pakistan), 188
Pakistan Law House (Pakistan), 189
Paradise Subscription Agency
  (Pakistan), 191
Sipra Book Company (Pakistan), 192

PANAMA
Fernando Garcia Cambeiro (Argentina), 1
Libros Centroamericanos (U.S.A.), 347

PARAGUAY
Fernando Garcia Cambeiro (Argentina), 1
Faxon Cono Sur (Chile), 41
Mayer's International (Paraguay), 194

PERU
Fernando Garcia Cambeiro (Argentina), 1
Editorial Inca (Bolivia), 27
Servicio de Extension de Cultura
  Chilena, SEREC (Chile), 42
E. Iturriaga & Cia. S.A. (Peru), 196
Libreria "Studium" S.A. (Peru), 198

PHILIPPINES
ESS Overseas, Inc. (Republic of
  China), 48

POLAND
Lange & Springer (Poland), 199

PORTUGAL
Puvill Libros (Spain), 211
Libros Latinos (U.S.A.), 351

ROMANIA
Slavic Verlag Dr. A. Kovac (Germany), 89

RUSSIA & THE COMMONWEALTH OF INDEPENDENT STATES
Troyka Ltd. (Canada), 38
Apollo Book Company Ltd. (Hong Kong), 96
East View Publications
(Russia & CIS), 199
Faxon International Moscow/ICSTI (Russia
& CIS), 200
Lange & Springer (Russia & CIS), 200
Collets Subscription Service
(United Kingdom), 233
East View Publications (U.S.A.), 309
Victor Kamkin Inc. (U.S.A.), 338
Russian Press Service (U.S.A.), 365

SAN MARINO
Casalini Libri (Italy), 139

SCANDINAVIA
Sautter & Lackmann Fachbuchhandlung
(Germany), 86
NEDBOOK International B.v.
(The Netherlands), 169

SIERRA LEONE
New Horizons (Sierra Leone), 201

SINGAPORE
ESS Overseas, Inc. (Republic of
China), 48
Pakistan Law House (Pakistan), 189
Academic Library Services
(Singapore), 202
Chopmen Publishers (Singapore), 204
Faxon Singapore (Singapore), 205
Intermail Enterprise Pte. Ltd.
(Singapore), 206
Parry's Book Center Pte. Ltd.
(Singapore), 206

SWITZERLAND (continued)

SYRIA

THAILAND

TURKEY

UNITED KINGDOM

402

UNITED STATES OF AMERICA (continued)

403

UNITED STATES OF AMERICA (continued)

URUGUAY

VATICAN CITY

VENEZUELA

VIETNAM

WEST BANK (OCCUPIED TERRITORIES)

WORLDWIDE

WORLDWIDE (continued)

WORLDWIDE (continued)

ZIMBABWE

SUBJECT INDEX

While many of the other agents listed in this directory also handle materials on subjects listed here, the agents below mentioned these as special areas of their business.

ASIAN STUDIES
Otto Harrassowitz (Germany), 73

DANCE
Broude Brothers Ltd. (U.S.A.), 290

EAST ASIAN STUDIES
Cheng & Tsui Company, Inc. (U.S.A.), 294

ENGLISH LANGUAGE SERIALS
Alfred Jaeger, Inc. (U.S.A.), 335
Research Periodicals and Book Services, Inc. (U.S.A.), 362

FRENCH LANGUAGE MATERIALS
Societe Internationale de Diffusion et d'Edition, S.I.D.E. (France), 66
Jean Touzot Libraire-Editeur (France), 68

MICROFORMS
Norman Ross Publishing Inc. (U.S.A.), 364

MUSIC
Broude Europa (Germany), 72
Otto Harrassowitz (Germany), 73
Neuwerk-Buch-und-Musikalienhandlung GmbH (Germany), 84
Broude Brothers Ltd. (U.S.A.), 290
Educational Music Service (U.S.A.), 311
Theodore Front Musical Literature, Inc. (U.S.A.), 327

MUSIC (continued)
Theodore Presser Company (U.S.A.), 358

UNITED NATIONS
Bernan/Unipub (U.S.A.), 278

U.S. GOVERNMENT PUBLICATIONS
Bernan/Unipub (U.S.A.), 278

WORLD BANK
Bernan/Unipub (U.S.A.), 278

DATE DUE

GAYLORD			PRINTED IN U.S.A.